D1599463

ROTH FAMILY FOUNDATION

Music in America Imprint

Michael P. Roth
and Sukey Garcetti
have endowed this
imprint to honor the
memory of their parents,
Julia and Harry Roth,
whose deep love of music
they wish to share
with others.

The publisher gratefully acknowledges the generous contribution to this book provided by the Music in America Endowment Fund of the University of California Press Foundation, which is supported by a major gift from Sukey and Gil Garcetti, Michael Roth, and the Roth Family Foundation.

LET'S GET TO THE NITTY GRITTY

LET'S GET TO THE NITTY GRITTY

THE AUTOBIOGRAPHY OF HORACE SILVER

HORACE SILVER

Edited, with Afterword, by Phil Pastras

Foreword by Joe Zawinul

University of California Press   Berkeley Los Angeles London

University of California Press, one of the most distinguished university presses in the United States, enriches lives around the world by advancing scholarship in the humanities, social sciences, and natural sciences. Its activities are supported by the UC Press Foundation and by philanthropic contributions from individuals and institutions. For more information, visit www.ucpress.edu.

University of California Press
Berkeley and Los Angeles, California

University of California Press, Ltd.
London, England

Unless otherwise noted, photographs are from the collection of the author.

Library of Congress Cataloging-in-Publication Data

Silver, Horace, 1928–.
Let's get to the nitty gritty : the autobiography of Horace Silver / Horace Silver ; edited, with afterword, by Phil Pastras ; foreword by Joe Zawinul.
p. cm.
Includes discography (p.), bibliographical references (p.), and index.
ISBN 0-520-24374-9 (cloth : alk. paper)
1. Silver, Horace, 1928–. 2. Jazz musicians—United States—Biography. 3. Pianists—United States—Biography. I. Pastras, Philip. II. Title.

ML417.S64A3 2006
781.65'092—dc22 2005021232
[B]

Manufactured in the United States of America

15 14 13 12 11 10 09 08 07 06
10 9 8 7 6 5 4 3 2 1

The paper used in this publication meets the minimum requirements of ANSI/NISO Z39.48–1992 (R 1997) (*Permanence of Paper*).

I dedicate this book to my mother,
Gertrude Edmonds Silver;
my dad, John Tavares Silver;
and my son, Gregory Paul Silver

I Speak Music

I speak music, the international language.
I speak and people everywhere understand me.
I speak and people listen.
I speak and people dance.
I speak and people sing.
I speak and people pat their feet and clap their hands.
Occasionally I speak and people cry, but more often when I speak
I bring joy, happiness, and uplift.
I speak music, the universal language.
I speak and the universe speaks to me.
I speak and the universe speaks through me.
I speak music, the personal language of my soul.
I seek music that will change the blues within my soul to
a rhapsody.
I speak the music of my thought.
I speak the music of my word.
I speak the music of my deed.
I speak the music of my soul, which is continually being composed
and de-composed, arranged and re-arranged
so that its melody, harmony, and rhythm may be in accord
with all people and the universe.

Horace Silver

CONTENTS

FOREWORD

JOE ZAWINUL

THROUGHOUT THE HISTORY OF MUSIC, there have been thousands of master players, artists, and composers. Yet each generation has produced relatively few individuals with something so distinctive, personal, and recognizable that when you hear the music not only do you know whose music it is but it also seems that you know that *person.* These are the ones who will always be remembered. In this very privileged group belongs the *hero* of this book . . . HORACE SILVER.

Enjoy his story!

PREFACE

IN WRITING THIS AUTOBIOGRAPHY, I tried to divide my life story into roughly chronological segments. I say "roughly" because, although I have a keen recollection for past events, my memory for dates is extremely bad. I do not believe that the dates are so important. But the stories are. I have tried to bare my soul in this book. I reveal things about myself that I've never revealed to anyone before, not even to my family members and close friends. I hope that it will give you, the reader, a keen insight into what I'm all about. Maybe it will help you to understand my dedication to this glorious music we call jazz. This autobiography should provide some historical documentation, but I also hope that it will be enjoyable and interesting reading. I'm trying my best to tell it like it is and like it was. In any event, it is as accurate a picture of my life as I can remember.

Sometimes when I was on tour and in my hotel room, I passed the time by writing poetry or just writing down some of my thoughts on certain topics. I kept these writings in a logbook and would like to share some of them with you. I've been so involved in writing lyrics for my music in recent years that I haven't written much poetry, but I would like to get back into it. I don't see much difference between a lyric writer and a poet. To me, they are opposite sides of the same coin: one creates poetry set to music, and the other creates poetry without music. I have included some of these writings as epigraphs to the chapters in this volume.

ACKNOWLEDGMENTS

AS I WROTE THIS BOOK, I reflected on five of the great friendships I've had in my life. Four of these individuals have made their transition and one remains. I've had many friends throughout my life, but these are the ones I remember and treasure the most, the ones who have been like brothers and sisters to me.

Bob Marshall and I met and became close friends when we were in high school. Bob was well read and well versed in worldly affairs. He also had a great vocabulary and was a good speller and knew the definition of many words, skills that I am rather weak in. Whenever I wrote a new tune and was pleased with it and wanted to share it with someone, I would often call him and play it for him over the phone. When I was writing my lyrics and didn't know the definition of a word and couldn't find it in the dictionary because I wasn't spelling it right, I would call him, and he would always come to my rescue. Bob has recently passed on. I miss him dearly.

I met Don Williams through trumpeter Blue Mitchell, and we became great friends. He loved my music and loved me. He was always concerned about my welfare. Since I live alone, he would call me at least twice a week to check on me and see if I was faring well. If I wasn't, he would always be there to assist me in whatever way he could. I am the godfather of his youngest daughter, Kimberly. For this I am very grateful. She is a joy to my heart. I miss Don dearly.

I met violinist and composer William Henderson through George Butler, who used to be an executive producer for Blue Note Records and then later for Columbia Records. Bill was the conductor of the Los Angeles Modern String Orchestra, which consisted of a group of string players who were composers and who wanted to get their compositions performed. I was commissioned by the ASCAP Foundation and Meet the Composer Inc. to compose a musical work in honor of the great Duke Ellington. I wrote a three-part suite for string orchestra called "Message from the Maestro," which was performed and recorded with the Los Angeles Modern String Orchestra. William Henderson conducted. (Trombonist and arranger/orchestrator Tom McIntosh, arranger/orchestrator Frank Kavelin, and Bill guided me in writing this suite, since I had never written for strings before.) Bill had a great classical background. Whenever I wanted some information about classical music or any of its composers, I could always rely on him to supply that information. He also knew a lot about Broadway composers and their compositions and shared that knowledge with me. Bill was a true friend, always there for me when I needed him. I miss him dearly.

I met Hank Perry when I was in my late twenties and had just started the Horace Silver Quintet. He used to hang out in all the jazz clubs where we performed, and he introduced himself to me. We discovered that we both had Cape Verdean ancestry. He was a lover of jazz and a fan of my music. We became close friends. He was very proud of me and my accomplishments. His mother was a great cook and would often invite me to dinner. I became the godfather of his daughter, Claudia. She has grown up to be a wonderful young lady, and I am very proud of her. "Perry," as I called him, was always there to encourage and support me. I miss him dearly.

I met Carol Forbes when she was eighteen years old. Her father, Graham Forbes, who was a pianist and conductor and had worked with singers Frank Sinatra and Roy Hamilton, brought her to the Cork and Bib, a club in Westbury, Long Island, where we were performing. I became friendly with Graham and his whole family. Carol is a great painter. I have many of her paintings displayed in my home. She is a lover of jazz music per se and a lover of my music in particular. Graham has passed on. Through the years, Carol has been a true friend. She lives in New York, and I live in Malibu. We phone each other frequently, and I see her when I am in New York. I treasure our friendship greatly.

I have recently acquired two new friends who have become a meaningful part of my life. They are Norman and Gail Jacobson. They have become like family to me.

One might say, "So what? What has all this to do with Horace Silver, the composer and musician?" I would like to give you a picture of myself not only as a composer and musician but as a total person. I would like to convey to you which things and which persons meant and still mean the most to me in my life. I think it has become fairly obvious by now that Lady Music was and is *the* thing that has been at the center of my life. The persons I hold most dear over the years include my mentors and my family and friends. I have been and continue to be a blessed man.

I am a family man. I love and enjoy family. I have only one son, whose name is Gregory Paul Silver. But I also have four young men whom I have accepted as unofficially adopted sons. Drummer Alvin Queen joined my band when he was eighteen years old. I've always tried to be a father figure to him, and he has treated me with the love and affection of a son. I would also mention pianist and composer Weldon Irving, who used to write me fan letters when he was a young man. I would answer them and try to give him guidance about music and the music business and the advancement of his career. Devre Jackson helped me greatly when I was operating my own recording company, Silveto Records. I know he looks upon me as a father figure, and I look upon him as a son. Actor Richard Chaves, who was in the movie *Predator*, which starred Arnold Schwarzenegger, has become an adopted son of mine also. All of my sons are doing well, and I am proud of them.

I have four goddaughters: Allison Lafontaine, who lives in Paris,

France; Claudia Perry, whose father was one of my very best friends; Michelle Hunter, whose father is my nephew; and Kimberly Williams, whose father was also one of my very best friends. I am blessed to have so many young people keeping tabs on me to see if I'm well. I know I can depend on them if I need them, and they can depend on me.

I've always looked on my various bands as family units. We strive to work together in harmony as families do. I think one reason that the Blue Mitchell, Junior Cook, Gene Taylor, Roy Brooks band stayed together for so long and enjoyed such success is because we were a family.

Three of my greatest piano-playing friends in the music world are Chick Corea, Joe Zawinul, and Herbie Hancock. They are always so kind to me and are always telling their friends that I was a major influence and inspiration to them when they started out on their musical journey. They are certainly among the giants of today's jazz piano players. It makes me feel good deep down within to know that I had a positive influence on them in their youth. Many of my musician and singer friends have passed on to the spirit world, but some of them still remain, especially tenor saxophonist Red Holloway, singers Bill Henderson and Andy Bey, and pianist David Garfield. Of course, I have several close nonmusician friends who bless my life with their presence. God has been kind to me.

Chapter One

CHILDHOOD

I've got to B natural
and have faith in what comes to me
and what comes through me.
I've got to B sharp
and be aware of all the possibilities that lie before me
so that I may take action in those specific directions.
I've got to B major in positivity
and B minor in negativity.
I've got to B diminished in the old
and B augmented in the new.
I must not B flat
and allow the light of my enthusiasm to fade.
I must B natural
and allow the sunshine of my positivity to nourish my ambitions.

I WAS BORN IN NORWALK, CONNECTICUT, on September 2, 1928. My parents are John Tavares Silver and Gertrude Silver, two of the greatest parents a guy could ever have.

Dad was born in the Cape Verde Islands, off the coast of west Africa, somewhat near Angola. The island where he was born is called Maio, or the Isle of May. Dad worked his way to the United States on a boat. I don't know just how old he was when he came to this country, but I do know he was a young man. He settled in Massachusetts at first and then lived a short time in New York City before finally settling in Norwalk, Connecticut, where he met my mom.

My father worked at the Norwalk Tire Company, a factory that made automobile tires and rubber soles for shoes. He was in charge of a small department that made rubber cement.

Dad spoke with a slight accent, but he spoke good English. When my uncles or some of his Cape Verdean friends who lived in our town would come by the house, he would speak Portuguese. Dad was one of four Cape Verdeans who lived in Norwalk—uptown, as they called it; South Norwalk was called downtown. There were a few other Cape Verdeans who lived in South Norwalk, namely, Nick Santos, the barber, who played music with my dad; and Mr. Perry, who managed a poolroom and also played music with my dad. You might say they were pretty enterprising in the black community. Dad returned to Cape Verde just once, but I don't remember him saying a hell of a lot about it.

Mom was born in New Canaan, Connecticut, and did domestic work. Several Hollywood movie stars had homes in Connecticut: Mom worked for Patsy Kelly, Boris Karloff, Bette Davis, and Ellery Queen, author of the popular mystery series.

My mother's marriage to my dad was her second. Her first was to a man named Fletcher. They had a son, Eugene, so I have a half brother named Eugene Fletcher. Gene, as we called him, was a grown man and married when I was just a little boy. My first recollection of him and his wife, Elizabeth, was when Gene, my dad, and my mom took me to the hospital to visit Elizabeth and their first baby boy, who was named Eugene Fletcher Jr. A few years later, they had a second son, Alfred Fletcher. I was the uncle of these two boys, but I was just a few years older than they were, and we often played together. When Alfred married, he and his wife had a daughter named Michelle, for whom I assumed the role of godfather.

Gene made his transition to the next life at the age of eighty-six. Because of our age difference and the fact that he lived in the neighboring town of Bridgeport and was busy with family responsibilities, we didn't see much of each other when I was growing up. He seemed more like a cousin than a brother to me at that time. After I reached adulthood, we got to know each other a little better. My dad loved him very much. Dad would always say to me, "If you grow up to be as good a man as your brother Gene, I'll be happy."

Two other children were born to my parents before me, a boy and a girl. John Manuel Silver lived six months, but he contracted pneumonia and died. Maria Silver was stillborn. I look forward to meeting them and getting to know them when I make my transition. I've always been a family person. I love my family dearly, and I was blessed to be born into what I think is one of the greatest families in the world.

Originally, Dad spelled his last name "Silva," which is the Portuguese spelling. When he married my mother, she changed the spelling to "Silver." I was baptized Horace Ward Silver. In Cape Verde, it is customary for a son to take on the father's middle name. When I was confirmed in the Catholic Church, I also took the name Martin for my confirmation name, after Saint Martin de Porres. Therefore, my full name is Horace Ward Martin Tavares Silver. I use only Horace Ward Silver when I sign documents.

I was named after my great-uncle Horace, my mother's uncle. He worked as a cook and candy maker. He was one of the few black people who owned their own home in those days. I enjoyed it when Dad took me to visit Uncle Horace, because he would always have homemade pie or cake and, at Christmastime, candy canes. He always had something good to eat in the house. He had a cherry tree in the front yard and a vineyard in the back. He had a little vegetable garden and raised chickens. He would feed us when we visited and give us plenty of goodies to take home.

I was a small boy when Dad's brothers, Uncle Charlie and Uncle Jack, entered the United States illegally. They were living in our apartment in the attic room. They both had jobs. One night, in the wee hours of the morning, when we were all asleep, there came a knock on our kitchen door. Dad, Mom, and I awoke but were hesitant to open the door at that time of the morning, not knowing who was on the other side. When Dad asked who was there, the reply came back, "This is the FBI—open up." Naturally, we were all very frightened. Dad opened the door, and they came in. They arrested my Uncle Charlie and Uncle Jack because of their illegal status and took them away to be deported to Cape Verde. Mom and I were very fearful that they would take Dad also, but he had entered the country legally, thank God. Although we were saddened to see them take Uncle Charlie and Uncle Jack away, we were relieved they didn't take Dad.

I WAS RAISED A CATHOLIC because my dad was a Catholic. I remained in the church until I was in my mid-twenties, when I became involved in the study of metaphysics and Spiritualism. The Catholic religion didn't seem to have the answers to a lot of spiritual questions that I was asking myself. I became and still am a dabbler when it comes to religion. I investigate as many religious concepts as I can, use what I can accept from each, and discard the rest. My mother was a Methodist. I attended her church occasionally and enjoyed the black gospel singing.

Dad played the violin, guitar, and mandolin, strictly by ear. He loved the folk music of Cape Verde. Mr. Nick Santos and Mr. Manuel Perry, friends of my dad who were Cape Verdean, played these instruments also. Occasionally, they would give a dance party in our kitchen on a Saturday night. The women fried up some chicken and made potato salad. The men would get whiskey and beer and invite all their friends, Cape Verdean and American blacks, to come and have a good time. They pushed the kitchen table into a corner of the room to make way for dancing, and Dad, Mr. Santos, and Mr. Perry provided the music, playing and singing all the old Cape Verdean songs.

I was a little boy and could not stay up late to witness the festivities. Mom would put me to bed before the party started. I would go to sleep, but eventually the music would wake me up, and I'd get out of bed, wearing my pajamas with the button-down flap in the back, and go downstairs to the party and sit on the steps, looking and listening. Usually, some of the women would see me, come over and embrace me, and bring me food to eat. Then Mom would take me upstairs and put me to bed.

MOM DIED WHEN I was nine years old. I loved my mom and my dad both, but Mom was always my favorite. I ran to greet her whenever she came home from domestic work with her shopping bag in her hand, for I knew she would have some goodies for me—cookies, candy, peanuts, sandwiches, left over from some white lady's bridge party. I could confide in Mom and tell her things I couldn't tell my dad, certain things I felt that he wouldn't understand or that would get him upset. I wasn't ashamed to tell anything to my mom, even my innermost secrets. I would sit at the kitchen table while she was cooking and pour my guts out to her. She always calmly listened and advised and comforted me if I had any problems or worries or doubts, and I would feel relieved.

Even though I loved Mom very dearly, I could be nasty sometimes, a real pain in the butt. When I went to St. Mary's School, we had to come home and get our lunch at twelve o'clock and then go back to school at one. One time, I came home for lunch and got into some kind of an argument with Mom. I was nasty—I mean, I wasn't cursing or anything, of course, I was just a kid—but I said some unkind things to her. And then it was time to go back to school. I got halfway there, and my conscience was bothering me so much. I wanted so bad to go back and say, "Mom, I love you. I'm sorry. Why did I say those things to you?" But if I'd done that, I would've been late and would have had to stay after school, so I kept going. But I felt terrible and guilty because I loved her so much.

The night she passed, she and I went to the Norwalk Theater to see a movie called *Ziegfeld Follies*, starring Fanny Brice. My brother, Gene, had come down unexpectedly to visit with us that evening, but we had already gone to the movies. My dad was home, so Gene visited with him but had to leave before we returned from the movies because he had to work the next day. When we came home, Dad told us Gene had been there. Usually, Mom and Dad slept in the same bed in the bedroom, and I slept on a couch in the living room, next to the bedroom. But on that particular night, for some reason or other, my mother slept on the couch, and I slept in the bed with my dad.

That morning, I woke up to hear my dad crying. He came into the bedroom and said, "Son, your mother has just died." I started crying and jumped up and ran into the living room. I knelt at the foot of the couch. She was dead. The next-door neighbors heard us crying, I guess, because they knocked on the door and came in, and we told them what had happened.

It was a big shock to both of us, because she hadn't been sick a day. She just—bam!—went in her sleep. It was a good thing, in a way, because, much later, I was told by a psychic person that Mom had had a stroke and that if she had lived, she would have been paralyzed. She was such an active person that it would've been a drag for her to spend the rest of her life on earth paralyzed. So thank God she went that way, quickly. But it was a hell of a thing for me and my dad, especially for me—for my dad, too, but for a nine-year-old boy who loved his mother so much, it was hard.

I became very bitter. I was mad at God for taking my mother away from me. I rebelled and was unruly in school. I got bad grades and stayed back a year. I used to have dreams that my mom was away but would be coming back soon. Then I would wake up and realize she was not coming back, and I would lie there silently crying.

Dad raised me with the help of my great-aunt, Maude, who took on the responsibilities of motherhood for me. Aunt Maude and her husband, Uncle Nate, were very helpful to me while I was growing up. Aunt Maude was a great cook and made all kinds of goodies for me. I was a skinny, rather weak kid, and I caught all the childhood diseases—chicken pox, mumps, measles, you name it. Aunt Maude took it upon herself to fatten me up. She gave me tonics and cooked good, wholesome food for me to eat. I couldn't have any dessert unless I ate all my dinner. She made some great desserts, so I forced myself to eat everything so I could get the dessert. Within a matter of weeks, I had gained weight and was no longer a skinny kid. She and Uncle Nate always had the family for dinner on holidays. She had a recipe for baked beans that all the family wanted, but she carried that secret to her grave.

Also, Aunt Maude would sit down with me and explain our family history and teach me right from wrong. She and Uncle Nate loved music, and they regularly took me to vaudeville shows in New Haven and Bridgeport, Connecticut. I was privileged to see and hear many of the big bands of that era.

WHEN I WAS A SMALL BOY—younger than seven, I believe—a white family moved next door to us. Mr. and Mrs. Parcell were hillbillies, real country folks. Their daughter, Alti, was a grown woman, but she was retarded and had the mind of a child. Mr. and Mrs. Parcell had day jobs. I don't remember much about Mr. Parcell, except that he stayed drunk most of the time. But Mrs. Parcell and Alti were the kindest and most loving people I've ever known.

When I or someone in my family got sick, Mrs. Parcell would fix an old country remedy. I remember having a bad chest cold with plenty of phlegm in my lungs. She gave my mom a bottle of skunk oil and told her to take a teaspoon of sugar, put a few drops of skunk oil on the sugar, and have me swallow it. After I did that, the phlegm in my lungs began to loosen up, and I could cough it up and spit it out.

Mrs. Parcell often cooked some good old country food and shared it with us. Alti frequently looked after me when Mom and Dad were working. She had no schooling except for what her mother taught her. She could not read or write, but she and her mom exemplified the true meaning of neighborliness—they judged people by their character and not their color or nationality.

A lady named Mrs. Cooper and her family lived down the street. She had four children, two girls and two boys, and no husband. The boys were much younger than I was, but the girls were my age and we often played together. Sometimes Mrs. Cooper would call the girls into the house and give them twenty-five cents to go to the local butcher shop for her, and I would go with them. They usually got a huge bag of either chicken feet (the claws) or neck bones. Mrs. Cooper would cook up a large pot of chicken feet with dumplings or a pot of neck bones with beans. She really knew how to cook—I would leave my mother's steak dinner to go down to the Coopers' house to eat chicken feet and dumplings or neck bones and beans. Although they were very poor, her children never went without food. As they say, necessity is the mother of invention. It's amazing how far you can stretch a few dollars if the situation necessitates it.

OUR OTHER NEXT-DOOR NEIGHBORS were the Griffin family. Mr. and Mrs. Griffin had two daughters, Dorothy and Mildred, and a son, Jimmy. Dorothy was around my age and Mildred was a few years younger, so I used to play with them. Jimmy was a grown man in his twenties who played ragtime piano at home and in local clubs and bars. I loved to listen to him practice. The wall between our living room and theirs was very thin, and I could hear everything he played.

Whenever Dorothy got a bike or a sled or a pair of skates, I'd ask my dad to get the same thing for me. So when Dorothy started piano lessons, I asked Dad if I could take piano lessons. It was not a case of my wanting to play the piano, but a case of monkey see, monkey do.

My Uncle Harry, my mom's brother, had worked as a gardener for some rich white folks out in the country. They were getting ready to move from Norwalk to somewhere in the South, and they wanted to get rid of an old upright piano. Uncle Harry told Dad about it, and they found someone with a truck, went and got the piano, and brought it home.

I started taking lessons, but after about four weeks I told Dad that I wanted to quit—I found the scales and exercises I had to practice very boring. Dad said, "No, you're not going to quit. You asked for this, and you got it, and now you're going to stick with it. One day, you'll thank me for this." I most certainly do thank him for making me stick with it. As Dad used to say, "There are only two professions a black man can be successful at in this country at this particular time, and they are sports and music."

I had three piano teachers. The first was Miss Elsie, who was my Uncle Louie's girlfriend. The second was Miss Tilley, and the third was Professor William Schofield. A friend of mine, Billy Booker, was taking lessons from Professor Schofield, and Billy took me to see him in the hope that he would teach me. Professor Schofield was a pianist and organist at one of the big white churches in Norwalk. He was a great classical pianist. He had also traveled abroad accompanying opera singers.

When I met him, he asked me to play something for him. I hadn't brought any music with me, and I told him that I couldn't play anything without the music except boogie-woogie. He said, "Play me some of that." I played a boogie-woogie tune I had made up called "Silver's Boogie." He liked it and agreed to take me on as a student. He charged all his white students eight dollars a lesson, but he knew that Billy Booker and I could not afford that, so he charged us each four dollars a lesson.

With all respect to my other two teachers, I learned the most from Professor Schofield. He was strict. If you didn't have your lesson prepared or if you made too many mistakes, he would holler at you or sometimes curse and crack your knuckles with a ruler. I was afraid to go to my piano lesson unprepared, for I knew he would get on my case.

As a means of earning some extra money, Dad used to cut men's hair in our kitchen on the weekends. He charged one dollar a haircut. One of his customers was a man named Bud Mills. Music was not his profession, but he played piano in the Harlem "stride" style of James P. Johnson, the great pianist and composer who mentored the likes of Thomas "Fats" Waller and Duke Ellington. After his haircut, Dad and I would ask Bud Mills to play the piano. He would oblige and then ask me to play. I was always embarrassed to play my little kiddie piano lessons for him after hearing him play à la James P.

I WAS QUITE A PRANKSTER when I was a young boy. I liked to play practical jokes on people. My dad used to take Doan's Kidney Pills to flush out his kidneys. I was in the bathroom one day when he was taking a leak, and I saw that he was pissin' green. I asked him how come his pee was green. He said it was because of the Doan's Kidney Pills he was taking. I immediately got a bright idea.

The next day, I took some of Dad's pills, drank a lot of water, and waited until I had to take a piss. I then called to one of the neighborhood boys to come into our apartment. I bet him a dime I could pee green. He didn't believe me, so he pulled a dime out of his pocket and put it on the kitchen table. I put up my dime, and we went into the bathroom. I pulled out my johnson and proceeded to piss green. He was shocked and said I was sick and should go see a doctor. I didn't tell him I had taken Dad's pills in order to piss green; I just picked up his dime from the kitchen table and put it in my pocket.

It's a good thing I didn't repeat this episode and try to take a dime from another kid. I might have damaged my young kidneys by taking this medication when it was not needed. But I got a big kick out of pulling off this practical joke. Dad never knew that I had taken some of his pills; if he had found out, I probably would have got a spanking.

I remember playing a practical joke on Dad one April Fool's Day. I emptied all the sugar out of the sugar bowl and filled it with salt. After he ate his dinner, he had his usual cup of coffee, but this time it was with salt instead of sugar. He took one sip and spit it out. I told him I did this as an April Fool's joke, but he didn't think it was funny. I had to do a lot of talking to convince him he shouldn't give me a spanking, because it was only a joke.

WHEN I WAS ABOUT ten years old, I fell in love with the movies, and I went to the afternoon matinee every Saturday. These matinees were geared toward kids. They always started off the program with a cartoon, followed by a feature film, usually with the Bowery Boys or the Dead End Kids. The middle of the program showed coming attractions, followed by an episode of a serial. Some of these were twelve episodes long, and some were fifteen. Among the serials I saw were *Drums of Fu Manchu*, *Dick Tracy*, *Captain Marvel*, and *The Lone Ranger*. They ended the program with a cowboy feature film. Hopalong Cassidy was my favorite cowboy.

Once, when I had seen fourteen episodes of a fifteen-part *Lone Ranger*, I was anticipating the last episode, in which he was to be finally unmasked—a big moment for Lone Ranger fans. I asked my dad for money to go see the final episode, but he said I couldn't go. I said, "Dad, I've seen fourteen episodes of *The Lone Ranger*, and today is the final episode, in which he is going to be unmasked. Can I go, please?" He still refused.

I was very angry with him and sought revenge. I had a BB gun, and Dad had just bought a brand-new set of bedroom furniture on the installment plan from Sears and Roebuck Company. I took my BB gun and fired it at the headboard of the brand-new bed. It penetrated and left a big hole in the headboard. When Dad discovered this, he called me and said he was going to give me a beating I would never forget. He made me take all my clothes off, and he beat my behind with a leather belt. I was determined not to give him the satisfaction of making me cry. It hurt like hell, but I gritted my teeth and held the tears back.

Years later, when I became a man, I asked him one day why he hadn't let me go see the last episode of *The Lone Ranger*. He said, "You should have asked me." I said, "I did ask, but you refused. I had been a good boy and hadn't done anything wrong, but you still refused to let me go." Dad was a good, kind, loving father, but maybe he had a rough day that day and took it out on me. In any event, I made my protest and took my punishment without a whimper.

Before the age of eleven, my ambition was to become a movie projectionist, to work in the projection booth and operate the camera and see all the movies free of charge. I've always loved the movies and still do. Dad bought me a 16-millimeter silent projector one Christmas, and I used to rent cowboy movies and cartoons from the local camera shop on weekends and show them to the kids in the neighborhood. When I went to the movies, I always sat way up in the last row of the balcony and tried to peep into the projection booth to see the projectionist loading the camera. I wished for an opportunity to go into the booth and watch the projectionist at work.

I finally got that opportunity in my early twenties, when I was working and traveling with Stan Getz. We played a week in Wildwood, New Jersey, and a projectionist who was a jazz fan came into the club to check us out. I met him and told him about my childhood ambition. He invited me to come by the cinema where he worked and watch him in the projection booth. I went, and it was very interesting to see him load a camera and switch from camera one to camera two when the film in the first camera ran out. For a smooth transition from one reel to another, a little dot appeared in the upper righthand corner of the screen notifying the projectionist to start camera two. In those days, they didn't have lamps in cameras—they used carbon rods to generate enough light to project the film. Carbon rods were effective, but they could be dangerous and could start a fire if not watched carefully.

AT THE AGE OF ELEVEN, my interest was diverted from becoming a movie projectionist to becoming a musician. It happened like this. On Sundays, Dad and I often went to an amusement park called Rowton Point, located in Rowayton, Connecticut, not far from where I lived. We had a great time, eating cotton candy and hot dogs and riding the merry-go-round, the bumper cars, and the roller coaster. We always made tracks for home when it started to get dark. I had to get to bed early because I had school on Monday.

There was a dance pavilion at Rowton Point, and every Sunday evening a famous big band would play there for dancing. One Sunday, when Dad and I were leaving the park, a big Greyhound bus with a sign that said "JIMMIE LUNCEFORD AND HIS ORCHESTRA" pulled up in the parking lot. I saw all these black musicians get out of the bus with their instruments in hand. I asked Dad if we could stay and hear them play, but he said no, because I had school the next day. I pleaded to stay and hear just one song. He consented, and we waited for them to set up and start to play.

We could not go into the dance pavilion because blacks were not allowed there. The pavilion was an enclosed structure overlooking the ocean, but it had open slats so that people outside could look through and hear the music. There were white people and black people outside, looking in and listening.

When I heard that band play, I said to myself, "That's for me. I want to be a musician." They turned me on. I was eleven years old when I heard the Lunceford band, and I made a vow that very night that music would be my life. I immediately became a big Jimmie Lunceford fan. I collected every record of his that I could get my hands on. I used to play his records and stand in front of the mirror in my living room with a big long stick in my right hand, pretending that I was Jimmie Lunceford leading his band. I was so wrapped up in the Lunceford band that I missed out on Duke Ellington and Count Basie and their great bands; I had to catch up with their work later on.

Although I still love the movies, there's nothing I love more than music. Since the moment I heard the Lunceford band, I have believed that God destined me to become a musician and composer, and I'm sure glad He did. Without music, my life would be empty and void of purpose. Music gives meaning to my life. And I hope my music will bring joy and happiness into the lives of all who listen to it.

NORWALK WAS A NICE LITTLE TOWN, but it was a prejudiced town. No one was burning a cross on your lawn or lynching anybody, but the white folks would let you know you were black and should stay in your place—or the place they had designed for you as a second-class citizen. I resented this. My dad always told me that God created everybody equal and that no man was better than another because of the color of his skin.

There was one black bar and restaurant in South Norwalk at that time, and one black restaurant in Norwalk. Blacks could not eat in white restaurants. The only other places that blacks could eat were the Woolworth's five-and-ten-cent store counter and a Japanese-owned restaurant. I liked the hot dogs at the Norwalk Diner, but if I wanted one, I had to order it to go; I could not sit at the counter and eat it there. And blacks had to sit in the balcony at the local movie house—they could not sit downstairs.

I remember my dad telling me that he took my mother to the movies one night and sat downstairs. My mother looked so much like a white woman that when I went shopping with her, white folks would stare, as if to say, "What is that white lady doing with that black boy?" Her complexion was white, and she had long, straight hair. An usher at the movies approached Mom and Dad and said that the lady could remain downstairs, but that Dad had to sit upstairs in the balcony. Dad asked for his money back, and they both left. Even after the theater's policy changed years later and blacks could sit anywhere, it took a lot of talking on my part to get Dad to go to the Norwalk Theater with me to see a movie.

The Catholic sisters and priests at St. Mary's Grammar School always treated me nice. I was the only black student in the whole school. It was rough growing up as a black kid in those days. Everything in your surroundings seemed to be telling you that you were inferior to the white race. I refused to accept that concept, so consequently I was always in conflict. One of the sisters at St. Mary's found out that I played the piano and played boogie-woogie, so she would ask me to play for the class on different occasions. I also sang in the St. Mary's Boys Choir. But the prejudice of Norwalk people was like a dark cloud over my head. I couldn't wait to grow up and get the hell out of there, to travel the world and be a great musician.

I was invited back to Norwalk in 1996 to be honored by the city and Norwalk High School as a graduate who had moved on to a successful life and career. I was amazed to find out that Norwalk High School now had a black principal and that his ancestry was Cape Verdean, like mine. This would never have happened in the days when I was a kid there. I used to think that the only good thing about Norwalk was that it was close to New York City—you could get to New York by train in an hour. I still carry with me a few emotional scars from Norwalk, but I have forgiven those who caused them. Norwalk and its people have grown, and I'm very proud of the progress they have made.

FROM THE TIME MY MOTHER DIED until I was twelve years old, I slept in the same bed with my dad. When I reached the age of twelve, Dad gave me my own room. I felt so grown up having my own room. Every Saturday, I would give it a thorough cleaning. I bought a little radio at Sears and Roebuck that cost me five dollars, so that I could enjoy some music and some of the great comedy programs, such as those with Jack Benny, Fred Allen, Eddie Cantor, Fibber McGee and Molly, The Great Gildersleeve, and Amos 'n Andy. I also enjoyed some of the dramas that came on, such as *Inner Sanctum*, *Gang Busters*, *The Fat Man*, *The Shadow*, *The Lone Ranger*, *Mr. Keen*, *Tracer of Lost Persons*, and *Lux Presents Hollywood* (Lux Soap was the sponsor).

In those days, big bands would broadcast late at night from different ballrooms and nightclubs throughout the country, bands like those led by Jimmie Lunceford, Glenn Miller, Count Basie, Tommy Dorsey, Jimmy Dorsey, Duke Ellington, Harry James, Gene Krupa, Buddy Rich, Guy Lombardo, Earl "Fatha" Hines, Stan Kenton, and Claude Thornhill. You could hear them on several of the major stations, so you could turn from station to station until you settled on the band of your choice. They usually started broadcasting at about eleven o'clock in the evening and went until about two A.M.

I wasn't supposed to be awake at that time of night. Dad always made me go to bed by ten P.M. at the latest. I would go to bed at ten but stay awake until eleven and then turn the radio on at a very low volume, so that Dad couldn't hear it, and scan the dial for some good music. His bedroom was on the second floor, and mine was on the third. Sometimes he'd hear my radio playing, and he would yell upstairs to me to shut it off and go to sleep. I would shut it off and wait a while, until I thought he'd gone to sleep, and then turn it back on very low, putting my ear to the speaker to hear the music.

The local Norwalk newspaper was called the *Norwalk Hour.* My family and I lived just in back of the newspaper building, at number 5 Brook Street, an old dirt alley. A brook ran through the alley, and my parents told me that if they caught me playing around that brook, I would get a spanking, because I would get hurt if I fell in. One day, I was playing with an older group of boys who were daring each other to jump from one side of the brook to the other. All of them had jumped and made it safely, and it was my turn. I was afraid, but I didn't want to be called chicken or a sissy, so I jumped, missed my footing on the other side, and fell in the brook on my back. My back ached me for about two weeks after that, but I didn't tell my parents because I didn't want to get a spanking. That fall was the cause of my spinal scoliosis, which has intermittently given me problems all my life. Chiropractic has helped me greatly through the years with this problem.

At number 5 Brook Street, we had no hot running water and no central heating. Heat came from a wood and coal stove in the downstairs kitchen and a potbellied wood and coal stove in the upstairs living room. In the winter, before we went to bed, we banked the stoves with ashes to keep the fires burning throughout the night. This kept the house reasonably warm as we slept, but often the fire would go out, and we would wake up to a freezing cold house. We'd have to start a brand-new fire with newspaper and wood and then heap on the coal. Sometimes the water pipes froze up, and Dad had to crumple up some newspapers, put them in the sink under the frozen pipes, and take a match and light the paper to get the water flowing again. As a small boy, I took a sponge bath at the kitchen sink every morning before I went to school. Every Saturday evening, I took a proper bath in a big tin tub. I had to boil the water on the kitchen stove, pour it into the tub, and then mix in some cold water to get a comfortable temperature.

Our apartment had three levels. The kitchen was in the basement. The living room and Dad and Mom's bedroom and toilet were on the second level. There were two bedrooms on the third level, one of which was mine. We had rats in the basement. They would stay out of sight in the daytime when we were active in the kitchen, but at night when we turned out the kitchen light and went upstairs to listen to the radio, they would come out. I was deathly afraid of them. If I had to go downstairs to the kitchen at night, for whatever reason, I first stomped hard on the steps until I heard them scattering across the floor. I then would turn on the light and cautiously go downstairs.

In the summer, we had bats in our roof. The bedbugs they carried would find their way through the walls and reach our mattresses. I often woke up in the middle of the night after they had bitten me and sucked my blood. I would turn on the light and see them crawling on the bed sheet. I squeezed them between my fingers until blood popped out. Dad burned a sulphur candle in the room to try to get rid of them. It helped some but did not solve the problem.

I remember the Salvation Army bringing food baskets to our house when I was a small boy. We were poor, but I never went without a meal or warm, clean clothes to wear or medical attention when I needed it. Dad and Mom saw to that. As I look back at my childhood and compare what I had then to what I have now, I realize how far I have come and how much God has uplifted my life and blessed me through the gift of music. I now live in Malibu, California. I own my own home, and I am financially secure. My music has been and still is going forth to bring pleasure to the people of the world.

What more could I ask for?

Chapter Two

DREAMING MY DREAMS
TEENAGE YEARS

No perimeters He.
All limits are imposed by me.
If I only knew what I could be,
I'd be working my way toward my destiny.
I must plan, work, envision my goals,
for with accomplishment of such
life's true purpose unfolds.

ST. MARY'S CATHOLIC SCHOOL only went through the eighth grade. I had to go to Center Junior High for ninth grade and then on to Norwalk High. Once I got into the public school system, I realized that you could sign up for band and orchestra and gain points toward your graduation. The schools let you borrow an instrument and gave you free lessons.

Being a great fan of tenor saxophonist Lester Young, I chose to play the tenor sax. I played the tenor from ninth grade to eleventh grade in the high school band and orchestra. During my twelfth year, the baritone saxophonist graduated, and the band and orchestra instructor took away my tenor and gave me the baritone sax to play. I really wanted to play tenor, though, so I bought my own. I was already playing some local gigs on tenor and some on piano.

The high school band and orchestra instructor was Mr. Alton Freiley. He was a good teacher. Much like Professor Schofield, he was strict but fair. He taught me how to breathe from the diaphragm. In Center Junior High, I had been breathing from my chest, and the instructor had never bothered to correct me.

I had two Caucasian buddies I hung out with who were in the high school band and orchestra: Lenny Swartz, who played trumpet; and Ernie Muro, who played tenor sax. Lenny's influence on trumpet came from Harry James, and Ernie's on tenor came from Charlie Ventura. We always sat together during lunch period and talked about music. After we graduated from high school, Lenny went with the bands of Victor Lombardo and Ray Anthony. Ernie went to West Point Academy. I lost track of Ernie after that, but Lenny and I would hook up on occasion. In later years, I ran into him sometimes while we were both out on the road.

As a teenager, I practiced every day on tenor and on piano. I'd get in the stairway going up to our attic and play tenor along with Lester Young's records, trying to cop his sound. The stairway acted like an echo chamber, and I could really hear what I sounded like. I was the teenage Lester Young of Connecticut. I had his sound down pretty well. As far as the piano was concerned, I listened to records upstairs on the electric phonograph and then took them downstairs to play on an old windup phonograph, where I'd slow the speed down so I could catch what the musicians were doing. That's how I learned the solo interlude chord changes to "Night in Tunisia." I learned a lot from recordings in my teenage years. Listening and then trying to analyze what the cats were doing was my thing. It was also a lot of fun.

While in high school, I met a drummer named Alan Burr, who had graduated a couple of years before I entered Norwalk High. He had a dance band consisting of musicians who had graduated around the same time he did. He heard about how well I played the tenor and called me to come to one of their rehearsals at a church basement to try out for the band. They liked what I did and asked me to join. We played stock arrangements of Glenn Miller, Tommy Dorsey, Count Basie, and others. The band was all white except for me. There was a girl piano player and a girl trumpet player. We played teenage YMCA dances, veterans' hospitals, high school dances, white country clubs, and things like that. The band members all treated me very nice and made me feel comfortable, although there were times at some of the gigs when the audience made me feel a little uncomfortable.

In addition to my music, I also had jobs all through high school. Another kid and I swept out the Norwalk Theater after school at five o'clock, when the afternoon matinee let out. We got no money for this, but our names were left at the box office so that we could see a free movie whenever we wanted. At different times, I had a paper route, was a pin boy at the Norwalk bowling alley, and worked in a shoeshine parlor. I also shined the shoes of golfers at the Westport Golf Course. I had a job working in the kitchen of a restaurant in Westport, washing dishes, peeling potatoes, cutting up string beans, and doing other kitchen chores. My Uncle Harry (my mother's brother), who was a janitor for two office buildings in Norwalk, paid me to give him a helping hand from time to time. I also worked at Woolworth's five-and-ten-cent store after school, sweeping and mopping the floors and putting out the garbage. It felt great to be a bit independent and not have to go to Dad all the time for money.

Even with my jobs, I would practice the piano and the tenor all week long and then hope and pray that I'd get a gig or two on the weekend so I could try out some of the things I'd been practicing. I often borrowed Dad's car and went down to Calf Pasture Beach on a hot summer night, where I parked and looked at the moon shining on the ocean, as I dreamed my dreams of becoming a great and famous musician, playing and traveling all over the world. I said to myself, "One of these days, I'm going to make records. And when the people put the needle down on the record and play about a quarter of an inch in, they will say, 'That's Horace Silver—I recognize his style.'"

AS SMALL AND DULL as Norwalk was, some great talent occasionally came to town. During World War II, actor Charles Laughton and actress Ann Rutherford came to Norwalk to promote the sale of war bonds. It was a thrill to see them in person after seeing them in so many movies. Norwalk people always loved to brag that actor Horace McMann was a native of the city. Benny Goodman played a concert at Norwalk High School, with Mary Lou Williams on piano. Jack Benny made an appearance with a symphony orchestra at Norwalk High, where he played the violin and did a comic routine. I believe the concert was to raise funds for some charitable organization. Al Cooper and the Savoy Sultans played a dance in Norwalk that was sponsored by a black promoter in the black neighborhood. I attended, not to dance but to stand near the bandstand and listen.

Every week, I listened to a dramatic program on the radio called *Casey, Crime Photographer.* The program always opened with Casey and his female assistant at the Blue Note Cafe discussing a murder case that they were assigned to cover. Pianist Herman Chittison played live in the background. I'd put my ear to the speaker so I could hear him more clearly. When he finished, I'd run downstairs to the kitchen where the piano was and try to copy some of what I had heard him play. Most times, I missed most of the story, but I made sure my ear was near the speaker at the end of the story when they were back at the Blue Note Cafe discussing how they had helped the police solve the murder. Herman Chittison once again played in the background, and again I'd run back down to the piano and try to copy him. There was a white restaurant and bar in South Norwalk that hired Herman to play solo piano during the dinner hour. I presume he commuted every night from New York to Norwalk for the gig. I would have loved to have gone there to listen to him, but I was too young to get in where they served liquor—plus blacks were not admitted. Herman Chittison is still one of my favorite swing-era piano players.

I remember an incident that happened one weekend in Norwalk when I didn't have a gig and wanted so much to go out and play somewhere. I was walking down the street on a Saturday afternoon, and I ran into a black drummer named Walter Truely, who played in an otherwise all-white band led by an accordion player, Woody Postiglione. Walter and Woody and the other band members were grown men. I was a teenager. Walter asked me if I had a gig that night. I said no. He said, "Why don't you come down to the Norwalk Yacht Club and sit in with Woody's band?"

I went home and practiced all afternoon and looked forward to sitting in with Woody and Walter and the rest of the guys. Woody's younger brother, Armine Postiglione, played alto sax, and he played it very well. He was a good improviser, and he knew his chord changes. He used me on piano sometimes when he had a gig, and I used him sometimes when I had a gig. (He later changed his name to Artie Post.)

I knew that the Norwalk Yacht Club did not admit blacks as customers, but I wasn't going as a customer—I was going as a musician, to sit in with Woody's band. The band was in the middle of playing a song when I walked in. I made it a point to have my saxophone case visible and to sit on the side of the room at a table near the bandstand until the band finished their song, when I could get my horn out and go up on stage and play with them.

Before they ended the song, a police officer came in and came over to my table. He said they had gotten a call at police headquarters that there was a black man in the club and they wanted him put out. I was so embarrassed. I walked outside with the police officer, who was very apologetic. He said he was sorry he had to do what he did, but that was his job. I was so belittled and hurt by this incident. I walked home and sat on my front porch and cried like a baby. I said to myself, "If I ever get out of this town, I'll never come back."

MY HOMETOWN HAD VERY LITTLE jazz activity. I had to commute to Bridgeport, New Haven, or Hartford from time to time in order to stay involved with the music. I had a few gigs in Stamford and Greenwich and some in Westchester County, New York. I worked gigs in Port Chester, White Plains, Tarrytown, and Mount Vernon. Thanks to Dad letting me use the family car, I was able to make these gigs. Sometimes I played tenor, sometimes piano. On some gigs, I was the leader of the band, and on some I worked with other leaders.

There was a club in Bridgeport called the Hollywood, where trumpeter and teacher Eddie Antalik held jam sessions on Sunday afternoons. When the Hollywood discontinued this policy, the 616 Club picked it up. Drummer Nate Sussman was the leader of the band there. Some of the fine musicians I jammed with at these two clubs included guitarists Pete Money and Harry Massameano, alto saxophonist Eddie Graff, tenor saxophonist Buddy Arnold, trumpeters Eddie Antalik and Howie Marks, and bassist Larry Marks.

In those days, the American Federation of Musicians, the national musicians' union, was not yet integrated. There were black locals and white locals throughout the country. The Bridgeport black musicians' local held Sunday jam sessions, which I used to attend. The president of the local was a tenor saxophone player named Saxie Ellis. The New Haven local had jam sessions, too, and I attended many of these. I looked forward to those Sunday sessions. It was a chance for me to try out some of the things I had been practicing all week on the tenor and on the piano. It was also a chance for me to play with older, more experienced musicians.

During my high school days, I met up with Larry and Howie Marks from Bridgeport. Larry played bass, and his brother, Howie, played the trumpet. They were grown men. They used me on some of their gigs, and I used them on some of mine. They offered me a lot of encouragement and support in those early days when I was developing my talents. I also met a young black pianist and vibraphonist named John Lewis (not the John Lewis of the Modern Jazz Quartet), a Norwalk resident who had just gotten out of the army. He heard me play, took a liking to me, and helped me a lot. He was the one who turned me on to Lester Young. He, like the Marks brothers, encouraged me. John and I went to a lot of jam sessions together.

There were very few places in Norwalk where we could go and sit in on a jam session. Often, I asked Dad to let me use the car so we could go to Bridgeport or New Haven. I met a very fine pianist from New Haven named Walter Radcliffe. He was a grown man, and I was still a teenager in high school, but we became very good friends, and he was very encouraging to me. He often engaged me to play tenor on weekend gigs with him in New Haven. I would get the train from Norwalk to New Haven after school on Friday, work with him Friday and Saturday nights, and return to Norwalk on Sunday. We played at the Recorders Club, Lillian's Paradise, the Musicians Club, and the Monterey, among others.

Walter lived with his parents, and he had the attic room. I slept in the attic room with him, and we sometimes sat up to the wee hours of the morning, talking about music before we went to sleep. His mother was a great cook, and I enjoyed the food. Saturday mornings we got up, washed up, and went straight to the piano to play for each other and exchange ideas. Then his mother fixed breakfast for us. Saturday afternoons we went to the movies. We both enjoyed cartoons; his favorites were *Looney Toons* and *Bugs Bunny.*

I also hung out and worked with a group of young musicians from Westchester County, New York: bassist Keter Betts, tenor saxophonist Carmen Leggio, drummer Junebug Lindsey, and a few others. Keter went on to work with Earl Bostic and Ella Fitzgerald. Carmen later worked with Gene Krupa. Junebug Lindsey died at an early age. A young alto sax player from Stamford named Clifford Bowen also started a teenage band, with me on piano, John Clayborn on tenor sax, Jimmy Harrison on trombone, Walter Lucas on drums, and some other players. We rehearsed and played stock arrangements bought at the local music store.

Buddy Lucas was a really fine tenor sax player from Stamford who played in Connecticut and New York. He was a great improviser—I always marveled at his improvising skill. He also played harmonica and made many rhythm and blues recordings as a sideman on that instrument. He played out of the Coleman Hawkins school. He often came by our rehearsals and helped us out. Buddy was related to Clifford Bowen and to drummer Walter Lucas. Walter and I were great friends, and I used him on some of the gigs I got with my combo.

When I gigged around Connecticut with some of the other teenage musicians, we got onto a kick of calling each other by our names spelled backward. Walter Bolden on drums was Retlaw Nedlob. Joe Calloway on bass was Eoj Yawollac. I was Ecaroh Revlis. Later on in life, when I started my own music publishing company, I named it Ecaroh Music Inc.

Soon after that, I formed H. W. Revlis Enterprises Inc., a management company to handle my band and its tours.

While in high school, I met Bob Marshall, a young black kid whose family had just moved from Greenwich, Connecticut, to Norwalk. He wasn't a music student, but he loved jazz and collected jazz records like I did. His talent was art, and he drew very well. He was from a large family, and two of his older brothers, Jimmy and Duane, were jazz lovers also. The four of us became real tight buddies, hung out together, and went to all the teenage parties and dances and jam sessions. We were all jazz record collectors, and whenever one of us bought a bunch of new recordings, we'd have what we called "reetee-vootee sessions," a nonsense term we made up ourselves, to listen to our new records at each other's pads. Duane made his transition some years ago. Jimmy lives in Maryland. Bob, who lived in Modesto, California, was my consistent friend and brother from high school onward, one of the four or five best friends I have had in the world. He made his transition recently. I shall miss him.

My friend Larry Marks from Bridgeport put on a jazz concert at Fairfield High School in Fairfield, Connecticut. He engaged some well-known jazz musicians from New York, including Kenny Dorham and Idrees Sulieman on trumpets, Big Nick Nicholas on tenor, Harold Cumberbach on alto, and Jack Parker on drums, as well as guys on bass and piano. He also engaged me to play tenor on this gig. It was quite a thrill for me to play with musicians of this caliber. It was also a bit frightening. Could I match up to their caliber of musicianship?

After the concert was over and all the musicians were waiting offstage to get paid, I walked over to the piano and started playing à la Bud Powell. All the musicians came over and stood around the piano and listened to me play. Kenny Dorham said, "Man, this kid plays the tenor like Lester Young and the piano like Bud Powell." Kenny gave me his address and phone number and told me to call him. He invited me down to New York some Sunday to hang out with him. He wanted to take me to the Audubon Ballroom on a Sunday night, where he played with a big band called the Messengers, led by Art Blakey. This band consisted primarily of musicians who were of the Muslim faith and who had changed their names to Muslim names.

I took him up on his offer and went down to New York to hang with him one Sunday. We had lunch and dinner together, and I went to his gig. I stood backstage in the wings, listening and enjoying the band. Kenny pointed out certain songs the band played that he had arranged. Walter Bishop Jr. was on piano, and I got a chance to meet him and Art Blakey during the intermission. It was a big thrill.

Some time after that, Jack Parker (the drummer from Larry's concert) invited me to play a weekend gig on piano in New York with him and Larry's brother, Howie, on trumpet. I was very excited about it. It was my first time playing in New York City. Howie was living in New York, so I stayed the weekend with him at his apartment. I didn't realize it at the time, but fate was drawing me step by step to eventually wind up living and performing in New York City.

As I mentioned before, the Jimmie Lunceford band was my favorite big band. I saw them at the Apollo Theater, at the Paramount Theater with tap dancer Bill Robinson, and at Loew's State Theater in New York. One day, I read in the Norwalk newspaper that the Lunceford band was to play a dance gig at the Ritz Ballroom in Bridgeport. That was only a half-hour bus ride from Norwalk, so I decided to go. By this time, black customers were allowed in, although they hadn't been when I was a child. The question of admittance now was not a question of color but of age. I was only sixteen years old. Would they admit me? I was tall; that was in my favor. I put on my zoot suit with the peg pants and padded shoulder jacket with the long chain hanging from my waist and wore my pointed-toe shoes and my wide-brim hat. I was looking as hip and as old as Cab Calloway. I got in without any problems.

I went to the Ritz Ballroom not to dance but to listen to the Lunceford band. I positioned myself on the side of the bandstand near the piano player, Edwin Wilcox. I knew the names of every member of the Lunceford band. During the intermission, I conversed with Mr. Wilcox. I told him that I was a piano student and that I loved jazz and wanted to become a jazz musician. He was very encouraging to me. We talked about Art Tatum. The next day, I read in the newspaper that Lunceford was to be interviewed on radio station WICC in Bridgeport. I took the bus over there and waited outside the radio station and got his autograph. My love for Lunceford and the Lunceford band is still intact. I still get inspired when I play some of their old recordings.

I recall playing a dance gig in Port Chester, New York, when I was about sixteen years old. I played tenor, Keter Betts was on bass, Junebug Lindsey was on drums, and Linton Garner (Erroll's brother) was on piano. We had a ball that night. I was so thrilled to be playing a gig with Erroll Garner's brother. Linton is a real fine pianist. He plays in his own style, not emulating his brother. As far as I know, he's still on the planet. I ran into him in Europe several years ago. I hadn't seen him since that night in Port Chester. We had a great get-together and talked a lot about Erroll. I was never influenced by Erroll's playing style, but his genius always inspired me and still does.

WHEN I WAS IN HIGH SCHOOL, I heard about Fifty-second Street in New York. Some simply referred to it as "the Street." One block on East Fifty-second Street had these little basement clubs, one right next door to the other, all up and down the block, where all the great jazz artists performed. They would open for business around ten in the evening and close at four in the morning.

I wanted very much to go and check out this scene, but I knew if I asked Dad, he would say no. I decided to skip school one day and go down to New York and spend the day and evening checking out some great music. I left a note on the kitchen table for Dad to find when he got home from work, saying that I had gone to New York to hear some music and would be back that evening. Although I knew I ran the risk of getting either a whipping or a scolding or both when I got back, I went anyway.

I must have skipped school and gone to New York two or three times during my high school years. I would leave Norwalk on an early morning train, arrive at Grand Central Station, and proceed to check out as many record stores as I could find that carried jazz records. The collection of jazz records in the Norwalk record stores was limited. I did more listening than buying, for my finances were also limited. You could listen to records in a booth before you bought them in those days.

There was a chain of cafeterias in New York called Horn and Hardart, where I always enjoyed eating. They had good food at a reasonable price. I loved their baked bean and hot dog casseroles; they were almost as good as the ones Aunt Maude used to make. I would spend the day in Manhattan record shopping. When evening approached, I'd go up to Harlem and check out a few more record stores before going to the Apollo Theater to catch a show. By the time the Apollo show let out, it was time to go back downtown and hit Fifty-second Street.

At the clubs on Fifty-second Street—places like the Onyx Club, the Three Deuces, the Downbeat, and Ryan's—you could choose to sit at a table or stand at the bar. I chose standing at the bar. It was cheaper. Each club had two bands. A bottle of beer was seventy-five cents. I made one beer last through both sets, and then I moved on to the next club and did the same thing. Some of the musicians I remember hearing on Fifty-second Street included the Lucky Thompson Quartet, the Dexter Gordon Quartet, the Don Byas Quartet, Henry "Red" Allen, Coleman Hawkins, the Charlie Parker Quintet with Miles Davis, Dizzy Gillespie's big band, and Art Tatum.

I especially recall hearing Art Tatum play solo piano at the Downbeat Club. It was obvious that even the bartenders, waiters, cigarette girls, and camera girls all had great respect for Tatum's genius. If people in the audience were talking a bit loud when Art was playing, all the help would ask them to quiet down. Tatum himself sometimes stopped in the middle of a song when the crowd got too loud. He'd just sit there until they realized that they were making too much noise, and then they quieted down. Once they got quiet, he resumed playing.

Watching and listening to Tatum was like watching and listening to a miracle in progress. It was hard to believe that any human being could play with such total mastery. After hearing him perform for the first time,

I got the train back to Norwalk, and all the way home I said to myself, "What am I doing trying to play the piano? I'll never be able to play like that. I might as well quit now." Luckily, I later realized that there were many fine pianists who were not the caliber of Tatum but had something valid of their own to contribute to the world. I made up my mind that I was going to be one of them.

WHEN I WAS A TEENAGER in high school, I came home after school and listened to Symphony Sid's *After School Swing Session* on the radio. He played all the hip jazz records of the day. His real name was Sid Torin. I later became personally acquainted with him when I played at Birdland in New York. He had a jazz program that was broadcast over radio station WJZ. It started at midnight and went to four in the morning. He eventually moved from the studio and did a remote broadcast from Birdland every night. In one corner of the club, they built him a little cubicle where he played records and did his broadcast.

I also listened to Martin Block and *The Make Believe Ballroom.* He broadcast over station WMCA and played mostly recordings of big bands. Another well-known deejay from that era was Freddie Robbins, who had a program known as *Robbins' Nest.* Pianist Sir Charles Thompson wrote a theme song for this show, called "Robbins' Nest," which became a big hit. Also, Al "Jazzbo" Collins had a program, *The Purple Grotto.* Mort Fega and Alan Grant each had a radio program, too. At present, we are blessed here in the Los Angeles area with radio station KKJZ-FM (formerly KLON). One of their deejays, Chuck Niles, reminds me of Symphony Sid. Sid had a deep, beautiful speaking voice, and so does Chuck. Jazz music has been blessed and perpetuated by all these great men.

In those days, the Apollo Theater had an amateur hour every Wednesday night between eleven o'clock and midnight, which was broadcast over the radio. The master of ceremonies was Willie Bryant, who was later replaced by Ralph Cooper. Whatever big band was playing at the theater that week would perform a couple of tunes at the half-hour mark. When a contestant wasn't making it, the audience got restless and sometimes booed. When that occurred, "Porto Rico" came out onstage dressed in some funny costume and danced around the contestant, shooting a blank gun at his or her feet until the contestant stopped singing and walked off the stage. At the same time, a siren screeched from offstage, and the band played some wild background music. Of course, I was not able to observe all this because I was only listening to the radio. But I eventually went to New York and caught the show in person.

One Wednesday evening, I was lying in my bed listening to the Apollo Amateur Hour with the volume on my radio turned down low so Dad couldn't hear it. A young female singer from Newark, New Jersey, was introduced. She sang and accompanied herself on piano. The song she sang was "Body and Soul." She moved the audience so much that they had her come back and sing the same song a second time. She won the contest and was offered a week's work at the Apollo at a future date. She went on to sing with the Earl Hines band and recorded with Dizzy, Tadd Dameron, Stuff Smith, and several others before venturing out on her own. Her name was Sarah Vaughan. The Apollo Amateur Hour was a great spot for unknown talent to be seen on stage and heard on radio. It was a great venue for amateurs to get their start in show business.

DURING WORLD WAR II, a lot of newspaper articles were written about "dive bombers," warplanes that would dive to drop their load of bombs. I decided to put together a four-piece combo and call it Horace Silver and the Jive Bombers. It consisted of John Clayborn on tenor sax, Jimmy Harrison on trombone, Walter Lucas on drums, and myself on piano. All the guys except me were from Stamford, Connecticut. Every Sunday evening in Stamford, there was a basketball game, followed by a dance for the teenagers, where we played. I remember one Sunday, after the gig, one of the big, robust basketball players asked me for a ride home, since he lived on my way home. I was driving, and he was sitting in front next to me. All of a sudden, he started to touch my leg. I was shocked. He was such a big, robust guy; I would never have suspected that he was gay. I explained to him that I had respect for gay people, but it was not my cup of tea. He understood, and everything was cool.

I also had a quartet that worked every Friday and Saturday evening for a while at a black-owned nightclub in South Norwalk called the Silent Four. Comedian Shorty Mathews brought in a floor show from New York every weekend that included a singer and an exotic dancer. Shorty did comedy and was the emcee. My band consisted of John Magruder (who was Caucasian) on tenor and clarinet, Walter Lucas on drums, a bass player, and myself. We had to get to the gig about two hours before it was time to hit, so we could rehearse the floor show. Occasionally these performers had music scores, but most of the time, they just told you what song they wanted you to play for them, what key they wanted it in, and gave you a tempo. This gig was a lot of fun. Shorty had some good jokes, and I remember many of them. I often tell them to my musicians when we are on the road and swapping jokes. Singer Etta Jones used to sing on these shows quite often.

After the Silent Four closed down, another black club opened up, called the White Swan, owned by Mr. Willie Russell. His youngest daughter, Mary, became my girlfriend years later. I also became the godfather of his oldest daughter Wilda's first child, whose name is Allison. She is now married and lives in Paris. Mr. and Mrs. Russell liked me very much. Mrs. Russell used to call me "Nature Boy" because I was into vitamins and health foods. Mary looked a lot like Diahann Carroll and used to get mistaken for her often.

As far as females are concerned, I've had four loves in my life. Two of them came later on, during my adult years. The first two were puppy loves. I was about eleven years old when I was smitten by Nancy Jones. She had buck teeth, but I thought she was the cutest thing in Norwalk. I took her to the Saturday matinee at the Norwalk Theater. We sat and held hands all through the movie. I was about sixteen and in high school when I met Carmel Lawrence. She originally lived in New York but had moved to Norwalk. We became a pair. I remember one day she asked me what I loved the most, music or her. I politely said I loved her, but deep down in my heart I knew that it was Lady Music that I loved the most.

AT THE AGE OF EIGHTEEN, I graduated from Norwalk High School. I worked weekend gigs on piano and tenor whenever they were available. Some weekends, I worked three nights; other weekends, it was only one or two nights. Some weekends, I had no work at all. Dad came to me one day and said that he was in favor of my pursuit of music, but that this meager money I was making on weekends was not enough to put food on our table and I would have to get a day job.

I got a job in East Norwalk at the Crawford and Knapp hat factory, which made felt hats for men. I worked there for several months, and then Dad got me a job at the Norwalk Tire Company, where he was employed. It paid a little more money, but it was much harder work. I came home from work with calluses on my hands and an aching back. I said to myself, "I've got to really get my musical skills together so that I can succeed in music, because I don't want to have to do this kind of work for the rest of my life." There was nothing wrong with this type of work—it was honest labor—but it was backbreaking and not gratifying. I looked at these jobs as temporary until my big break came along and I could immerse myself totally in the big-time music scene.

Although we worked in the same factory, Dad's job started a bit earlier than mine. One morning after Dad left for work, I received a phone call from my good friend drummer Walter Bolden. He was calling from Hartford. He said that a black nightclub there called the Sundown needed a piano player to work with the house trio, because their piano player had quit. Harold Holt was on tenor, and the drummer's name was Smitty. The gig paid fifty dollars a week, not a bad salary in those days. I would work Tuesday through Saturday and have Sunday and Monday off. Walter said that his mother would rent me a room in their home for ten dollars a week.

I said, "Tell them I'll take it." I rushed right to the factory and told them I was quitting my job and then rushed home to rejoice and thank

God for the opportunity to earn my living by doing the thing I enjoyed most—playing music.

Before Dad left the factory for home, someone told him that I had been there and quit my job. He was furious when he came home and started chewing me out. I said, "Before you get all upset, let me tell you that I got another job." I told him the whole story, and he was greatly relieved. All he wanted was to ensure that I was not shiftless and lazy. As long as I had a job, he was happy. I moved on to Hartford around 1946, with his approval. I lived in Hartford for about a year and a half with Walter and his mother and another elderly lady, who also rented a room from Mrs. Bolden.

I look back at my months in Hartford as a happy time. There was a piano in the living room, and Mrs. Bolden allowed me to practice on it. Often on the way home from a gig, I'd buy a pizza and bring it home with me. Mrs. Bolden and the other lady would be sleeping, but Walter would be up. We'd close the kitchen door so we wouldn't wake the two ladies, and we'd listen to Symphony Sid's radio show into the wee hours of the morning, while enjoying a cup of tea and some pizza. Sid played all the hip records of the day. We listened and were inspired by the music and shared our dreams about getting out of Connecticut and going to New York to make it in the big-time music scene.

Chapter Three

LADY MUSIC AND THE MESSENGERS
EARLY ADULT YEARS

To venture forth into new perspectives
takes a bit of courage and some definite objectives.
To keep remaining in the same old rut
can dull your mind and put calluses on your butt.
That initial move is often difficult to make
until some incident helps you to awake
to the fact that there's more living in which you can partake.
So get to crackin', for goodness sake.

MOVING FROM NORWALK TO HARTFORD represented a step upward on the ladder of my career, especially since the musicians in Hartford were more involved in jazz than those in Norwalk. The next step upward on the ladder was to be the Big Apple—New York City.

Several Hartford talents had made it to the big time. Singer Arthur Prysock, who performed with the Buddy Johnson big band, was from Hartford. After he left the band and went out on his own, another Hartford singer, Nolan Lewis, took his place with Buddy's band. Nolan was a fine vocalist, but he had a drug problem, which led to his death. Singer and lyricist King Pleasure was from Hartford, and so was alto saxophonist Gigi Gryce.

Drummer Walter Bolden (whose mother rented me a room), bassist Joe Calloway, and I formed a trio and worked on Sunday afternoons at the Officers' Club at Westover Field in Springfield, Massachusetts, and on Mondays at the Elks Club in Hartford. At the Officers' Club, we backed up singers Larry Darnell and Wynonie Harris. Pianist Mary Lou Williams performed there one Sunday afternoon.

The Sundown Club in Hartford had a floor show on Fridays and Saturdays, usually consisting of a comedian, a singer, and an exotic dancer. Singers Ruth Brown and Little Jimmy Scott appeared frequently. Comedian Spoodee Oddee also performed there quite often. There were a few pimps and prostitutes and drug dealers who hung out in the club. I liked them, and they were very nice to me. King Pleasure also hung out there. He sold drugs and had a lady trickin' for him. I always remembered what my mother once told me. She said, "Don't hang out with people of questionable character, but don't snub them or stick your nose up in the air at them. Always have a smile, a handshake, and a friendly hello for them, and then go on your merry way." This I always did, and they all liked me.

One evening during intermission, I went to the bar to get a Coke, and one of the drug dealers came over to me and said, "Why don't you go out to my car and say hello to Charlie Parker?" I said, "You're puttin' me on. What would Charlie Parker be doing in Hartford?" I went out to his car and, sure enough, Charlie Parker was sitting in the front seat. I went over to the car and introduced myself. He had a stack of Art Tatum records on his lap. We talked for a while, and then I had to go back in the club to play another set. He never came into the club. I presume he just drove up from New York to Hartford with this drug dealer to cop some drugs. It was a thrill to meet him.

Occasionally, they had big bands at the State Theater in Hartford. Lionel Hampton's band played there one week. Every night after his last show at the State Theater, he came to the Sundown Club and sat in and jammed with us. Hamp sure loved to play.

The Sundown engaged tenor saxophonist Lucky Thompson to come up to Hartford as a single attraction, which meant that my trio backed him up. He liked us and said he wanted to use us sometime on one of his gigs. A few weeks later, we received a nice letter from him, but no gig materialized.

About a month later, the Sundown brought tenor saxophonist Stan Getz to Hartford, with my trio backing him up. He also said he'd like to use us sometime. We thought that he was only being polite, like Lucky Thompson. But two weeks later, we received a phone call from him, asking us to join his band in Philadelphia at the Club Harlem.

We were elated. The regular salary for sidemen in those days was one hundred and twenty-five dollars per week. Getz was offering us seventy-five dollars a week. We didn't care. We just wanted to get out of Hartford and get into the heavyweight music scene. We would have paid him for the opportunity to play with him and further our careers if we could have afforded it. This was our introduction to the big time.

Stan Getz was a junkie, a mainliner—he injected heroin directly into a vein ("shooting up," as it's called) instead of "snorting," or inhaling it through the nose. I had been around people who used drugs before, but I had never seen a guy shoot up until I worked with Stan. His wife, Beverly, was a sweet and gentle lady, but she also was hooked on drugs. On the first gig I played with Stan, he borrowed fifty dollars of the seventy-five he paid me and used it to cop some drugs. I never got that money back.

I remember a weekend gig we had sometime later, on Long Island. It was Stan, J. J. Johnson, Walt, Joe, and myself. J. J. met us at the club, and Stan drove me and Walt and Joe to the gig in his station wagon. Every night before the gig, Stan had to stop off in Harlem to cop some drugs. We were late each night because of this. One night, Stan asked Walt to drive, and he got in the backseat and tried to shoot up.

Stan had been advanced most of the money for the gig, but on closing night, he did not have enough money to pay the band. J. J. Johnson was having difficulty getting work in those days. It's a mystery to me why such a great musician would have trouble finding work, but he had a day gig in a defense plant to ensure that he could support his wife and kids. When Stan came to the guys in the band on closing night and said he didn't have enough money to pay us, J. J. became furious. He grabbed

Stan by the neck and shoved him up against the wall and said, "You pay me my money, or I'm gonna kick your ass. I got a wife and kids to support." Stan was frightened. He drove us all to his father's house on Long Island, woke his father up at four o'clock in the morning, and got some money from him.

He paid J. J., but we never got paid. We didn't quit, though; we stayed on because this was our connection to the big time, and we enjoyed playing with Stan. He was a beautiful person and a great musician. He just happened to be hooked on drugs.

Anyhow, Walter, Joe, and I joined Stan Getz in 1949 for our first gig at Club Harlem in Philadelphia. There was a black minister, an evangelist, named Father Divine who had a church in Philadelphia at that time. He did a lot of good for poor people, finding jobs for them and providing them with food and clothing and medical attention when needed. A lot of people didn't like him, though, because he claimed that he was God. He owned two hotels, one called the Divine Tracy, and the other called the Divine Lorraine. In these hotels, all the men were housed on one side and all the women on the other—no intermingling in the rooms. If men and women wanted to intermingle, they had to meet in the lobby or in the cafeteria. Men and women were housed dormitory-style. All slept on cots. Rent was three dollars a week, and you could get a full-course meal in the cafeteria for twenty-five cents.

Walt, Joe, and I stayed at the Divine Tracy during the week we played in the Club Harlem with Stan. The hotel had an old upright piano in the vestibule, right off the lobby, and I practiced there. I met some very interesting people there that week, including a young black girl named Penny, who was studying to become a nurse. I was smitten by her charms and wrote a song for her, which I called "Penny." I recorded it with Stan some months later. My first week in the big time with Stan Getz in Philadelphia was a memorable one.

I RECALL PLAYING A weeklong gig with Stan in Philadelphia at the 421 Club. We opened on a Monday and closed on a Saturday and were scheduled to open at the Flame Show Bar in St. Paul, Minnesota, on Monday of the next week. We closed at midnight on Saturday at the 421 Club, packed our luggage into Stan's station wagon, and proceeded to drive to St. Paul for our Monday opening. We stopped only to get take-out food and gas. We were riding almost constantly for about two and a half days. By the time we arrived in St. Paul, we were exhausted, and we all had sore asses. We had about three hours to check into the hotel, wash up, change clothes, and make it to the gig.

We had a two-week engagement there. I enjoyed the gig, but the weather in St. Paul was brutally cold. Except for going out to eat, I stayed in the hotel all day every day in order to keep warm. George Shearing was working a gig in Minneapolis at that time, and he came over to St. Paul to check us out on his off night. I'll always remember that, because Stan told me that George had liked one of my compositions that we played; it was called "Yeah!" That made my day.

During the two weeks we played there, I couldn't get anything started with any of the chicks. All the young chicks that I hit on were married. I asked one of them why all the young chicks in town were married. She said, "You know, we have some very cold winters, and we need someone to keep us warm."

In those days, none of the jazz groups made enough money to fly a band to a gig. We had to travel by car or station wagon. It was a hard life, but we had plenty of fun. We swapped jazz stories about other musicians and told jokes to pass the time as we drove. We were happy because we were doing the thing we loved to do most—playing jazz music. Of course, every city we played in held the possibility of introducing us to a nice young lady who would help us enjoy our stay there. What more could a young man ask for?

Later on, when I worked at New York's Birdland, after my days with Stan Getz, there were many women, both black and white, who hung out in the club and made themselves available to the musicians. I sampled some of each. I noticed that some of the white women only went for really dark-complexioned black musicians. They didn't go for light-complexioned black musicians who had straight hair, like myself. They wanted a "real nigger," not one that was mixed with other races and had straight hair. I missed out on several nice-looking white ladies that I would have liked to have got next to. Nevertheless, I got my share. I also noticed that some of the black musicians only went out with white women. The black women liked light-complexioned black musicians with straight hair like mine. It seemed that everybody wanted to experience the opposite of what they were.

Interracial couples had been nonexistent in Norwalk. In Hartford, there were a few. In New York, interracial couples were more common. A fine mama was a fine mama to me, white or black. I didn't have any preference and still don't.

I had had sexual relations and had gone steady with many black women, but I had no sexual relations with a white woman until I was in my early twenties and had moved to New York. My first white girlfriend's name was Lauren. Her mother used to go with Dixieland saxophonist Bud Freeman. Lauren was a nice person, and I liked her, but I wasn't in love with her. I had many one-nighters with white women in New York, but I chose Lauren to experience what it was like to go steady with a white woman. There was no physical difference, aside from one's skin being black and one's skin being white. But there was a vast difference in the way you were treated, especially by white society. The majority of white people did not approve of mixed couples and would try to make things as difficult as possible for them. Black society was a bit more liberal about the situation, but not totally.

WHEN WALT, JOE, AND I were working with Stan, we played a week at the High Hat Club in Boston. Alto saxophonist Gigi Gryce, who was also a composer and arranger, was living in Boston at that time. Gigi had lived in Hartford before I arrived on the scene, and both Walt and Joe knew him. They arranged for the three of us to stay at Gigi's pad for the week, rent-free. It was the dead of winter—snow on the ground and temperatures down to almost freezing. On the third night at Gigi's apartment, the central heating system broke down. The only heat we had was from the oven of the gas stove in the kitchen. We kept the stove lit and the oven door open, and we all huddled around it to keep warm.

We told Stan about Gigi being a fine composer and arranger. Stan called a rehearsal that week and told us to have Gigi come by and bring some of his music. Gigi made the rehearsal with us and brought several of his tunes. Stan tried them out and liked them. He eventually recorded some of them.

Gigi and I were great friends. Gigi and Lucky Thompson were the only black musicians who had their own publishing company in those days. Gigi turned me on to publishing, and I immediately started my own company, calling it Ecaroh Music Inc. Whenever I had a publishing or copyright problem, I'd call Gigi, and he'd tell me what I should do. I own one hundred percent of the rights to all my compositions, except for three: "Opus de Funk," "Buhaina," and "Silverware." I hope I'll be able to get those three back into my possession in the future.

Fellow musicians, please be alert when signing contracts. Be sure to read the fine print. Have a lawyer look over the contract before you sign it. The music business is filled with unscrupulous people who are out to take advantage of you. Be alert—don't be paranoid, but be alert. Stand up for your rights, but by no means allow yourself to become bitter when they are abused. To become bitter is only to hurt yourself. Do the best you can to protect your rights, and forgive those who abuse them. Have sympathy for them, for they are building bad karma for themselves. We reap what we sow.

AFTER PHILADELPHIA AND ST. PAUL, one of the first gigs I worked with Stan Getz was at the Blue Note Club in downtown Chicago, in a section they call the Loop. We worked there for two weeks. It was a five-day week, with Monday and Tuesday off. Eddie South, who was called the "Dark Angel of the Violin," played opposite us. He was a great violinist, a great technician, and classically trained. I always liked his playing, but it was

Stuff Smith's violin that knocked me out the most. Stuff was more nitty gritty, more down to earth.

Walter, Joe, and I took advantage of our two days off to go hang out on the South Side, where all the black nightclubs were. Chicago was really jumpin' in those days. Great music all over town. We heard Stuff Smith and his group. He invited us to sit in with him. We heard Sun Ra, Johnny Griffin, and Horace Henderson's band with Floyd Smith on guitar. Floyd later joined Wild Bill Davis's organ group. We went to the Saturday night–Sunday morning breakfast show at the Club De Lisa. Drummer Red Saunders had the band there. I met and became friendly with his pianist, Earl Washington.

When I returned to Chicago some years later with the Jazz Messengers, I met pianist and composer Ronnell Bright, and we became good friends. I also met John Pate, a bassist and arranger; bassist Wilber Ware; tenor saxophonist John Gilmore; Clifford Jordan; Eddie Harris; and many other great Chicago musicians. I don't know what the jazz climate is like in Chicago today, but it sure was on fire in the early 1950s.

WHEN I PLAYED THE APOLLO THEATER in Harlem with Stan Getz, he had to put together a big band for the occasion. Our regular working band was only a quintet. Harry "Sweets" Edison and Al Perchino were in the trumpet section of the big band Stan assembled. The saxophone section had Al Cohn and Zoot Simms on tenors and Gerry Mulligan on baritone. Jimmy Raney was on guitar.

In those days, some of the older, more experienced musicians gave the younger, inexperienced musicians a hard time, especially if the younger guys fell a little short in their performance. For the Apollo gig, the band had to play for a Chinese juggling act. Walter had never had this type of experience before, and he was missing a lot of cues he was supposed to catch. Sweets Edison loud-talked him in front of all the other musicians and embarrassed him. Drummer Shadow Wilson was working with Erroll Garner on the show. Because he was an older, more experienced drummer, they got him to play behind the Chinese juggling act. While the movie was being shown, I happened to walk backstage and caught Walt crying. He was so embarrassed, and his feelings were hurt.

The Apollo had a theme song, which was "I May Be Wrong, But I Think You're Wonderful." I was trying to learn how to arrange but had no formal training in arranging. I decided to arrange one chorus of this tune and bring it in to see whether Stan would try it out. He decided to use it. We played it as an opening theme during the list of coming attractions on screen. Sweets said to Stan, "Man, why do we have to play this arrangement? Everybody else jams this tune when they play here." Stan said, "Play it. I want it played."

There was a trombone player in the band named Mr. Chambers—I didn't know his first name—who had worked with many of the great black big bands of that era. He came to me backstage one afternoon while the movie was showing and took me over to his music stand. He said, "Horace, you've written the trombone out of its range in this measure. The trombone doesn't go down that low." I thanked him and made the correction on his part. He could have loud-talked me in front of the whole band and embarrassed me like Sweets did to Walt, but he was kind and considerate. He knew that we were just youngsters on the scene getting our feet wet, and he wasn't about to dampen our spirits. He was there to help us and encourage us and share his knowledge with us.

Often, as a young musician in my early twenties, I would get real nervous when one of the great piano players would come into a club where I was playing. I would say to myself, "Aw, shit, so-and-so is in the house listening. I've got to try to play my best." Consequently, I would tense up and not play as well. I wasn't cured of the affliction until years later, when both Bud Powell and Erroll Garner came into Birdland one night while I was playing. I got all tensed up, and I couldn't play relaxed. Then, at one point, I happened to look up from the piano and gaze over at the bar. They weren't even listening. They were hittin' on some chicks at the bar. Tryin' to cop. That cured me. From that moment on, I said to myself, "If they like what I'm playing, fine. If not, screw 'em." That was my attitude then and still is. I meant no disrespect, but I resolved not to allow the presence of an older, famous pianist to interfere with the caliber of my performance.

STAN GETZ WAS one hell of a musician. When one of the alto players in the band was late for our rehearsal, Stan transposed the alto part, playing it on his tenor, and didn't miss a note. He could play his ass off in any key. He had great harmonic knowledge and a command of the horn from top to bottom. He also had great technique.

On one of the record sessions I did with Stan, he was lacking a tune to complete the session. I suggested a song written by a piano player friend of mine from New Haven named Count Steadwell. When I played it for Stan, he liked it and recorded it. The tune didn't have a name, so we called it "Tootsie Roll." However, Stan got sole composer credit on the recording, a common practice in those days. Count Steadwell could have made it in the big time. He had that kind of talent, but he got married too young and had kids and was obligated to support them. He wound up working in the post office. When I saw what happened to him, I said to myself, "I've got to make my mark in music first before I marry and raise a family." Lady Music always came first in my life.

During the time I worked with Stan, he recorded three of my tunes. One was "Split Kick," which has a straight-ahead kind of melody, but with a Latin beat, and the solos are all straight-ahead 4/4. That's why I called it "Split Kick." "Split Kick" and "Penny" featured Stan on tenor, Walter Bolden on drums, Joe Calloway on bass, and myself on piano. "Potter's Luck" featured Stan on tenor, Jimmy Raney on guitar, Tommy Potter on bass, Roy Haynes on drums, and myself on piano. The tune was dedicated to bassist Tommy Potter.

Walt and Joe left Stan after about six months with the band. I stayed on for another six months, during which I got a chance to play with a lot of other great musicians who came into the band, such as Jimmy Raney, Tommy Potter, drummers Tiny Kahn and Roy Haynes, and bassist Charlie Mingus.

I remember an incident that happened in Birdland when Mingus was the bass player in Stan's group. Stan was taking a solo when all of a sudden he injected a quotation of the verse from "Ol' Man River"—the words go, "Darkies all work on the Mississippi, / Darkies all work while the white folks play." Stan played that in his solo, not thinking about a racial thing, but Mingus was supersensitive about race, so he took offense. While the other band was on, he went across the street to Colony Records and asked the guy behind the counter to play a recording of "Eli, Eli," a Jewish folk song. The guy played it for him, and Charles memorized it and came back to Birdland. In the next set, he included that in his solo, as if he was getting even with Stan for playing "Darkies all work on the Mississippi." I don't think he mentioned it to Stan, and I don't think Stan even noticed.

THE UPPER EAST SIDE of Manhattan, where the wealthy resided, was considered the "high society" part of New York. Stan wanted to get a gig there, at a jazz club called the Roundtable, which featured mostly piano trios—soft, polite jazz that people could talk over. The music was background for talking and dining. The gig paid pretty good money.

The Roundtable's regular band or trio was off on Sundays, so Stan got a gig there on a Sunday night. He called me to make the gig with him. It was sort of like an audition for the band—if they liked us, they would hire us for a two-week engagement. Stan asked me to call Art Blakey and see if he would play with us. I called Art, and he agreed to make it.

I remember that there were several famous actors in the house that night, among them John Carradine, Cesar Romero, and Sir Cedric Hardwick. Stan tried to subdue the volume of his playing all night long. He even stuffed a towel into the bell of his horn so he wouldn't sound too loud. He really wanted to get that gig. But he could never subdue his great ability to play the horn, for he was a natural-born genius.

However, anybody who knew Art Blakey knows he never subdued his playing for anybody. He cooked wherever he played—east side, west side, Greenwich Village, Harlem—he took care of business and cooked, no pussy-footin' around. Needless to say, we didn't get that gig. The band was too loud.

I, for one, was glad we didn't get the gig. Although the money was good, it would have been a miserable two weeks for me if we had had to subdue our music to accommodate the talking in the audience. There were several clubs in New York during those days that catered to soft, watered-down jazz. People came there to talk and eat, not to listen to the music. I played a few of them but never enjoyed it. I preferred to play at a club such as Birdland, where people came to hear the music.

One day, Stan came to me and said that pianist Al Haig was coming back with the band. I was put on two weeks' notice. I didn't feel bad about it. By this time, I had met a lot of great musicians in jazz and become friends with many of them, so I knew I would get another gig.

I decided to make my home in New York City and apply for my Local 802 union card. I started looking for a place to live. John Tucker, a friend from Norwalk who was a big jazz fan, had a sister named Laura who lived in the Bronx. He asked her to rent me a room in her apartment at 189th Street and Boston Road, and I ended up living there for the next few years.

In those days, you had to show proof of residence for six months in New York City before Local 802 would issue you a union card. During that time, you could play only one night a week. I had a little money saved up for this, and I was lucky enough to get a gig in Carteret, New Jersey, at a little hole-in-the-wall black club with a guitar player named Billy Avant. We worked weekends, and the gig paid ten dollars a night. I made thirty dollars a weekend. Billy took two dollars of that from each band member for gas. He drove us from Manhattan to Carteret and back, with a tenor player named Bow McKane and a drummer named Chink. We had to play floor shows. Billy did the comedy and emcee bit, and we had a singer and an exotic dancer. This little bit of money kept me from having to dig too deeply into the money I had saved to get me through the waiting period. Anyway, I had a reputation for being rather tight with a buck in those younger days. I'm a Virgo, and Virgos are rather frugal. Art Blakey used to say, "Horace don't spend nothin' but a lovely evenin'."

Bow McKane was working on and off with Art Blakey's little nine-piece dance band. He came to me one day and said that Art was looking for a new piano player for the band and that he had told Art about me. I was very nervous at rehearsal, so nervous that I was sweating. I could read music, but my reading was slow. I wasn't a hell of a sight reader. In later years, whenever I'd work with Art, he'd tease me about this. The band consisted of Ray Copeland on trumpet, a cat named Rasheed on trombone, Sahib Shihab on alto, Bow McKane on tenor, a cat named Fletcher on baritone, Gary Mapp on bass, Sabu Martinez on conga, myself on piano, and Art on drums. Ray Copeland did most of the arrangements. We were a good band, and the arrangements were good, but we couldn't get much work, except for a few ballroom dances around New York. The band eventually broke up because of lack of work.

Between the time I left the Stan Getz band in 1951 and eventually joined the Jazz Messengers in 1954, I played many gigs around New York City, with many different musicians. Those were happy days. All my days were happy as long as I was playing with the cats and I was playing the music I loved. I enjoyed working with tenor saxophonist Big Nick Nicholas at the Paradise Bar on 110th Street and Eighth Avenue. Berney Peacock, an alto saxophonist, had a quartet that included Teddy Stewart on drums (Teddy used to work with Dizzy Gillespie's big band), Ted Sturgis on bass, and myself on piano. Tenor saxophonist King Curtis, bassist Jimmy Lewis, a drummer, and I worked for a while at a bar located on Sixth Avenue near Forty-second Street. The bar featured B-girls, and we played for dancing. Many soldiers and sailors came in to buy these girls drinks and dance with them.

I played a weekend gig in Newark, New Jersey, with Lou Donaldson and another weekend gig on Long Island with Johnny Hodges, Sonny Greer on drums, and Lloyd Trotman on bass. I worked a variety of weekend gigs in Brooklyn with Brooklyn-based musicians such as trumpeter Kenny Dorham, baritone saxophonist Cecil Payne, alto saxophonist

Ernie Henry, trumpeter Ray Copeland, and drummer Willie Jones, to name a few.

Around that time, I met a young black soldier named Fred, who had just gotten out of the army. He lived in the Bronx. He was a jazz fan and often hung out at some of the clubs where I worked. He was dating a very pretty eighteen-year-old girl named Diahann Carroll. Her mother had strict rules about him taking her out; he had to agree to bring her home at a very early hour. I was working with Big Nick Nicholas at a club located somewhere in the forties off Broadway, and Fred and Diahann came by to check us out. Diahann sat in and sang a few numbers. She broke it up. She was completely unknown at that time, but the audience loved her. I knew that night that she was destined for stardom. She had that certain something, that indescribable something that said "Star." And, of course, she did later become a big star as a vocalist and an actress. She married Monty Kay, who used to manage the Modern Jazz Quartet.

DURING THIS PERIOD, I had the honor of working with the great tenor saxophonist Coleman Hawkins on a few occasions. I played with him twice at Birdland in September 1952 and did a few dance gigs with him around New York. One of the weeks at Birdland included Roy Eldridge on trumpet, Curly Russell on bass, and Art Blakey on drums. The other week included Howard McGhee on trumpet, Curly Russell on bass, and Arthur Taylor on drums.

I would often quote other songs in my solos. I got this from hearing Art Tatum do it on his trio recordings. I remember that on one of the gigs I played with Hawk, I quoted an old Fletcher Henderson song in my solo. Hawk was quite surprised that a young man in his early twenties would know that song. What he didn't know was that I was an avid listener of all the older jazz recordings and had a pile of old tunes stored in my head.

In the following year, 1953, I also had the honor of working with the great Lester "Prez" Young, my model on tenor sax. Prez was an innovator on the tenor, but he also created many of the slang words and phrases that a lot of jazz musicians later used. He was the most unique and original man I ever met. Thelonious Monk was unique and original, but I think Prez was even more so. His playing, his speech, his dress were all unique.

When I worked with Lester Young, he told me some stories about when he worked with Fletcher Henderson's band. He said that when he stood up to take a solo, some of the other musicians in the band whispered behind his back and made fun of him because he didn't have that Coleman Hawkins type of big, heavy tone. His sound and approach were lighter. This really hurt Lester. Fletcher Henderson's wife, who played trumpet, woke Lester up every morning at nine o'clock and played Coleman Hawkins records for him, telling him that this was the way he should sound. Prez would say, "That's all right for Coleman Hawkins, but this is Lester." Thank God, he had enough faith in himself to stick to his approach to the horn. If he hadn't, we would never have enjoyed the talents of his disciples, musicians such as Stan Getz, Gene Ammons, Dexter Gordon, Al Cohn, Zoot Simms, Allen Eager, Brew Moore, Lee Konitz, Gerry Mulligan, and many more. Prez was and still is a source of great inspiration to me. He was one of my main mentors.

He also had a great sense of humor. He kept his sidemen laughing all the time. Prez told me a story about when he was in the army. He and some other privates were standing at attention while their sergeant was chewing them out. When the sergeant finished, he said, "Anyone who doesn't agree with what I just said, take two paces forward." Prez was the only one to do so. As a result, he was put into detention barracks. Many of the men had been in there for quite some time and were sex-starved, so much so that some of them were having intercourse with each other. He said, "But not me, Prez. I'd get up in my little upper berth and crawl under the covers and get myself a deuce of helpings of hand."

When I worked with Prez, Jessie Drake was on trumpet, Franklin Skeets on bass, and Connie Kay on drums. Prez called everybody "lady," both men and women, except on occasions when he called people by his own nickname, Prez. Of course, he was the first to call Billie Holiday

"Lady Day." Jessie was "Lady Drake," Connie Kay was "Lady Kay." He called Franklin Skeets "Mrs. Mirrortop" because he had a bald head. He called me "Lady Horoscope." When I started my first quintet, I told the guys in the band that Prez used to call me "Lady Horoscope." They used that name for a while and then they shortened it to "Scope." One night when Prez wanted Skeets to take a bass solo, he looked over at him and said, "Put me in the basement, Prez." Skeets proceeded to solo and then started to sum up his solo and go back to playing time. Prez must have liked what Skeets was playing, because he looked over at him and said, "Don't stop now, Prez, take another helping."

Birdland's doorman and master of ceremonies, Pee Wee Marquette, always expected the musicians to tip him on pay night for announcing their names on stage throughout the week. Pee Wee was a midget. Harold Nicholas, of the Nicholas Brothers tap dancing team, who was a short man, used to give Pee Wee all his old clothing, and Pee Wee had it altered to fit him. Anyhow, some of the musicians would try to sneak out after they got paid and not give Pee Wee a tip. If he caught you sneaking out, he would loud-talk you. One night, Pee Wee was hassling Prez for a tip. Prez said to him, "Get away from me, you little half-a-motherfucker."

I have a cassette copy of a 1957 interview Prez did in his hotel room in Paris. He didn't usually grant interviews to the press. The interviewer asked Prez if he enjoyed doing a guest solo spot in front of the Count Basie band at the Newport Jazz Festival. His reply was, "I always bust my nuts when I play with them." If you weren't familiar with his slang terminology, you often wouldn't know what he was talking about. He always remained himself, never altering to fit convention.

Prez never called tunes by their original names—he always retitled a song. He called "Three Little Words" "Three Little Turds." He called "All of Me" "Oil of Me." He had a tune that he wrote and recorded called "D.B. Blues." The D.B. stood for "Dirty Bitch." When Prez said, "I feel a draft," that meant he felt uncomfortable about something. When he was preparing to go to Europe on a tour, he would say, "I'm goin' across the pond, Prez." He called a chorus a "lung"; "two lungs" meant he was going to play two choruses. He called pot "Edis," and he called a woman's vagina her "hat."

I recall playing a week in Cleveland with my quintet at the Modern Jazz Room some years later. Prez was an added attraction on the bill. The quintet played twenty minutes, and then my horn players (Hank Mobley and Art Farmer) stepped down, and Prez came up and played twenty minutes with our rhythm section. The club had a tiny little dressing room for the band. There was not room enough for six people. Prez had his horn lying on a small table in the room. Hank Mobley came into the room, looking for a place to lay his horn down. After observing that there was no place for it, he turned and started out of the room. Prez said to Hank, "Lady Hank, come on and lay your peoples next to mine." Prez was so soulful.

Pianist Bobby Scott told me another story about Prez. Bobby was doing a tour with Jazz at the Philharmonic, and Prez was on tour. Prez was on stage with the Oscar Peterson group, and they were playing "I Can't Get Started." Oscar started using substitute chord changes that the beboppers used on this tune. Prez was not familiar with these changes, so he leaned over into the curve of the piano and said, "Lady Pete, where you motherfuckers at?" Prez didn't realize that there was a mike in the piano, and it picked up everything he said. The audience heard his comment and burst into laughter.

MANY OF MY MUSICIAN FRIENDS had nicknames for me back in the old days. Stan Getz used to call me "Funky Butt" because I played funky. Bassist Major Holly called me "Cooker and Burner" because I cooked and burned at the piano. Bassist Percy Heath still calls me "Horatio Piano Blower." My friends Red Holloway and Cedar Walton refer to me as "Horatio," and some of my Latin friends use "Horacio." Whatever my friends call me, I know they all love me, and I love them.

I also had nicknames for some of them: "Arturo Tosca Farmer" for Art Farmer, "Wado" (short for Edwardo) for Eddie Harris, "Red Man" for Red Holloway. All the cats used to call Kenny Dorham "K. D." and

Oscar Pettiford "O. P." Of course, everybody knows that Charlie Parker was called "Bird." Lester Young was called "Prez," and Coleman Hawkins was called "Hawk" and sometimes "Bean." Milt Jackson was "Bags," and Kenny Clarke was "Klook." Jazz musicians always found a loving nickname for you if they liked you and had respect for your talent.

All the cats dug the way I comped behind them. I always tried to get up under them and push them, to provide a great rhythmic and harmonic background that would inspire them to play their best and, above all, to swing. Many fine piano players of that era gave weak support to soloists, preferring to save most of their energy for their own solo spot. I wanted to put all of my energy in the song we were playing from start to finish, not just when it was time for me to solo. Rhythm and blues saxophonist Wild Bill Moore, who played the saxophone on Marvin Gaye's record "What's Goin' On," used to hang out at Birdland. He was always on the scene when we played there. When we got to cookin' and burnin', he would come over to the piano and holler, "Give 'em hell, Silver, give 'em hell!" That always inspired me to pump a little harder.

My piano influences started with boogie-woogie and the blues and then went on to include Art Tatum, Teddy Wilson, Nat "King" Cole, Bud Powell, and Thelonious Monk. I then blended some of Hawk, Prez, Bird, Diz, and Miles into my piano concept. In 1988, I interviewed the Modern Jazz Quartet on a one-hour radio program I had in Los Angeles every Friday evening, called *Music and Metaphysics*. I asked John Lewis how he came to formulate his unique piano style. What piano players influenced him? He said none. He wanted to play the piano like Lester Young played the saxophone. It's interesting to note how some horn players have influenced piano players and helped them to create a totally different concept on the piano: Louis Armstrong and Earl Hines, Charlie Parker and Bud Powell, Lester Young and John Lewis, John Coltrane and McCoy Tyner.

I do a lot of quoting in my solos—that's the one thing I got from Art Tatum. I loved Tatum's playing, but he was so swift, technically, that I couldn't copy a lot of his shit. With other piano players, like Teddy Wilson, for instance, I could copy their shit off of records, but I couldn't copy

Tatum—he went by so fast I couldn't catch it. But the quotations, that's the one thing I got from him. Especially when he had the trios, like the one with Tiny Grimes on guitar and Slam Stewart on bass, he quoted a lot of other songs in his solos. That was the first time I had ever heard anyone do that.

I don't think about it or plan it when I quote other songs. When the chord changes come up and I hear something that fits, I just play it. I won't mention any names, but I had a trumpet player once—a good player, too; I wouldn't have hired him if he wasn't good—who did a summer gig with us. He heard me doing a lot of that stuff, so he tried to do it, too. But he would goof it off—he would play the quotation but wouldn't make it fit the chord. He'd play the quotation straight, even if the whole thing wouldn't fit the chord changes, so it would sound out to lunch. If you're going to quote another song in a solo, either it's got to fit the changes completely, or, if it doesn't, you've got to alter it to make it fit, and that's what he didn't do.

I love Latin music, black gospel music, and Broadway show music. These also influenced my piano style and my composing, which are a conglomeration of many different influences.

I love the pianistics of Ahmad Jamal. When he interprets a standard composition, he really gives it a thorough workout. When he finally finishes his interpretation of it, there's not much more that can be done with it. Another thing I like about Ahmad is that he has a great deal of technique but doesn't flaunt it. He leaves space in the music.

I first heard Oscar Peterson on a record on a jukebox at the Open Door Club in Greenwich Village. I used to play there with various groups on Sunday nights. Oscar had a hit recording of "Tenderly" that just knocked me out. My quintet played opposite his trio at a jazz festival in Pittsburgh once. He had Ray Brown on bass, and they were burnin'. I've always admired Oscar's mastery of the instrument. He's a great musician and a great guy.

The first time my quintet played opposite Bill Evans and his trio was on a gig at a club in Newark. We later played opposite him and his trio several times at the Village Vanguard in New York City. I've always admired his playing and his style. I love the way he voices his harmony. He's one of the great ones.

My friend Dick La Palm, who used to be Nat Cole's road manager, told me that Nat loved a song I wrote called "The Jody Grind." This knocked me out because Nat was one of my piano influences and an inspiration. When I was a teenager, I copied his solo on "Body and Soul" note for note and played it at all the jam sessions I attended.

I can recall going to the Village Gate with my wife, later in my career, to catch the piano duo of Willie "the Lion" Smith and Don Ewell. They had two grand pianos back to back, and they were cookin'. Roy Eldridge came in, pulled out his trumpet, and sat in with them. Don Ewell evidently was familiar with me and my music—after spotting me in the audience, he went to the microphone and asked me to come up and play a tune. I went up and played "Serenade to a Soul Sister." After the set was over, I got a chance to meet the Lion. He asked me if I had ever met Duke Ellington. I said, "No, but Duke has always been one of my inspirations." He said that I should meet Duke because both Duke's music and mine were very spiritual. I was thrilled to be compared to the great maestro. I have tried and will continue to try to live up to that comparison.

I should add that I have always had certain favorite pianists, even though they may not have influenced my style as directly: bebop pianist Al Haig was certainly one, along with Hank Jones, Tommy Flanagan, Ray Bryant, Barry Harris, Duke Jordan, Hampton Hawes, and Cedar Walton. There were also some excellent female jazz piano players back in the old days, namely, Beryl Booker, Patty Bowen, Mary Lou Williams, Marian McPartland, Dorothy Donegan, Hazel Scott, and Valerie Capers. There were others, but these are the ones I knew and remember. Marian McPartland and Valerie Capers are still with us; I'm not sure about Patty Bowen. There were so many great piano players in those days. They all deserve to be remembered for their contribution to the music. There are quite a few great ones today also. Thank God for all the great musicians and composers who have given and continue to give us so much.

WHILE LIVING IN THE BRONX in Laura Tucker's apartment, I often worked at Birdland on Monday nights, which was their off night. Birdland was a cellar club located on Fifty-second Street and Broadway. The regular show ran from Tuesday through Sunday. Monday night was the off night when they put together different musicians to jam. I played in many of these jam sessions. I had to take a bus across town to the subway and then take the train downtown. There were four musicians I often ran into on the train on my way home from the gig. One was Tiger Haynes, guitarist and singer, who later became an actor. He used to work in the Village with a trio called the Three Flames. We talked music from Manhattan up to the Bronx. Another was Eugene Cedric, who once played tenor and clarinet with Fats Waller. I'd run into Ray Barretto on the train many mornings, and we would also talk music. I also used to see guitarist Jimmy Shirley, who worked with the Herman Chittison Trio.

Oscar Goodstein, the manager of Birdland and also Bud Powell's manager, liked me because I was a disciple of Powell, because I played well, and because he was fascinated to find that I was a clean-cut young man who didn't smoke, drink, or do drugs—unusual for a jazz musician in those days. (My only vice was the ladies, and I had plenty of them.) Oscar and his wife took a liking to me and treated me very kindly.

There was no piano at Laura Tucker's apartment in the Bronx, so I asked Oscar if I could come down to Birdland during the day and practice there. He said yes but told me to call first and ask the cleanup man if any band was there rehearsing; if not, I could come down and practice. I would practice amid the clamor of the cleanup man vacuuming and throwing out empty beer and whiskey bottles. Years later, I read an article by Chick Corea in a jazz magazine in which he said he was walking down Broadway one afternoon during this period and passed by Birdland and heard someone playing the piano. He walked in and sat at the back of the club and listened to me practice. I was totally unaware of his presence.

Whenever there was an opening in one of the bands at Birdland, Oscar tried to fit me in. I am very grateful for all the help he gave me during those early years of my career. I worked at Birdland with Slim Gaillard's group and Chubby Jackson's group, which included Serge Chaloff on baritone sax, Bill Harris on trombone, Ed Shaughnessy on drums, myself on piano, and Chubby on bass. I also worked there with a group led by baritone saxophonist Gerry Mulligan and tenor saxophonist Brew Moore. Gerry and Brew were into the beatnik thing in those days. They both had long hair and were unshaven and dressed in a beatnik manner. One night, Oscar told them that if they didn't get a haircut and a shave and wear a tie, not to bother coming in the next night. They complied.

When I played Birdland with Slim Gaillard, singer Arthur Prysock was also on the bill. He had a young bebop piano player accompanying him. Arthur had a blues number in which his pianist was playing the bebop turnaround, which Arthur didn't want. He asked me to play for him on that particular song every show, which I did. He was a great singer and a wonderful person.

I met singer and guitarist Jackie Paris, and we became friends. He liked the way I comped. We used to hang out after my gig at Birdland and go to the Ham and Eggery to have breakfast and talk music until the sun came up. My quintet played opposite the Billy Taylor Trio several times at Birdland. Billy had Earl May on bass and Charlie Smith on drums. Charlie and I also hung out at the Ham and Eggery after hours. As for Billy Taylor, I've always admired his mastery of the instrument. He also has become an ambassador of our music, speaking out for the cause of jazz throughout the world. We all owe him a debt of thanks for this.

I miss hanging out after the gig in New York and unwinding and having breakfast with a fellow musician and talking music. In L.A., where I live now, we can't do that. There's nowhere to hang out. You have to go straight home.

Birdland always featured two groups and sometimes three on their weekly program. Sometimes they ran a show for two weeks, but they usually changed shows every week. I worked there frequently during the summer months. Often, after my set, when the other band took over, I walked up and down Broadway to stretch my legs and get some fresh air. I recall doing this one evening and running into bassist Charlie Mingus and two white policemen having a confrontation. Mingus had been stopped by the policemen not because he had broken any law, but because he and several of his black male friends were in his car with a white woman, who happened to be Mingus's wife. Mingus saw me and shouted, "Horace Silver, I want you to witness that these men are un-American. They want to arrest me because my wife is white."

I knew if I got involved in the situation, I probably would wind up at the nearest precinct station along with them and would miss my next set at Birdland, so I ignored him and kept walking. Mingus held that against me for about two years after that. Every time he saw me, he would say, "You didn't support me when I needed your help." He finally forgave me. Mingus was very adamant about racial situations and was very outspoken about the way he felt. This put him in jeopardy when confronted by the police, because he didn't bite his tongue about the way he felt.

Sunday night was pay night at Birdland, and all the musician junkies in town knew this. Besides having Pee Wee Marquette, the master of ceremonies and doorman, hit on you for a tip for announcing your name from the stage every night, you had to face all these junkies outside the club at four A.M., asking you for money. They would always say, "Can you loan me five or ten dollars until my check comes in? I'll pay you back." I knew I would never get paid back if I loaned them any money, but I would usually give them something anyway. They were a pathetic lot, and I felt sorry for them. Once, I happened to tell Pee Wee that the band and I were getting ready to do a European tour and that we had several gigs in Italy. He asked me to bring him back an Italian switchblade knife for protection when he left the club at four A.M. I brought one back and gave it to him as a gift.

Bassist Curly Russell told me a story about Pee Wee Marquette. When Pee Wee lived at the Theresa Hotel in Harlem, Curly lived there, too, and had the room next to Pee Wee. Curly said that one night he heard some banging up against the wall coming from Pee Wee's room. He put his ear to the wall and heard Pee Wee say, "Put me down, bitch, I'm gonna pay ya."

When I couldn't practice at Birdland, I would go down to Harlem to a little dumpy place called Newby's Studio. Newby's had three or four little rooms with old, beat-up upright pianos in them. They charged fifty cents an hour for practice time. It was at Newby's Studio that I met Arthur Woods. We became great friends. He was not a professional musician, but he loved jazz and tried to play the alto sax. He worked a day gig downtown in a motion picture distributing company. He knew all the cats personally and hung out at all the jazz scenes. He hung out with Bird, Sonny Rollins, and Bud Powell. He and Bud used to go to the movies together. He said Bud liked cowboy movies. Art and I had one thing in common: we both loved jazz with a passion. Art often came by my pad to listen to records, or we'd go out to hear some live music or go to dinner and a movie. Our conversation was always about jazz and jazz people. We had a lot of fun together. I've lost contact with him through the years, but wherever he is, I wish him well.

I remember hearing Harry Belafonte sing at Birdland years ago. This was before Harry got into singing calypso music. He was singing standards at that time. Bud Powell accompanied him at the piano. One of the songs he sang was called "Say It Over and Over Again." It was from an old Jack Benny movie. Jack was one of my favorite comedians. I loved his radio programs and his TV programs, but somehow his movies didn't make it for me. Harry Belafonte and Sidney Poitier had a barbecue rib joint uptown in Harlem in those days, and I went there one night and had dinner. Harry was behind the counter, serving ribs.

LIVING IN THE BRONX at 189th Street and Boston Road was nice, but it took too long to get downtown to Manhattan and the Village, where most of the happenings were. I decided I wanted to move downtown. I happened to be walking across West Twenty-fifth Street one day in 1954 and spotted the Arlington Hotel. I went in and inquired about their rates and found them within my means. I moved into the Arlington and lived there for about four years. Many of my early compositions were written there, such as "Doodlin'," "The Preacher," "Room 608" (which was my hotel room number), "Nica's Dream," and many more.

Pianist Duke Jordan and his wife, Sheila, a jazz singer, lived around the corner from the Arlington. When they separated and Duke moved out, Sheila bought a new piano and wanted to get rid of her old upright. When she offered it to me, I gratefully accepted. I went to the hotel manager and asked him if I could have a piano in my room. He said yes, as long as I didn't practice after nine P.M. I hired a piano mover and had the piano moved in.

I introduced several of my musician friends to the Arlington Hotel. Bassist Doug Watkins and trumpeters Art Farmer, Donald Byrd, and Miles Davis all stayed there at some point. Miles used to come to my room and show me certain voicings on the piano. The first two chords of "Nica's Dream" came from some voicings he showed me. I've learned something from every one of the great musicians I've had the privilege of working with, but I can honestly say that I think I learned more from Miles than from anyone else. Some things he showed me, and some things I learned just by observing. He was a great teacher.

I'll always remember two great compliments that Miles Davis paid me. My quintet was playing Birdland, and Miles came in to check us out. The quintet was cookin', and the rhythm section was on fire. When we came off the bandstand, Miles came over to me and said that drummer Louis Hayes and I were thoroughbreds. Miles's father owned and bred horses, and Miles knew a lot about the subject, so that was a great compliment. Another time, the quintet was playing at Basin Street, and Miles came in. I had just written "Doodlin'," and we played it for the first time that night. Miles came up to me after the set and said, "Man, that tune 'Doodlin'' is so funky. If I was a bitch, I'd give you some pussy."

Miles had a great sense of humor. I think God has endowed all great musicians with a sense of humor. I had another good friend named Jules Columby. He was not a professional musician, but he tried to play the trumpet, and he knew Miles quite well. He loved jazz and eventually wound up working for a record company as a producer. He had two brothers: Bobby Columby played drums with Blood, Sweat, and Tears; and Harry Columby managed Thelonious Monk and comedian George Carlin. Jules came to most of my gigs. Afterward, we'd have breakfast, and he'd drive me home to the Arlington, where we'd park out front and talk music until the sun came up. Later on, Jules married and had two children. He eventually contracted multiple sclerosis and was confined to a wheelchair. He told me that one day he was talking to Miles on the phone and telling him about all his physical problems. Miles listened and asked him if he could still fuck. Jules said yes. Miles said, "You're all right then. Ain't nothin' wrong with you."

At one time, Miles Davis was one of the highest-paid artists in jazz. He made big money. He invested some of this money in an electric company that supplied New York with electricity. Every time he phoned me, his opening remark was, "Have you got your lights on? Go turn your lights on."

I did one quartet session on Blue Note Records with Miles, drummer Art Blakey, and bassist Percy Heath. I also did three different sessions on Prestige Records with him, one with Dave Shildkraut on alto, Kenny Clarke on drums, and Percy Heath on bass. I remember that Klook (Kenny Clarke) forgot to bring his hi hat cymbal to the session. He's such a master drummer that when you listen to the record, you don't even miss it. The *Blue Haze* session featured Art Blakey, Percy Heath, and myself. In the cab on the way to the studio, I asked Miles what we were going to record. He said, "I'll think of something when we get there." While Art was setting up his drums, Percy was tuning up his bass, and I was limbering up my fingers on the keyboard, Miles took a chair and sat in a corner. He put his hand on his chin as if he were in deep thought. When he came out of the corner, he had a whole head arrangement put together. He told us what to play and told the engineer to turn out all the lights in the studio. Only the light from the control room was visible. It created a mood, and out of that mood came "Blue Haze."

I remember the *Walkin'* session on Prestige Records that included Miles, J. J. Johnson on trombone, Lucky Thompson on tenor, Percy Heath on bass, and Kenny Clarke on drums. Miles had asked Lucky Thompson to write some music for this session, which Lucky did. We got to Rudy Van Gelder's studio and started to rehearse the music. We made a couple of takes, but Miles wasn't satisfied with the way it was coming off. So he told everybody to put the music aside, and we proceeded to jam two blues tunes. One was "Blue 'n Boogie" and the other was "Walkin'," which became a classic. We did two takes on "Blue 'n Boogie" and one take on "Walkin'," and that was it.

Working with Kenny Clarke was a unique experience. When I played with Art Blakey, I had to play very hard because Art played so hard and full of fire. If you didn't play hard, he'd wipe you out and make you sound like a weakling. When I played with Kenny Clarke, I had to adapt to his style of playing. Percy Heath told me to listen carefully to Klook's cymbal beat so that I would be turned on and be able to groove with him. I did, and I was.

Some years later, I ran into Miles, and we reminisced about when we both lived at the Arlington. He told me about an incident that went down there. I had gone to Baltimore to play a week at a club with a quartet that included Cecil Payne on baritone sax, Arthur Edgehill on drums, and a bass player whose first name was Zade. Miles had a drug habit at that time and needed money for a fix. He told the desk clerk at the Arlington that he had left something in my room and needed to get in to get it. The desk clerk gave him the key to my room. Miles went in and took all my suits and pawned them to get money for drugs. The beautiful part is that he was able to get some money from somewhere and get my suits out of the pawn shop and back into my room before I returned from Baltimore. If he hadn't told me about it, I would never have known. To me, it shows that he had some respect for me.

As far as Miles's electric fusion stuff, I couldn't get with it too much, to be honest. I mean, he played such great music in his earlier career—all the bebop stuff he did was just fantastic. Well, the man was a genius, let's face it, early career or late, and I always admired him for striving to do something different. He didn't stick with the same old shit over and over. He was always striving to forge ahead. Regardless of what I or some of his fans or some of the other musicians might have thought about the music in the latter part of his life, when he went into his fusion thing, you've got to take your hat off to him and admire him for having the courage to make a change, because everyone loved what he was doing before so much. But I didn't particularly care for the direction he took.

Now that I reflect on it, though, I think it was a wise decision on his part, because at his age I don't think he could have kept up with the early part of his career, musically, as far as soloing, because he had so much chops, earlier on. You get older, your chops get weaker. What he was doing in the latter part of his career was better for him because he didn't have to use the pressure and the energy he used in the early years. Of course, he still had to have his chops to some degree, but they didn't have to be up to where they were when he was young. So I respect what he did, though it wasn't exactly my cup of tea.

Another great trumpeter I had the privilege of working with was Clifford Brown. Clifford was from Wilmington, Delaware. Many of the musicians in New York had heard about this great trumpet player from Wilmington, but nobody had heard him play. He had never gotten to New York. Blue Note Records owner Alfred Lion had heard about Clifford, so he and Art Blakey went to Wilmington to find him and engage him for a recording session.

They decided they wanted to do a live session with Clifford at Birdland in New York. They engaged Lou Donaldson on alto, Curly Russell on bass, and me on piano to round out the group. I had played with Curly several times before at Birdland with various groups. I was introduced to Lou Donaldson by my good friend Arthur Woods, who knew all the cats. I met Lou at the Paradise Bar in Harlem, where I worked for several months with tenor saxophonist Big Nick Nicholas. Lou used to come in and jam with us. Except for Clifford, I had worked with all these guys before, so I felt very comfortable doing this gig.

When we heard Clifford play, we were blown away. Miles came by to observe one of our rehearsals. Before he left, he said jokingly, "Clifford, I hope you bust your chops," and then he laughed and left. After he left, Curly Russell said, "He wasn't joking when he said that. He really meant it." Clifford Brown was not just a great trumpet player; he was a wonderful person. For one who played so great, he was very humble, a very lovable guy.

That group lasted only three weeks. In February 1954, we played two weeks at Birdland and made a series of two recordings there called *A Night at Birdland.* Then we played in Philadelphia for one week. We couldn't get any work after that. Max Roach came along and swooped up Clifford and took him to California with his group. Clifford made a lot of records with Max, but those *Night at Birdland* records will always remain classics. They sound as great today as they sounded years ago when we made them. I am proud to have been part of it all.

A few years later, when young trumpet player Lee Morgan came to New York as part of the Dizzy Gillespie trumpet section, he was about eighteen years old and playin' his ass off. Although he had great technique and knew his chord changes, I always thought that he played too many notes in those days and didn't leave enough space in his playing. As he got older, he began to utilize the value of space and became a more proficient soloist. Booker Little was another wonderful young trumpeter who I thought played too many notes. He was a great player, but I think he would have been even greater if he had utilized space. Unfortunately, he didn't live long enough to come to this realization. I always remembered what Miles told me about leaving some space in the music.

IN THE 1950S, some of the great trumpet players of all time lived and worked in New York. Roy Eldridge—"Little Jazz," we called him—was one of the greatest. When I think of Roy, I often remember something that happened years later, around 1972 or '73. My quintet was playing at the Half Note Club in New York, which had moved from the Lower West Side of Manhattan to the Upper East Side. We played there for a week opposite the Kai Winding Quartet. One night after our last set, I went upstairs to the dressing room to change my clothes. I always perspire so heavily that I have to change clothes after every set. The dressing room was right over the bandstand, and I was listening to Kai and the band play as I was changing clothes. All of a sudden, I heard a tenor sitting in with Kai—and I recognized that it was Stan Getz. They were wailin'. Then I heard a trumpeter sitting in, and he was burnin'. I rushed downstairs to see who it was. It was Roy Eldridge, and he was on fire. Stan and Kai had stepped down from the bandstand and were sitting at a nearby table, observing Roy, who was takin' care of business. He lit the whole joint up. When he finished, Stan and Kai went over and gave him a big hug.

Drummer Eddie Lock used to work with Roy at Ryan's back in the late 1950s. Eddie told me that when Dizzy Gillespie had a week or two off the road, he would come into Ryan's and jam with Roy to keep his chops up. Roy was Dizzy's trumpet mentor. According to Eddie, Dizzy and Roy were at the bar one night, and Dizzy said to Roy, "Do you mind if I go up on the bandstand first and play a few tunes by myself? 'Cause I don't feel like fightin' with your ass tonight." When Roy got on the bandstand with another trumpet player, he was always competing, trying to outdo the other trumpeter. Roy was the link between the swing-era trumpet players and the bebop trumpet players. No one played with more fire and feeling than Roy Eldridge, although Charlie Shavers ran a close second.

In the mid- to late fifties, Charlie Shavers was a regular at the Metropole Cafe, a great place. One weekend, after visiting my dad up in Connecticut, I came back to New York in the late afternoon, about five o'clock. I got off the train at Grand Central Station and walked across Forty-second Street and up Seventh Avenue toward the Metropole. About three or four blocks away, I could hear Charlie Shavers's trumpet—this motherfucker had such a great big sound, I could hear him cooking three blocks away. The doors of the Metropole were always open, and the music would flow out onto Seventh Avenue. So I walked up, and, as always, a bunch of people were standing in front of the doorway, looking in. The musicians were playing on an elevated bandstand behind the bar, with Coleman Hawkins and Charlie Shavers fronting the group. When they saw me, they motioned for me to come in, and I went up and played with them a little.

The Metropole was something else. Trumpet player Henry "Red" Allen used to play there a lot, too. He tickled me, the way he counted off his tunes. He'd say, "Wamp! Wamp!"

BIG NICK NICHOLAS had a gig at the Paradise Bar with a trio that included Kahlil Madee on drums and a piano player. They worked there five nights a week, Tuesday through Saturday. They played for dancing and floor shows on Friday and Saturday, but on Tuesday through Thursday, they could play anything they wanted. This became a popular place where cats could sit in and jam. I used to go by and sit in from time to time, and when the piano player left, Nick called me to join the group.

This was a great learning period for me. I got a chance to play with many of the great jazz musicians who came by to jam with Nick. Nick had played with many of the name black big bands of that era, including Dizzy Gillespie's. All the musicians knew him and respected his musicianship. Trumpeters Joe Newman, Harold "Shorty" Baker, and Hot Lips Page; tenor saxophonists Ike Quebec, Sonny Stitt, Gene Ammons, and Bud Johnson; alto saxophonists Charlie Parker and Lou Donaldson—all used to come by to jam with us on Tuesdays, Wednesdays, and Thursdays. Betty Carter often sang on some of the weekend floor shows. She was known as Betty "Bebop" Carter in those days and had just left the Lionel Hampton band.

Someone told Nick that I also played tenor. He asked me to bring my tenor in one night and play some with him. I was reluctant because I didn't think I could keep up with him. I decided I would do it on a night when attendance was low and not many musicians would be coming in to jam. I had my tenor case up on the stage. Sonny Stitt happened to come in that night, and he asked Nick whose tenor was on the stage. Nick said it was mine. Sonny asked me to get it out and play some with him. I said, "Man, are you kiddin'? I can't keep up with you." He went and opened the case, assembled the horn, put the strap on it, and put the strap around my neck. I had no choice but to go ahead and play with him. We started playing, and he proceeded to crucify me. I couldn't keep up with him.

I was a little embarrassed, but this incident helped me make an important career decision. I was trying to play both the piano and the saxophone along with composing and arranging. I felt I had to lessen my load. I didn't want to give up the piano, and I didn't want to give up composition and arranging. Although I truly loved the tenor saxophone and was a disciple of Lester Young, I decided that if I had to give up something, it would be the tenor. That's when I packed the tenor away in the closet. Years later, I gave it to a deserving young student who didn't have a horn.

When I worked with Stan Getz, he also heard that I played the tenor. We played a dance gig one night in Hartford, Connecticut, and he asked me bring my tenor and play some with him. I was reluctant, but he was kind. He didn't put the pressure on me like Sonny Stitt did, although he very well could have if he had wanted to.

Nick was a lover of Broadway show tunes. He used to bring in sheet music for some of the beautiful, obscure Broadway show tunes, and we would play them. Working that gig really expanded my repertoire of Broadway standards. One night, Nick brought in the sheet music to "The Song Is You." We learned it and played it often. When Bird came in to jam with us, Nick started playing it. Bird didn't know the tune, but while Nick was playing, Bird asked me to call out the chord changes to him, which I did. When it came time for his solo, he stepped up to the mike and played his ass off. Several months later, I heard a brand-new Charlie Parker recording on the radio. The song he had recorded was "The Song Is You." Nick had turned him on to this tune at the Paradise Bar.

I HAD THE GOOD FORTUNE to play with Bird on five occasions, all one-nighters. The first was a dance gig in Stamford, Connecticut. My quartet, featuring Hank Mobley on tenor, Doug Watkins on bass, and Arthur Edgehill on drums, was booked for the gig with Charlie Parker and blues singer Annie Laurie as added attractions. What a soulful night that was! I wish I could have caught it on tape. The second time was when the Jazz Messengers played a Friday night gig at the Open Door in Greenwich Village. Bird came in and sat in with us.

The third time was when I played a dance gig with him in Buffalo, New York. Walter Bishop Jr. was his regular piano player, but "Bish" got sick and asked me to sub for him. The band was made up of Little Benny Harris on trumpet, Charlie Mingus on bass, Kenny Clarke on drums, myself on piano, and Bird. I met Little Benny Harris at the information booth at Grand Central Station and went up to Buffalo by train with him. We arrived there in the early afternoon. The dance didn't start until early evening, so we went by the apartment of one of Benny's musician friends in Buffalo to kill some time. While there, Benny and his friend started to shoot up some heroin. I thought to myself, "Oh, God, suppose the police come in here now and bust us all." We made it to the gig, and the band was on fire.

The fourth time I played with Bird was at the Baby Grand in Harlem, where he had a quartet with Walter Bishop Jr. on piano, Roy Haynes on drums, and a bassist. They played three sets a night. I came in to listen to them on their second set and stayed for the third. Walter Bishop asked me to sit in on the third set. Naturally, I said yes. Miles Davis and Gerry Mulligan also sat in on that set. At the end of the set, Bird came over to me and said, "Man, you sure are comping your ass off." I was very elated to get this compliment from Bird. I was walking on a cloud for the next two weeks.

I played with Bird for a fifth time at Minton's Playhouse in Harlem, where he sat in with my quartet. We were on intermission, and I was standing at the bar when I saw him come in. He walked straight up to me at the bar. It was obvious that he was high.

He started pushing me. I said to myself, "Why is he pushing me? I haven't done anything to him." He kept pushing me backward until he got me up against the kitchen's swinging doors, and then he pushed me into the kitchen. The kitchen was closed at that time, and no one was in there. I didn't want to try and fight him. I had too much respect for him to do that. Besides, I didn't think I would come out the winner. I said to myself, "He's gonna punch me and lay me out right on this kitchen floor." All of a sudden, he lunged at me, put his arms around my neck, and said, "Man, where am I?" He was so high he didn't know where he was.

Bird was playing his white plastic saxophone in those days. He came up on stage to sit in with us. He called the tune "Laura," which was written in the key of C. I started the introduction in the key of C, and he started to play in a different key. He couldn't seem to get with it. He got disgusted with himself and raised his horn in the air and started to throw it out into the audience. Luckily, he held back. That was the only time I've ever seen Bird when he couldn't get his shit together. I don't know what drugs he had taken earlier, but they sure fucked him up.

Art Blakey told me some stories about when he worked with Charlie Parker in the Billy Eckstine band. Art said that the whole saxophone section was using heroin. They all had empty Maxwell House coffee cans under their music stands so that when they had to puke, they could just duck their heads under the music stand and puke into the can, and the audience would not be aware of it. Art said that Billy Eckstine used to jokingly call him "Baa." Billy pronounced it just like the noise a sheep makes. He said the initials stood for "Black Ass Art."

According to Art, the band was playing a song that Bird was to solo on. Bird was high and had fallen asleep in the middle of the tune. Everyone in the band was wondering if he would wake up in time to come in on his solo. He woke up just in time, jumped out of his seat, went to centerstage to the mike, with the spotlight on him, and played a phenomenal solo. However, he had taken his shoes off beforehand and was centerstage in the spotlight in his stockingfeet with holes in both socks. Charlie Rouse was also in the saxophone section at that time. Rouse was so awestruck at what Bird played that he sat there with his mouth wide open and missed his own cue to come in when the section was to hit.

ART BLAKEY INTRODUCED ME to Thelonious Monk. They were good friends. Monk and his family lived in the projects somewhere on the west side of Manhattan. I knew that Monk liked wine, so I would buy him a bottle of wine and go by his pad and lay it on him and ask him to play for me. He would, and I was always amazed at his harmonies and his unique approach to the piano. He and Bud Powell, Teddy Wilson, Nat "King" Cole, and Art Tatum were my piano inspirations.

I worked for a short time with tenor saxophonist Flip Phillips, who gained prominence with the Woody Herman band and Jazz at the Philharmonic. He led a trio that included me on piano and J. C. Heard on drums. Since we had no bass player, I had to use my left hand a bit more than I did when I worked with a bass player, to keep the rhythm flowing. This was not exactly foreign to me, because I had done the same thing when I worked at the Paradise Bar with Big Nick Nicholas, who had the same instrumentation.

J. C. and I worked a couple of weeks with the Flip Phillips Trio at a club called Basin Street, right off Broadway in Manhattan. Minton's Playhouse, where all the beboppers cultivated their talents, was located uptown in Harlem. Regular working hours at Minton's Playhouse were nine-twenty P.M. to four A.M. They had a private club downstairs in the basement that opened up at four A.M. and stayed open until noon. J. C. and I went there one morning after our gig with Flip downtown. A bass player named Chocolate had a trio playing there. Ben Webster came in that morning, and I had a chance to jam with him and J. C. and Chocolate. I wish I could have gotten that on tape. What a cookin' session that was. I'll always remember that morning. We set that place on fire.

I worked occasionally with Lucky Thompson in and around the New York area. He had a quartet that featured himself on tenor, Beverly Peer on bass, Kenny Clarke on drums, and myself on piano. Beverly Peer was also working with pianist and singer Bobby Short at that time. Lucky was a great friend of boxer Archie Moore. Archie was a great jazz fan, as was Joe Louis. Joe used to come into Birdland quite often when I was working there. He'd always have a foxy young lady with him. I never got the chance to meet him. Sugar Ray Robinson was a jazz fan also. Sugar Ray had a wife who was so beautiful she could stop traffic. I remember seeing them drive down Broadway in his purple Cadillac with the top down. People would stop in their tracks to look and check them out. They came down to Birdland one night when I was playing there, and although people turned to look at Ray, it was his wife who got most of the attention. I never got to meet Ray, either. I did get to meet and know Archie Moore. He was a great boxer and a beautiful person. He was also a frustrated bass player. He could play only one song on the bass, and that was "St. Louis Blues" in the key of G.

Archie's training camp was in the Catskill Mountains in upper New York State. He often had Lucky's quartet come up to the camp to play for him and his trainers. We would drive up from New York and get there in time for supper. We ate with Archie and his trainers and performed for them after supper. Every time we played there, Archie sat in on bass and played the one tune he knew, "St. Louis Blues" in the key of G. Archie wound up getting married to a very nice young lady who had been a bar maid in a bar located close to where I used to live, on 189th Street and Boston Road in the Bronx. She was quite a bit younger than Archie, but I think they made a beautiful pair and had a very happy marriage.

Bassist Curly Russell told me a story about Joe Louis and tenor saxophonist Ben Webster. Curly was working with Ben at one of the clubs on Fifty-second Street. Joe often came in and stood at the bar to listen. Ben was one of the sweetest guys in the world when he was sober. But when he was drinking, he could become a little raunchy. Ben would come off the bandstand after his set, walk over to Joe, and say, "How you doin', champ?" and give him a blow to the stomach. I'm sure this was done in jest on Ben's part, and he was usually smashed at the time he did it. Eventually, Joe got tired of this shit. One night when Ben gave Joe his friendly blow to the stomach, Joe retaliated with a blow to Ben's stomach. Ben fell over backward, and before he hit the floor, he regurgitated everything he had to eat and drink for supper. That was the end of Ben's friendly blows to Joe's stomach.

J.J. Johnson also told me a story about Ben. J.J. was doing an all-star recording session for jazz critic Leonard Feather, and Ben was one of the stars. Everybody was ready to record, but Ben hadn't shown up. They waited for about an hour, but no Ben. So they started without him. Finally, Ben showed up drunk. Everybody was pissed off at him, but when they played a ballad and he soloed on it, they all forgave him. Everybody went over to him and gave him a hug. I've never heard anyone play a ballad more soulfully than Ben Webster.

I also worked with the Terry Gibbs Sextet, which featured Terry on vibes, Don Elliot on melophone, Phil Urso on tenor, Curly Russell on bass (who was later replaced by George Duvivier), and Sid Bulkin on drums. Terry, like Prez, had a great sense of humor and always kept the guys in the band laughing. Birdland always had a sign outside the club listing the names of all the performers who were working there. One time when I was playing there with Terry, the sign painter listed me as "MORRIS SILVER" on piano. Terry was greatly amused at this. He's been calling me Morris, not Horace, ever since. He says he's made me an honorary Jew.

Mel Torme was a good friend of Terry's and used to sit in on drums with us sometimes. I have the greatest respect for Mel as a singer, songwriter, arranger, author, and actor. He was one hell of a talent. My two favorite scat singers are Ella Fitzgerald and Mel Torme. But Curly, George, and I used to call Mel "Old Club Foot"—not to his face, though. The problem was that he played the bass drum too loud. When we saw him come into the club, we used to say, "Aw, shit, here comes Old Club Foot. Hope he don't sit in." But he usually did. He never sat in singing, though.

I had the pleasure of working with the great jazz bassist Oscar Pettiford at a club called Snookie's in New York. I can't remember the exact location of Snookie's—it was somewhere between Forty-second Street and Forty-seventh Street, a block east of Broadway. We worked there six nights a week for about three months. It was an eight-piece band: Leonard Hawkins on trumpet, Kai Winding on trombone, Lee Konitz on alto, Rudy Williams on tenor, Cecil Payne on baritone, Osie Johnson on drums, myself on piano, and Oscar on bass. We played a lot of Duke Ellington's music, most of it arranged by Tom Tolbert and Tom Whaley. One night, bassist Ray Brown came in to check us out, and Oscar invited him to sit in on bass while he got out his cello. That was a memorable night. I wish it had been recorded. Two masters of the bass at work.

Oscar was a great bassist and a beautiful person, except when he got drunk. When he was drinking, his whole personality changed, and he became quite nasty and obnoxious. We worked from nine at night to four in the morning. Sometimes when Oscar got drunk during the course of the evening, he would complain that the band wasn't playing the music right. Then he had us rehearse from four to six in the morning. The guys in the band got so mad at him. They were all tired and wanted to go home. Most of the time, I couldn't hear anything wrong with the way the band was playing the music, but it was his band and his gig, so we all went along with the program. It was a real good band, and I had a lot of fun working with them.

By about 1955, the musicians in New York had heard about Cannonball and Nat Adderley from Fort Lauderdale, Florida, and how well they played. I was working at the Cafe Bohemia with Oscar Pettiford, Jerome Richardson, and Kenny Clarke, and the Adderleys came in to hear us. They had driven to New York to spend a weekend and check out the jazz scene. Someone told Oscar they were in the house, and he invited them to come up and sit in with us. They went out to their car and got their horns out of the trunk and sat in. They broke it up. Everyone was impressed with their playing. Soon after that, A&R (artists and repertoire) man Ozzie Cadena, who worked for Savoy Records, engaged them to do a record, along with Paul Chambers, Kenny Clarke, and myself. We recorded one of Oscar Pettiford's tunes, "Bohemia after Dark."

WHILE I WAS WORKING a gig with Oscar Pettiford at the Cafe Bohemia in Greenwich Village, I met a lady who became one of the two major loves of my life. A large party of white people came in as we were playing, and I noticed a particular girl in the group. She was very attractive, and she seemed to be giving me the eye. The group left before we finished our set. When we went up to do our next set, I looked out in the audience and saw this girl sitting at a table by herself. She had left whoever she came in with and had come back to meet me. When I came off the bandstand, I went over to her table and introduced myself. We talked, and after the gig we had breakfast together and went straight to the Arlington to room 608. I was about having a good time. I was not about getting serious with any woman. Music was my woman, and I had married her at the age of eleven.

This girl's name was Shirley Swift. She was from Flint, Michigan. She had three kids by a previous marriage. Her ex-husband played trombone in one of the Woody Herman bands. I had no intention of getting serious with her, but she was different from all the others. When I was sick with the flu and had a temperature of 104 and was confined to bed, other ladies would call and offer their sympathies and say they would call back in a few days to see how I felt. When Shirley called and found out that I was sick, she said, "Hold on, I'll put my kids to bed and get my neighbor to look in on them, and I'll be right down to look after you." She came down from the Bronx with hot soup, aspirin, and Vicks VapoRub and tended to me. She also was a great cook. I went up to her apartment on Sundays and visited with her and her kids, and she cooked a great meal. Her kids really liked me, and I liked them.

I tried to hold back, but I finally weakened and fell in love with her. She was a fine-looking woman and a beautiful person. I took her to a family reunion dinner in Norwalk one day to meet my family. They all liked her very much. A couple of weeks later, my brother, Gene, came to me and said, "Horace, we all like Shirley very much. She's a fine person, but have you thought about the responsibility you would be taking on if you were to marry her? You would start out with a ready-made family. Starting out with a wife and three kids is a bit much for a young man at your stage of life."

I had thought about that, and it weighed heavily on my mind. I was then twenty-seven years old. I did love her, but I hadn't yet made my mark in music. If I were to marry her, I thought, I might wind up like my friend Count Steadwell, working in the post office to support my family. In addition, Shirley's ex-husband heard that she was going with a black man and threatened to take the kids away from her. Her mother had no problems about our going together, but her father did. Eventually, Shirley and the kids moved back to Flint because she was having financial difficulties in New York. We remained in contact with each other, and I would fly her to New York to spend weekends with me. Little by little, though, we began to drift apart, not because there was any friction between us, but because I think we both began to realize that the situation was impossible.

WHEN I FIRST STARTED going with Shirley Swift, I lived at the Arlington Hotel. She thought I should have my own apartment, so one week when I was out of town on a gig, she went apartment hunting for me. She found a nice little one-room kitchenette apartment at 23 West Seventy-sixth Street, between Central Park West and Columbus Avenue. She called and told me how nice it was, and I wired her some money to pay for the first month's rent. She signed the lease in my name, gave the landlady the money, and got a receipt.

Shirley told the landlady that she was getting the apartment for a friend. Since Shirley was white, the landlady assumed that her friend was white also. The day I moved in, the landlady was sweeping the steps of the apartment building. She asked me where I was going. I said, "I'm going to my apartment."

She asked, "What apartment?"

I replied, "Apartment 4A."

"Are you Mr. Silver?"

"Yes, I am," I told her.

She looked startled. She was expecting a white man. She was a very prejudiced woman and didn't want any blacks in her apartment building. She tried to make things as difficult as possible for me in the hope that I would move out. When things needed repair, she would either take a long time to fix them or not fix them at all. Shirley had her own apartment in the Bronx, but she visited me often. The landlady didn't like that, but there was nothing she could do about it. I had a signed lease, and I always paid my rent on time. I lived there for about three years. It was a nice apartment. The rent was reasonable, it was centrally located, and I wasn't about to give her the satisfaction of forcing me to move out because of her prejudiced ways. The things that a black person had to endure in those days were a pain in the ass.

In the early 1960s, I moved to a place called Park West Village, at 400 Central Park West and One Hundredth Street. The tenants were interracial, and I encountered no prejudice there. A lot of celebrities were living in Park West Village at that time. The list included Coleman Hawkins, singer/actor Bill Henderson, singer Miriam Makeba, drummer Specs Powell, actress Claudia McNeil, pianist Ray Bryant, trumpeter Hugh Masakela, drummer Sonny Greer, Duke Ellington, and Famous Amos, the chocolate chip cookie guy. Max Roach and Abbey Lincoln, Art Blakey, and Babs Gonzales all lived in the same neighborhood. Max and Abbey were married at that time.

New York had a lot of thrills for me in those days. I used to see actor Basil Rathbone walking his dog up and down Central Park West. He lived in an apartment building at Seventy-second Street and Central Park West. For my taste, no one could play Sherlock Holmes like Basil, and no one could play Dr. Watson like Nigel Bruce. I met actress Gale Sondergaard one day on Central Park West and got her autograph. One day when the buses were on strike and taxis were hard to get, actress Betsy Palmer picked me up on Central Park West and gave me a ride downtown. I saw Myrna Loy walking down Fifth Avenue to window-shop and Carol Burnett stopping at the corner of Central Park West to get a cab. New York was loaded with great and famous people in those days; I have many fond memories of living there.

THE MUSIC CALLED BEBOP had its inception at Minton's Playhouse in Harlem. Dizzy, Monk, Bird, and Bud Powell all formulated their music at this club. I had heard about Minton's Playhouse when I was in Hartford but never dreamed I would work there one day. In fact, I ended up working there on four occasions. My first week with Lester Young was at Minton's. I later played there for several months with Tony Scott's group, with Tony on clarinet, Arvell Shaw on bass, and Osie Johnson on drums.

I later worked at Minton's for several months with tenor saxophonist Eddie "Lockjaw" Davis and his group, which included Arvell Shaw and Osie Johnson. Lock sometimes called tunes that I didn't know. I'd say, "Lock, I don't know that one." He'd say, "That's all right, you'll hear it." Then he would stomp it off at a breakneck tempo. I'd be scuffling for the first two choruses, trying to find the right chord changes. I'd finally find them and be able to provide him with the proper harmonies before he took the tune out. I was always embarrassed when this happened.

Years later, when I got my own band and was appearing at Birdland, Lock came in to hear us. After our set, I went over to say hello to him, and I reminded him of how he'd call a tune I didn't know and how I'd be scuffling, trying to find the chord changes. He laughed and said, "That's how you learn. They used to do that to me when I was a youngster just coming on the scene." I later worked Minton's for several months with my own group: Hank Mobley on tenor, Doug Watkins on bass, Arthur Edgehill on drums, and myself on piano.

There was an alto saxophone player whose name none of us knew. We all called him "the Demon." He had absolutely no harmonic knowledge, and his improvising was terrible. He would want to sit in and jam with us. We'd see him sitting in the audience with his horn on his lap, but we never invited him up to play with us, because we knew how badly he played. He'd sit there and wait to be invited, and when we didn't ask, he'd get out his horn and play from his table. We all cringed when we saw him come in, because we knew that he was going to mess up the groove we had going.

Much like the Sundown Club in Hartford, Minton's had its share of prostitutes, pimps, drug dealers, and boosters, guys who sold stolen clothes. I always remembered my mother's advice not to hang out with people of questionable character, but always to have a friendly hello and a handshake for them and then go on my way. This I did, and they all liked me. I liked them also. I knew that if anyone ever threatened me with physical harm, these people would come to my rescue. I bought a lot of my clothes from some of the boosters who came into Minton's. I'd go into the men's room with them, and they would open up their overcoats and show me suits they had wrapped around their bodies and clothes stuffed into their pockets. I saved a lot of money this way. I have fond memories of working at Minton's Playhouse, as well as at the Paradise Club and Birdland. I gained much valuable experience working at all three of these places.

I'VE DONE RECORD SESSIONS led by Stan Getz, Terry Gibbs, J.J. Johnson, Gigi Gryce, Art Farmer, Sonny Rollins, Milt Jackson, Al Cohn, Lou Donaldson, Coleman Hawkins, Hank Mobley, Art Blakey, and Miles Davis. I've been blessed to walk among these great ones. There are many other great musicians that I've been blessed to work with but never got the chance to record with. I am grateful that I was born at a time in history when so many great jazz musicians were located in New York and that I had a chance to be cultivated there among them. What an inspiration they were and still are to me! I've always dug the blues, black gospel music, and Latin music. I always enjoyed it so much when we worked Birdland opposite Machito or Tito Puente.

I also got some gigs of my own from time to time in those days. One time I'll never forget. I was scheduled to work a Saturday night gig in Brooklyn with a drummer friend of mine, Al Dreares, who used to work with Dizzy Gillespie. We both lived in Manhattan, and we met to take the subway to Brooklyn for the gig. Al brought his drums on the train, and I helped him carry them. Unknown to me, Al had asthma, and he suffered an attack on the train. We had to get off at the nearest stop, drums and all, and get a cab to the nearest hospital emergency ward, where they treated him for several hours. We never did make that gig in Brooklyn. I thought he was going to die that night. He might have, if I hadn't got him to the hospital. Thank God I was able to do this. I don't know where Al is today, but I wish him well, wherever he is. He was a good drummer and a nice guy.

I had the pleasure of knowing John Coltrane, and we worked together on two occasions. I did a recording led by Donald Byrd for Blue Note Records that Trane was on. I had a two-week engagement at the Cafe Bohemia in Greenwich Village with a quintet that included Art Farmer on trumpet, Clifford Jordan on tenor, Teddy Kotick on bass, and Louis Hayes on drums. On the third night of the gig, Clifford Jordan received a telegram saying that his father was dying and that he should rush right home to Chicago. Coltrane was working with Miles Davis at the time, but they had a week off and were at home in New York. I called him, and he agreed to finish out the gig with us. Needless to say, we had a ball working with him.

Some of my favorite jazz composers are Duke Ellington, Billy Strayhorn, Thelonious Monk, Bud Powell, and Tadd Dameron. Of course, I love all the great Tin Pan Alley composers such as Irving Berlin, Cole Porter, George Gershwin, Jerome Kern, Harold Arlen, and many others. In particular, I was always inspired by Tadd Dameron's compositions and arrangements. He had such a definite style. Whenever I heard Tadd's music, it seemed like he was opening his arms and asking you to come and let him give you a big hug. Tadd had a drug problem; he had been busted and served time. Trumpeter Blue Mitchell engaged Tadd to orchestrate some music for a string section he was doing for Riverside Records. Tadd was in jail at the time but was allowed to do this work from there. One of the tunes he orchestrated was my song called "Strollin'."

I got a chance to meet Tadd when he got out of jail. He was a beautiful, warm person. He became ill at one point and was in and out of the hospital. He married his nurse, who was a Caucasian lady from Europe. I don't know what country she originally came from, but she now lives in London. I visited Tadd and his wife in their apartment in New York a few weeks before he died. I've written two songs dedicated to Tadd. One is called "Dameron's Dance," which I recorded; the other I haven't recorded yet.

I have always admired the talents of George Shearing. He's a great pianist and a fine composer, too. George recorded four of my compositions: "Señor Blues," "The Outlaw," "Peace," and "Strollin'." George asked me to come by his apartment in New York and bring him some lead sheets to some of my tunes. Since George is blind, I presumed that his wife, who also plays piano, would read and play some of these lead sheets for him. George had a grand piano in his living room, but in another room he had two upright Yamahas standing side by side, on which he and his wife would play classical duets. He invited me into that room and asked me to play something for him. I sat down and played a brand-new composition that I had just written. After I had played it through once, he sat down at the other piano and played it along with me, making all the right chord changes and melody first time down. George Shearing can hear around the corner—a great musician and a great guy.

AFTER HE HEARD LOU DONALDSON play at one of the jam sessions at the Paradise Bar, Alfred Lion of Blue Note Records engaged Lou to do a quartet session for him. Alfred was always hanging out on the jazz scene, searching for great new talent. Lou engaged me to play piano on the session. I did a second session with Lou for Blue Note Records that started out as a quartet. But someone brought Blue Mitchell by the session to check us out. Lou knew Blue and dug his playing, so he asked him to play on a few tracks. That was the first time I met Blue.

I was supposed to do a third session with Lou for Blue Note, but three days before the session was scheduled, Alfred called to say that Lou couldn't make the session and to ask whether I could make a trio album for him. Naturally, I accepted. Luckily, I had plenty of material. I was always composing. I had three days to pick the material I wanted to record, get in the woodshed and practice, and get my shit together.

I went into the studio three times to do trio recordings for Alfred. I used Art Blakey on drums for all three sessions, with Gene Ramey on bass for the first, Curly Russell for the second, and Percy Heath for the third.

When Alfred asked me to do a fourth trio session, I said, "Alfred, if you don't mind, I would like to use some horns on this session." He said, "Okay, who would you like to use?" I said, "Kenny Dorham on trumpet, Hank Mobley on tenor, Doug Watkins on bass, and Art Blakey on drums." We got together and rehearsed and did the session. It came off great.

Alfred decided to record us a second time. After making these recordings, all the cats in the band said, "Man, we sound good together. We should try to keep this band happening." These recordings were first released on two different ten-inch vinyl records under the name of the Horace Silver Quintet. They were later compiled and released on a twelve-inch vinyl called *Horace Silver and the Jazz Messengers.* Some of the tunes included were "Doodlin'," "The Preacher," and "Room 608." Out of these sessions in late 1954 and early 1955, the Jazz Messengers were born, most definitely one of the greatest groups I've ever had the privilege of working with.

I always had a good relationship with Alfred Lion and Frank Wolff, co-founders and directors of Blue Note Records. They liked me, and they liked my music and my writing. I never had to fight to get any of my compositions recorded. I do remember one incident, though, during the recording of *Horace Silver and the Jazz Messengers.* The day before the session, we rehearsed "The Preacher." Alfred and Frank said it sounded too much like Dixieland music. They suggested that we delete that tune and jam a blues in its place.

Art Blakey pulled me aside and said, "Horace, there ain't nothin' wrong with that tune. You should insist on doing it." I went back to Alfred and Frank and told them I didn't want to delete "The Preacher" and jam a blues in its place. I suggested that we cancel the session until I could write another tune that they would like and then reschedule the session. They both went into a corner to discuss the matter and decided to let me record "The Preacher."

Upon release of the album, "The Preacher" became quite popular and was recorded by many other artists. I was speaking to producer Michael Cuscuna some years after Alfred's and Frank's deaths. Michael said that Alfred had told him he still didn't like "The Preacher," even though it was a hit. He may not have liked it, but he made a lot of money from it. That was the one and only conflict I had with Alfred Lion and Frank Wolff. They were great guys, and they really and truly loved jazz music.

I heard Herbie Hancock being interviewed on the radio one day. He was speaking about Blue Note Records and Alfred Lion. He said that Donald Byrd had arranged an interview for him with Alfred. Herbie wanted to do an album as a leader, although up to that time, he had been a sideman only. Donald told Herbie to prepare six tunes to play for Alfred at the interview, three standards, and three originals. Herbie met Alfred and played three standards and three originals for him. Alfred approved the whole program, but he asked Herbie if he had any more originals. Alfred Lion gave a lot of young musicians and composers a chance to get their original compositions recorded. Of course, he made a lot of money doing this, because many of the original compositions became very popular. The standard compositions were tried and true, and it was safe to go with them. But Alfred wasn't afraid to take a chance, and it paid off for him and many of the composers whose originals he recorded.

I WORKED AND TRAVELED with the Jazz Messengers for about a year and a half before I left the band. I left not because I didn't like the music or because of any personal friction with anyone in the band. I left because of the drug addiction that was prevalent among the band members. Bassist Doug Watkins and I were the only ones that didn't have a drug habit. Almost everywhere we played, the vice squad came to check us out for drugs. I was always worried that they would catch one of the guys holding and we'd all get busted. It seemed the word had gone out from police department to police department in all major cities that the Jazz Messengers were drug addicts.

I didn't smoke, drink, or use drugs, although I had tried some of these things on occasion. I had started smoking cigarettes when I was sixteen years old and smoked until I was nineteen. At nineteen, smoking started to make me nauseated. I switched from one brand to another, but I still got nauseated every time I smoked. I decided that someone was trying to tell me something, so I kicked the habit. It was a blessing in disguise. If I had kept on smoking, I probably would have been dead long before now. And I never could handle hard liquor. I tried it a couple of times, but it always made me sick—another blessing in disguise. I could handle a little wine or beer, but hard liquor didn't agree with me.

I had tried smoking pot a few times, but it always made me feel paranoid. I had one embarrassing experience that made me say, "This is not for me." Anyone who has ever been around heroin users knows that often, after taking the drug, they have to puke. I remember one evening eating a big meal and then smoking a joint with a friend. We then had to run to catch a bus to the Apollo Theater. We went backstage to say hello to some musicians we knew. When we got there, I started feeling nauseated and puked all over the sidewalk, right outside the stage door entrance. People were watching, and I knew they were thinking that I was on heroin. I was so embarrassed that I never smoked pot again after that. From my early twenties on, I became a straight-lifer. But that wasn't true for most of the other guys in the group.

Just like Stan Getz when I was working with him, the Jazz Messengers were often late for gigs because the guys had to cop some shit. When we were late, the club owner would deduct money from our salary. I was getting a bit fed up with this situation. We opened in Washington, D.C., for a week's work and were two hours late on opening night because the guys had to cop some drugs. Before we started to play that opening night, I said to myself, "I'm going to put in my two weeks' notice. I'm tired of this shit." Kenny Dorham had left the group by then, and Donald Byrd had replaced him and was playing his ass off. Donald was not a drug user. When we finally got set up and started to play, we were cookin' so tough, I thought to myself, "I can't quit this band. Where else am I gonna go and get this great feeling?" So I stayed on until the situation got so bad and the heat from the various vice squads became so intense that I quit.

I recall playing a week with the Jazz Messengers at a jazz club in Youngstown, Ohio. Art Blakey, Kenny Dorham, and Hank Mobley drove back to New York every other night after the gig to cop some drugs. On their return to Youngstown, they would be an hour or an hour and a half late for the gig. Doug Watkins and I stayed in Youngstown. Doug didn't use any heavy drugs. He smoked a little pot from time to time and took an occasional drink. I didn't drink or use any kind of drugs. Business was not good that week at the club; I don't think Youngstown was ready for a hip bebop band. On closing night, Art went to the club owner's office to get paid. The club owner refused to give him any money because the band had started late several times and we hadn't drawn a crowd. Art didn't argue with him because he knew that the club was gangster-operated, and he didn't want to get roughed up. Maybe Art got some advance money from the club owner during the early part of the week, but if he did, I never got any of it.

Anyhow, there we were in Youngstown, Ohio, with a week's hotel bill to pay, and none of us had any money. I could just picture myself being put in jail because I couldn't pay my hotel bill. But Art called the Baroness Pannonica de Koenigswarter, and she wired us some money so we could pay our hotel bills and return to New York. Once again, we were befriended by Nica, as jazz musicians called her. She was a great lover of jazz music and a wonderful person. She did so much to help the Jazz Messengers. The Messengers were scuffling in those days. When we didn't have money to buy uniforms, she bought us three different uniforms. They were Ivy League suits with shirts and ties to match, and shoes to go along with them. We were looking good and sounding good. Pannonica had a brother in London who played the piano and was also a jazz fan. He used to come all the way from London to New York to get a piano lesson from Teddy Wilson.

Nica lived at the Stanhope Hotel, a plush hotel on the east side of Manhattan. Doug Watkins and I would often go by to visit her. She had a huge record collection, and Doug and I made it a point to visit her around dinner time, because she always invited us to eat. We ordered filet mignon from the restaurant downstairs, and the waiters wheeled the meal in on a trolley and served it to us. We laid back and grooved with the food and the music. Nica owned a Rolls-Royce. I remember one night after Doug and I had dinner at her place, the three of us decided to go to Birdland. We got in her Rolls-Royce, with her driving, and proceeded down Broadway. I remember all the white people staring at us as if to say, "What are those niggers doing in a Rolls-Royce with that white lady?" I wrote the tune "Nica's Dream" for her, and it became one of our jazz standards.

THE JAZZ MESSENGERS played a club in Chicago called the Bee Hive. Sonny Rollins was living in Chicago at that time. He used to practice in the park every day. He came by the club to check us out one night. He stayed through the whole evening and hung out with us during intermission in the dressing room. Before he left, he handed me a note, which I opened and read after he left. It read as follows:

> Dear Horace,
>
> You are the living (in flesh) representative of all that modern progressive musicians should be. Continue to play and to live the life that your talents are worthy of.
>
> *(Signed) S. R.*

I have kept this note in my scrapbook for many years. The paper it is written on is now turning brown and is very fragile. I treasure it. Sonny is one of the true masters of the saxophone. Coleman Hawkins and Lester Young were the innovators and leaders of the swing era. Sonny Rollins and John Coltrane were the innovators and leaders of the bebop era. As far as the bebop school of saxophone players is concerned, Sonny is my favorite after Charlie Parker. I had the privilege of recording with Sonny three times: once on an Art Farmer session, once on a Miles Davis session, and once on one of Sonny's sessions, on which Thelonious Monk also played. Sonny has been a source of inspiration to me, along with many other jazz giants.

When I was working with the Jazz Messengers at the Stage Lounge on the South Side of Chicago, I took the El, the overhead train, back to my hotel every night after the gig. I noticed a young black man on that train every night with his tenor saxophone, coming home from a gig. One night, I started up a conversation with him. His name was Eddie Harris. Eddie patterned his sound after Stan Getz. When he found out I used to work with Stan, he pumped me for all the information I could give him about Stan. He came by to check out the Jazz Messengers, and we became friends. Years later, he moved to California. When I moved there too, we reactivated our friendship. I used him on three of my Silveto recordings: *Guides to Growing Up*, *Spiritualizing the Senses*, and *There's No Need to Struggle*. I also used him on my two Sony/Columbia recordings *It's Got to Be Funky* and *Pencil Packin' Papa*. Eddie was one of the most creative and inventive musicians I've ever met. He was always stretching his imagination to come up with something new and different. I miss him.

Chicago gave us a lot of great jazz musicians. Wilber Ware, Clifford Jordan, and John Gilmore all sat in with the Jazz Messengers when we played Chicago. I recommended Clifford Jordan and John Gilmore to Alfred Lion of Blue Note Records, and he recorded them. I was privileged to meet and hear Chicago pianists Jody Christian, Chris Anderson, and Ronnell Bright as well as bassist and arranger Johnny Pate and drummer Wilber Cambell. When I got my own band, we used to play at the Southerland Lounge and McKee's on the South Side. Eventually, we started playing at the Plugged Nickel in downtown Chicago. When we played there, I would stay at the Croyden Hotel on Rush Street. Drummer Barrett Deems, who worked with Louis Armstrong for many years, lived there. I would meet him in the coffee shop downstairs for breakfast or lunch. I always enjoyed listening to the stories he told about his experience in the music business.

THE JAZZ MESSENGERS also played Storyville in Boston for a week's engagement. One night, we were on stage performing, and George Wein, who owned the club, came up to the side of the piano and told me that Art Tatum was in the house. As I sometimes did in those days, I got real nervous and couldn't relax and play my normal shit. The thought of this super-genius out there checking me out made me freeze up. When we finished the set, George introduced me to Tatum. Every pianist—not just jazz pianists but classical pianists also—who has ever heard Art Tatum play is in awe of his genius.

Many stories about the genius of Art Tatum have been passed around. I have two that were told to me, which I'd like to pass on to you. I met the great composer and arranger Sy Oliver on a plane years ago on the way to Cleveland. He was one of the fine arrangers who had written for the Jimmie Lunceford band, and Lunceford was my idol. As Sy described the story, he had arranged some music for a singer and was in the control booth, getting prepared to record. Johnny Guarnieri, a real fine pianist whose work I always admired, was the piano player on the session. Johnny was playing some runs on the piano while the rest of the band was tuning up. Sy turned on the intercom and said, "Hey, Johnny, that sounds like a Tatum run."

Johnny came into the control booth and said, "You know, Sy, it took me six months of practicing that run before I could play it right. When I ran into Art, I asked him to listen to me play it and tell me if I was playing it right. I played it for him, and he said, yes, it was right. Then he sat down and played the whole run with his left hand only."

Pianist Earl Washington, who worked with Red Saunders's band at the Club De Lisa in Chicago, told me another story about Art Tatum. He used to hang out with Tatum when he came to Chicago. Tatum always had a suite with a piano in it. One day when Earl visited him in his suite, Tatum went to the bathroom, and Earl sat down at the piano and started to play. Tatum yelled out from the bathroom, “Hey, fourth finger on that B-flat.” There are geniuses and then there are super-geniuses. We’ve had many geniuses in the jazz world, but I believe that Art Tatum and Charlie Parker were super-geniuses.

DOUG WATKINS AND I were good friends. We hung out together. One week when the Jazz Messengers were playing at the Cafe Bohemia in Greenwich Village, we met two fine brown-skinned young ladies from Florida. He hit on one, and I hit on the other. They were girlfriends who had driven to New York for a week’s vacation. We took them for breakfast after the gig and then to the Arlington Hotel. Doug and his lady went to his room, and my lady and I went to room 608. On awakening, I called Doug and suggested that we all go to lunch together.

When we returned from lunch, Doug and his lady went to his room, only to find a detective there, going through his belongings. My lady and I went to my room, where we found another detective going through my belongings. The scene was clean. Nobody was dirty because we didn’t use drugs. I asked the detectives, “Why us?” They said they had received an anonymous call at police headquarters saying that Doug and I were drug users.

The Jazz Messengers also played Philadelphia several times. After one of those weekly gigs, I was packing and getting ready to go back to New York by train. I called Art’s room to let him know I was leaving. He said, “Why pay train fare when you can go back with me in my car? I’m leaving in a few hours.” I said, “Okay, I’ll wait and go with you.”

Besides Art and myself, the Baroness Nica’s daughter Janka and Art’s band boy, Ahmed, were in the car. Ahmed used to travel with Art and set up and break down his drums, run errands, and cop drugs for Art. Ahmed was a user also, a mainliner. We got in the car, and Art started driving. Before we could get out of Philly, we were stopped by a motorcycle cop. We weren’t speeding or breaking any traffic rules. The cop saw three black men in a car with a white woman, and that was reason enough for him to stop us.

If Art had been cool, the cop might have let us go. But Art was high and acted belligerent and indignant. The cop told Art to follow him to the local precinct. The cop took us into the precinct and then went outside to search Art's car. He found a loaded gun and a box of shells and a box of Benzedrine tablets in the glove compartment. Art had no permit for the gun. The Benzedrine belonged to Janka, the baroness's daughter. Ahmed had track marks on his arms.

We were all booked. Art and I were put in a cell together at the precinct. Janka and Ahmed were taken somewhere else. I was going to call my dad to come down from Norwalk and get me out. Art said, "Don't worry your dad. I'll call Nica, and she'll get us out." Art called Nica, and she engaged a lawyer to get us out. However, when the lawyer found out that three of us were black, he didn't want to get involved with us. He did get Janka out, but he left us in jail.

Art and I stayed in the precinct over the weekend and then were transferred to the city prison on Monday. When we arrived at the city prison, I was put in a cell with two other black inmates, and Art was taken to another section of the prison. The two guys I bunked with were seasoned criminals and had been in many different prisons before. They were also jazz fans and knew all about Art and me.

One night while I was asleep, the guard woke me up at about three o'clock in the morning and said that I was wanted in the warden's office. When I arrived there, two FBI men were waiting to question me. One of them said, "I'm going to ask you some questions, and if I catch you in a lie, I'm going to kick you right in your balls." I said, "I've been questioned several times before, and I'm telling the truth. I don't use drugs. I work with these guys, but I'm clean."

When I got back to my cell, I couldn't go back to sleep because some crazy guy on the first tier was yelling and screaming and waking up all the other inmates. The guards came and gave him a shot and put him in a straitjacket.

The police allowed you to make one phone call only. Instead of calling my dad direct and taking a chance on not catching him at home, I called Ida Cox, who ran a boardinghouse in Philly, where I sometimes stayed when I was in town. I asked her to call my dad and tell him to come down to Philly and bail me out of jail. Dad came down and bailed me out.

I felt so bad about this situation. I didn't want Dad to think that I was a drug user. When I got out and Dad and I returned to my New York apartment, I sat down and explained everything to him. I broke down and cried. He believed me when I told him that I did not use drugs. There was to be a hearing within a few weeks, and Dad engaged a Philadelphia lawyer on my behalf. When we met with this lawyer, we asked him what chance I had of getting this charge dropped. He said that I had a fair chance, but that if I wanted to be certain, I could grease the palm of the magistrate judge, by paying him six hundred dollars, and the charge would be dropped. We gave him the money.

The hearing was a farce. Janka was giving all the wrong answers when she was being questioned, but the judge and her lawyer were putting the right answers in her mouth. When she made a mistake, they would say, "Oh, you mean so-and-so, don't you?" The hearing was very brief, and everybody was acquitted. Evidently, everybody paid off the judge. This was a very harrowing experience for me. I had nightmares about it for about two years afterward.

IN SPITE OF SUCH EXPERIENCES, I can say that the Jazz Messengers were the greatest band that I've ever played with—and I've played with some great ones. Some nights, we'd be cookin' so tough it would seem like we were floating in space. I've never grooved with any group of musicians so consistently as I did with the Jazz Messengers. I believe that these guys didn't play great because of their use of drugs. Drugs are a handicap; they played great in spite of their use of drugs.

Kenny Dorham and Hank Mobley are two of the most underrated musicians in jazz. They worked so well together. They were both giants. They sure played some slick shit when they improvised. I remember baritone saxophonist Charles Davis asking Kenny to show him some of that slick shit that he played. Kenny's reply was, "Man, it's all on my records.

If you can cop it, go on and get it." Good advice, I would say. I learned much in my formative years by listening to records and analyzing what I heard and using it in my playing. It's good ear training. You don't have to use it exactly as you got it from the record. You can turn it around to fit your style and your concept.

Art Blakey is one of the great jazz drummers of all time. He and Doug Watkins and I used to lock in rhythmically and swing so tough that we'd inspire the horn players to greater heights. We were constantly kickin' them in the ass rhythmically. With all that fire we were puttin' up under their asses, they had to take care of business and cook. And they sure did just that.

I recall Art Blakey calling the Jazz Messengers together to give us a lecture after a set we had played at the Cafe Bohemia in Greenwich Village. Evidently, he wasn't pleased with how the band was sounding that night. He said, "I don't care if you've had a fight with your wife or your girlfriend or what kind of problems you have at home. When you come to this gig, leave that shit outside, and come in here with the intent to cook. If you want to pick those problems up again when you leave, that's your business. But when you come in here, be prepared to cook." Art always gave one hundred percent of himself to the audience. I've seen him when he was sick or when he had hung out for three days gettin' high and hardly had any sleep. But he always gave one hundred percent of himself when he got on the bandstand. We used to refer to him as the "Little Dynamo."

The original Jazz Messengers were one hell of a band. I love and miss all of these guys.

Chapter Four

THE QUINTET

Pillars of thought that I can hold on to,
to keep myself from fallin'.
For years I've sought a different direction,
to walk instead of crawlin'.
The poets bring a new introspection
that speaks of wings and flyin'.
I'll flap my arms and open my mind
to a different way of tryin'.

I WAS TWENTY-SEVEN years old when I started my quintet, just after I left the Jazz Messengers. The quintet came about as a result of several albums I recorded for Alfred Lion and the Blue Note label. I did not have a regular working band at the time. I just got the guys together, rehearsed them, and made an album. One day in 1956, I received a phone call from Jack Whittemore, a booking agent. He said that the Showboat, a Philadelphia nightclub, wanted to book my quintet for a week's engagement. The owner of the Showboat told him my recordings were receiving a lot of airplay in Philly, and he thought we could make him some money. I said to Jack, "I don't have a steady working band." He said, "Why don't you put one together and go on down there and make that money?" I thought about it and decided to do just that.

I got hold of trumpeter Art Farmer, tenor saxophonist Hank Mobley, bassist Doug Watkins, and drummer Arthur Taylor, and we rehearsed and made the gig. With the exception of Arthur Taylor, these were the musicians who would become the first Horace Silver Quintet. We packed the house every night. At the end of the week, the owner said that we had made money for him and that he wanted us back in about four months. In the meantime, other offers started to come in through Jack Whittemore. All of a sudden, I was a bandleader with a steady working band. Jack Whittemore became my booking agent and remained so until he died. He was a good agent and a nice guy.

Arthur Taylor was with us for that one week only—he had committed himself to work with someone else after that. Doug Watkins and Donald Byrd recommended Louis Hayes to take his place. Louis, who was eighteen years old at the time, was living in Detroit. I had never heard him play, but based on Doug's and Donald's recommendation, I called him and offered him two weeks' work with the band. If he worked out to my satisfaction, he would remain our drummer. He worked out beautifully and remained with us for several years.

When we made the album titled *Six Pieces of Silver* for Blue Note later that year, Art Farmer was signed with Prestige Records. Bob Weinstock of Prestige and Alfred Lion of Blue Note were always feuding. Alfred claimed that Bob was trying to steal his artists, and Bob claimed that Alfred was trying to steal his. A few days before the session, Bob notified Alfred that Art couldn't make the session, that he was exclusive to Prestige Records. So I called Donald Byrd. Donald was attending the Manhattan School of Music and subbed for Art Farmer from time to time. Art worked both with our group and with Gerry Mulligan's band. Gerry got more work than we did and made more money, so when Gerry had a gig for Art the same week we did, I got Donald to sub for Art. Donald would always come in and take care of business. The group included Donald, Hank Mobley, Doug Watkins, and Louis Hayes. On this album, we introduced "Señor Blues," which went on to become a jazz standard.

After "Señor Blues" became popular as an instrumental, I decided to rerecord it with a vocal in 1958. I chose Bill Henderson to sing it because he had style and great feeling. In those days, he was not an actor; but through the years, he has become a fine actor as well. We've been friends for over thirty-five years. I met Bill through a mutual friend named Don Newey, a pianist and a fine composer. Don and Bill, who are both from Chicago, shared an apartment in New York, just around the corner from where I lived at 23 West Seventy-sixth Street. I recorded a couple of Don's compositions on one of my Blue Note albums.

When I lived in New York, I often visited with Don and Bill. One evening, we were listening to records and having a piece of cake and a cup of tea. Don asked me if I had ever seen anyone light up a fart. I said no. I didn't believe this could be done. He said, "I feel a fart coming on—would you like to see me demonstrate?" I said, "Yeah." He turned out all the lights and bent over and struck a match. He held it a few inches from his butt and farted. A blue flame shot out across the room. He turned the lights on, and the three of us had a good laugh. He cautioned us that if we were to try this, we should be very careful not to hold the match too close to our butt or we could burn our butt hole. This goes to prove that gas is flammable no matter where it comes from. What a great scientific discovery!

PHILADELPHIA WAS A TOUGH TOWN to work in back in the fifties if you were a jazz musician, especially if you were a black musician. The police thought that every jazz musician was a drug addict. True, many were, but many were not. The ones who were not were subjected to the same indignities from the police that the users faced.

My quintet played the Blue Note Club in North Philadelphia for a one-week engagement. We had a four o'clock matinee on Saturday. We stayed at a black-owned hotel near the club. After the gig on Friday night, I hung out late with some friends and got to bed late. I intended to sleep late on Saturday because I knew we had a matinee at four o'clock, and I needed my rest.

Around nine o'clock Saturday morning, there came a knock on my door. I asked who it was, and a voice said, "It's Willie Baby. Willie from the Blue Note. Open up."

I answered, "I don't know any Willie from the Blue Note. If you want to talk to me, you'll have to see me at the matinee. I've got to get my rest."

The voice at the door sounded like a white man trying to imitate the sound of a black man's voice. Then the voice said, "Open up; it's the police."

I opened the door and let him in. I was dressed only in my undershorts. He picked up my phone and told the operator to send the other detective up. The other detective was keeping an eye on the switchboard operator to make sure she didn't inform me that the police were coming to my room and give me a chance to get rid of any drugs that I might have on hand.

Both detectives searched my room and found nothing. Then they told me drop my drawers and bend over and hold up my testicles. They shined a flashlight under my testicles to see if I had any drugs taped there. Then one of them went to the phone, called his captain at the police station, and told him that I was clean. His captain told them to bring me down to the station anyway, that he wanted to talk to me.

I said, "Am I under arrest? If so, please let me notify the club owner, because I'm supposed to play a matinee at four o'clock" They said, "No, you're not under arrest. The captain just wants to talk to you."

I had to walk through the hotel lobby with these guys and get into the police car with them. The lobby was filled with people, all curious to see what was happening. It was very embarrassing. The captain was an elderly man. He told me to empty everything out of my pockets and put it all on his desk. I took wallet, comb, pen, handkerchief, coins, and everything out of my pockets and laid them on his desk. He then laid out a sheet of white paper and told me to empty the corners of my pockets onto this paper. He was looking for remnants of pot or pot seeds. He was going to send everything in my pockets to the lab to check.

I asked him, "Why are you harassing me? I'm not a drug user." He said that someone they had busted claimed that he had bought drugs from the piano player at the Blue Note.

"The Blue Note changes bands every week. He could have bought his drugs from the piano player who was there last week," I said.

The captain said, "I'm the guy who busted Gene Krupa when he played at the Earl Theater in Philly. I can look in your eyes and tell you're using something. I'd advise you not to come back to Philly—because if you do, we're going to get you next time."

It was a long time before I would accept a gig in Philadelphia after that incident. Eventually, the owner of the Showboat convinced me that it would be safe to come back to Philly and work for him. He admitted that he could not stop the police from coming into his club and interrupting our performance to take us in the dressing room and search us and our belongings, but he promised that he would be there with us at all times to see that they didn't mistreat us or plant any drugs on us. The things one had to endure to play jazz music in those days!

I recall the Horace Silver Quintet playing an all-star jazz concert at a convention hall in Philadelphia some years ago. Four or five name jazz groups were in the show, including Dizzy Gillespie and his big band. As the bands approached the backstage door, they were greeted by members of the Philadelphia vice squad. Every musician who played a horn had to open up his horn case so that the detectives could search for drugs. Everyone had to roll up their shirt sleeves on both arms so that the detectives could examine their arms for track marks. Of course, you were also personally searched. The scene was clean. Nobody was dirty. Nobody got busted.

They used to call Philadelphia the "City of Brotherly Love." Maybe it was for some people, but it sure wasn't for a jazz musician, especially a black musician. A black jazz musician in those days was considered by the Philadelphia police to be guilty until proven innocent. Thank God, Philadelphia has mellowed considerably since then.

IN THE FORMATIVE YEARS of the quintet, we used to drive to all our gigs because we couldn't afford to fly. We drove to Chicago, Detroit, Pittsburgh, Philadelphia, Boston, Baltimore, and Washington, D.C. We often ran into Ray Charles and his group on the Pennsylvania Turnpike at one of the Howard Johnson restaurants and gas stations.

My first car was a Plymouth station wagon. We had a one-night concert gig in Indianapolis, and we drove there in the station wagon. We had heard about this great guitar player, Wes Montgomery, who lived there. He was playing at a local black-owned barbecue rib joint. After our gig, the band and I went by to eat and listen to Wes play. Our instruments and my change of clothes were locked up in the station wagon outside the restaurant.

We were enjoying the food and the music when someone came in and said that some guys were breaking into our station wagon and trying to steal our instruments. We got outside just in time. They had broken the window and had their arms full of my clothing. They saw us come out of the restaurant, and they ran off with my clothes. They didn't have time to steal the instruments, thank God. We had to drive all the way back to New York with a broken window, in the dead of winter. Even though we had the heater turned up all the way, we froze our asses off during that trip back to New York.

What a relief it was, years later, when we started to make enough money to fly the band to our various gigs. We would arrive fresher and more rested and more energetic, ready to take care of business and cook. But we always took care of business and cooked, no matter what our mode of transportation. This was an attitude Art Blakey instilled in me when I was with the Jazz Messengers, and I don't intend to ever relinquish it. The bandstand is sacred ground. No place to be messin' around. We gotta take care of serious business when we get up there. No bullshittin'. We give one hundred percent of ourselves to the music and to the people.

When we traveled, we used to rehearse during the day at the club where we were performing that night. When we were off and in New York, we would rehearse at Nola's Studio on Broadway or at Lynn Oliver's Studio on Broadway. I always believed in a lot of rehearsal, and I still do. Although the rehearsals are great to help get the band tight, there's nothing like performing before a live audience to loosen up everybody and get deeply into the music.

IN MY LATE TWENTIES and early thirties, most of the jazz record companies wanted their artists to record standard compositions that people were familiar with. They would allow you to record some original compositions, but their main thrust was the standards. I recorded an album called *Silver's Blue* for Epic Records in 1956. George Avakian was the producer. I approached him with six originals that I wanted to record. He wanted me to do three standards and three originals. I reviewed some of my favorite standard compositions and chose three to arrange for the session. The session came off well, and I am proud of it.

The quintet that included Art Farmer on trumpet, Clifford Jordan on tenor, Teddy Kotick on bass, and Louis Hayes on drums was a fine group. Louis, Teddy, and I could really get some great grooves going. We'd kick ass. We'd prod the horn players and make them stretch. We got to make only one more album with this band before it broke up. That album, recorded in early 1958, was called *Further Explorations.*

Sometime during that period, alto saxophonist Lee Konitz called me and said he would like to work with my band. I was flattered. He's such a great musician. At the time, I had a real good tenor sax player working with the quintet, and I wanted to hold on to him. I wasn't making enough money to afford to expand the group to a sextet, so I respectfully declined Lee's offer. I often wonder what the band would have sounded like if I could have added him to the group. I'm sure he would have brought another dimension to my music.

One of the cities where we often worked was Detroit, where I met a young eighteen-year-old singer named Freda Payne. She was the toast of Detroit at that time. I was invited to her home to have dinner with Freda, her parents, and her younger sister.

When she was approximately nineteen years old, Freda came to New York to further pursue her career. We met once again and started going out together. She was a real fine singer and a very pretty young lady. But neither of us was ready for any serious involvement at that time because both of us were busy trying to move forward with our careers.

Aside from being a fine singer, Freda is also a good actress. She was an understudy for a role in a Broadway play. One night when the primary actress got sick, Freda was called on to take over the part. She called me and invited me to come and see the play. I did and was greatly impressed with her acting ability.

Some of the musicians who worked with my quintet back in the first couple of years but never recorded with me were drummers Alvin Queen, Harold White, and Jeff Brillinger; tenor saxophonists Ronnie Bridgewater and Vincent Herring; bassists Chip Jackson, John Burr, Mike Richmond, and Will Lee; and trumpeters John McNeil, Dave Douglas, and Barry Reese. During those years, we also played a one-week gig at the Village Gate in New York City opposite Aretha Franklin. She was eighteen years old then, and this was her first gig outside her hometown of Detroit. She had a trio and was singing and accompanying herself on piano. It was evident to me that she would eventually become a big star, because she had all the qualifications. She played good piano and had good stage presence, and she sang her ass off.

In the early part of my career as a bandleader, sometime between 1958 and 1960, the quintet and I played opposite Ornette Coleman and Don Cherry at Storyville in Boston for a week. All week long, I was listening and trying to figure out what these guys were doing. Finally, I cornered Ornette and asked him to explain it to me. He gave me a lengthy explanation, which I couldn't seem to understand. I guess I'm just an old-fashioned guy who loves a good melody, some nice harmony, and a beat that swings. Ornette and Don were swingin', but I couldn't figure out their approach to improvising. I was used to following a form, and their music seemed to be formless. There is something about this type of music that I enjoy when I see and hear it performed live, but when I try to listen to it on records, I find that it doesn't hold my attention. Don't ask me why, 'cause I don't know.

I have a great deal of respect for Ornette and Don. They are innovators. I have respect for anyone who is daring enough to come up with a totally different concept and stick to their guns about it even though the concept is not widely accepted by the establishment. We need more artists like these in music, artists who are willing to sacrifice for what they believe in. Lester Young and Thelonious Monk were such musicians.

Harry Belafonte discovered a great South African singer named Miriam Makeba and brought her to the United States to tour with his group. She eventually started touring on her own and became quite successful. She had an apartment at Park West Village when I lived there. One night when my quintet was working at Birdland, she came in with some of her friends, and I was introduced to her. There were some sparks between us, and we started seeing each other regularly.

She was busy touring and I was busy touring, but when we were both at home in New York, we spent time together. As well as being a great talent, she was a very warm and lovable person. She cooked many great South African meals for me and introduced me to many beautiful South African people. But I was married to Lady Music, who still had top priority. I wasn't ready to make any serious commitment. I felt that I hadn't securely established myself in the music business at that time, and I needed more time to do that before considering a serious relationship with any woman. However, my memories of our times spent together are beautiful ones.

The quintet often played in Chicago at the Southerland Lounge, which was located in the Southerland Hotel on the city's South Side. We all had rooms in the hotel. One evening, I went downstairs to the lounge about an hour before our gig to check out the piano and see if it had been tuned as I had requested. While I was checking out the piano, the phone rang, and the bartender answered it. He said that it was for me. I went to the phone to discover that it was actress Diana Barrymore, calling to see if I could make reservations for her and a party of her friends to attend that evening's performance. I made the reservations, and she and her friends arrived that evening.

I met her during intermission, and we had a long talk. She told me that her first husband had turned her on to jazz and that she had been a jazz fan and a follower of our music ever since. She was appearing in the Tennessee Williams play *Sweet Bird of Youth* at one of the downtown Chicago theaters. She invited me to come and see the play on my off night and to come backstage and say hello after the show. I went and enjoyed the play and went backstage afterward. We went to a club in downtown Chicago where Ramsey Lewis was performing that night. Diana and I exchanged phone numbers. We both lived in New York, and we occasionally called one another.

She called me one day and said that Tennessee Williams was at her apartment and that he had heard some of my music and wanted to meet me. It just so happened that my Uncle Nate had called from Norwalk about an hour before to tell me that my Aunt Maude was very sick and near death and that she was asking to see me. He asked if I would come right away. So I had to decline the invitation to meet Tennessee Williams and go to Norwalk to see Aunt Maude. My aunt eventually recovered from her illness and didn't die until years later. I don't regret going to see Aunt Maude, for I loved her very much. She was like a second mother to me after my mom died. But I do regret not getting to meet Tennessee Williams, because I am a great admirer of his talent. The poem that he wrote for the motion picture *The Night of the Iguana* so moved me that I saw the movie twice on TV and taped and memorized it. That poem helped me get through a difficult period later on, right after my divorce. I can still recite it from memory:

How calmly does the olive branch
Observe the sky begin to blanch
Without a cry, without a prayer,
With no betrayal of despair.

Sometime while night obscures the tree
The zenith of its life will be
Gone past forever, and from thence
A second history will commence.

A chronicle no longer gold,
A bargaining with mist and mould,

And finally the broken stem
The plummeting to earth; and then

An intercourse not well designed
For beings of a golden kind
Whose native green must arch above
The earth's obscene, corrupting love.

And still the ripe fruit and the branch
Observe the sky begin to blanch
Without a cry, without a prayer,
With no betrayal of despair.

O Courage, could you not as well
Select a second place to dwell,
Not only in that golden tree
But in the frightened heart of me?

One of the times we played the Blue Note Club in Philadelphia, Bud Powell came by to check us out. Philadelphia was his hometown. We were in the middle of a set, and the doorman came up to me and said that Bud was outside in a taxi and didn't have any money to pay the cabbie. I gave him some money to pay for the cab. A few moments later, I saw Bud walk in. He sat in the rear of the club and listened. As soon as we finished our set, I rushed over to talk to him, but he had split. I thought to myself, "I hope he didn't split because he didn't like what I was playing." Bud came by another time when we were playing at a club in the Bronx. We were in the middle of a set when I saw him walk in and sit in the rear of the club to listen. When the set was over, I rushed to talk to him, but again he had split.

The next time I saw Bud was when he returned from his stay in Europe and opened at Birdland for a two-week engagement. My quintet worked opposite his trio. We used to play a tune called "No Smokin'," which was very Bud Powell influenced. One night after playing "No Smokin'," I came off the bandstand and walked by Bud's table. He stopped me and said he liked the tune and asked me how I came to write it. I said, "Man, you know that's some of your shit." He laughed and said he would like to get a lead sheet of the tune and perform it. I mailed him a lead sheet the following week. He never got around to performing it or recording it, but I was honored that he liked it.

During that same engagement at Birdland, a funny thing happened between Bud and a young lady who was hanging out on the scene at that time. Drummer Bobby Thomas had gone to Europe with some band on a tour. In Sweden, he had met a fine-lookin' young lady and had an affair with her. I guess to Bobby it was just a one-nighter, so to speak, but she fell in love with him. She followed him back to New York in the hope of maybe hooking him and marrying him or something, but he just turned his back on her. I met her and hit on her myself, but I couldn't get to first base with her because she wasn't giving up any of that pussy to anyone but Bobby Thomas.

Anyhow, during that week at Birdland, she was hanging out with Bud. During the intermission, when there was a lull of about five or ten minutes between the time I came off and Bud was supposed to go back up, he was sitting with her at a table. I was sitting about three tables away from them. I wasn't eavesdropping on their conversation, but I couldn't help overhearing them talk. Somewhere in the middle of the conversation, I heard him say, "Yeah . . . Yeah . . . But when you goin' to give me some of that pussy?" I laughed and said to myself, "People say Bud Powell's crazy, but he's not crazy. He knows when he wants some pussy to ask for some."

Bud was in and out of several mental hospitals during his life. He had received shock treatments, and his behavior was erratic from time to time. His playing might have deteriorated a bit in his later years because of this, but he left us a beautiful legacy of recorded music that will continue to inspire me and many others.

AFTER A NUMBER OF personnel changes, Blue Mitchell and Junior Cook eventually replaced Art Farmer and Hank Mobley in the quintet, and Gene Taylor replaced Doug Watkins. Around 1960, Cannonball Adderley lured Louis Hayes away from us with an offer of more money. I have always made it a practice to pay all my sidemen the same salary; no one gets paid any more than the others. If I had given Louis a raise, I would have had to raise the salary of everyone in the band. This I could not afford to do at the time. Once again, I looked to Detroit for a replacement. Roy Brooks was recommended. I called him and offered him the same deal I offered Louis. Roy joined us and remained with us for several years.

The Blue Mitchell, Junior Cook, Gene Taylor, Louis Hayes/Roy Brooks band was one of the best bands I ever had. We stayed together for about six years. We were real tight, musically and personally. We were a family, like brothers. We played well together and looked out for each other like family members do. We got along well together. We were very compatible as musicians and as people. There were two differences between the band members and myself: they all liked to drink, and I was a nondrinker; and I was into health foods and vitamins, and they were not. In spite of their drinking, they never got so wasted that they couldn't play well. We rocked many a nightclub with that band.

Blue Mitchell and I used to compete for some of the fine ladies we saw seated at the bar in some of the clubs we played. We would spot a fine-looking lady, and after the set it would be a mad dash to see which one of us would get to her first. We had mutual respect for each other. If he got there first, I bowed out. If I got there first, he bowed out. If he couldn't get to first base with the lady and bowed out, I tried my shot at her, and vice versa.

The six years that group spent together were happy ones for me. I hope they were happy for the rest of the band also. We made a lot of great recordings together and made a lot of people happy through our music.

The term "funky" in the jazz vocabulary means bluesy or down-to-earth. My music has been termed "funky" by jazz critics and fans. I remember showing my dad an article written about me in *Downbeat* magazine, which said that I was funky. Dad read this and was greatly offended. He said, "What do they mean, you're funky? You take a bath every day." He didn't know the jazz meaning of the word. One thing I liked and appreciated about the Blue Mitchell–Junior Cook band was that they could play bebop *and* they could play funky. Some musicians in those days excelled at bebop but couldn't play funky. Other musicians excelled at playing funky but couldn't play bebop. The Blue Mitchell, Junior Cook, Gene Taylor, Roy Brooks band played well in both idioms.

I recall the band playing a concert in the late 1950s in Paris. After the gig, we went to a club to hear the Lou Bennett Trio—Lou on organ, Jimmy Gourley on guitar, and Kenny "Klook" Clarke on drums. After they finished for the evening, I asked Klook how he came to invent the bebop style of drumming. Klook is from Pittsburgh. He said he used to practice with a bass player in Pittsburgh who always told him to stay out of his way when they played together. I presume the bass player meant for him to let the bass notes come through and not to cover them up by playing the bass drum too loud. Anyway, that's how bebop drumming was invented. Kenny Clarke was the daddy of it all. Max Roach and Art Blakey came later and added their contributions, but Klook started it all.

Drummer Philly Joe Jones sat in with us several times. Whenever I'd see Philly Joe in the audience, I'd say, "C'mon, Joe, sit in on a couple of tunes for us," and he would. Drummer Roy Haynes sat in with us once in London at Ronnie Scott's club and played his ass off. When he accompanies horn players that play with fire, he'll bash and kick the cats in the ass and make them blow and bear down. But when he's playing with singers like Sarah Vaughan, he's very delicate. Philly Joe's the same way. When he'd play with us, he'd be bashin' and cookin'. But when he came out here to the West Coast in the Bill Evans Trio at the Lighthouse, I said, "I've got to see this, because Philly Joe is too heavy for Bill Evans. He's the kind of drummer who would drown him out." But when I went to see them, Philly was playing so tasteful and delicate—it sounded great. I complimented him when he came off the bandstand. A good drummer exercises taste. He can fit the situation.

AMONG THE MANY PLACES where we appeared in the States and around the world, the quintet worked Los Angeles and San Francisco once a year. One time when we were playing in Los Angeles at the It Club, trumpeter Carmell Jones and drummer Frank Butler sat in with us. I was impressed with their talent. Carmell was cookin', and Frank and I were very compatible. We seemed to anticipate each other's moves. It was like we had been playing together for years and knew just what the other was about to do.

Once, while we were performing in Paris, a friend took me to see and hear pianist Joe Turner. Joe had been a friend of James P. Johnson and played in that style. He had a great left hand. He was one of the great stride piano players. Bud Powell was living and working in Paris at that time, and he would often go to catch Joe perform. Joe played solo piano at a club in Paris and rocked the joint every night. I was introduced to Joe during intermission, and we talked about various piano players. I told him that pianist Herman Chittison was one of my favorite swing-era piano players. He said that he and Herman had been buddies and had shared an apartment together in New York.

My quintet also played a two-week engagement at Ronnie Scott's in London some years ago. While we were there, I barely averted a situation that could have become very unpleasant. At Ronnie's, we worked from Monday through Saturday, with Sunday off. In those days, London was pretty much shut down on Sundays. There was nowhere to go except to the movies and a few restaurants. On my first Sunday off, I decided to get up early and go to Piccadilly Circus and Trafalgar Square, check out what was playing at some of the movies, and do a bit of window-shopping at some of the department stores.

As I was looking at men's clothing in some of the shop windows, I spied a beautiful brown-skinned lady checking out some women's clothes about a block away. She appeared to be alone. I started to approach her to hit on her and invite her to Ronnie Scott's to hear the group. As I started toward her, out of the corner of my eye I saw a black man come around the corner and head toward her. As I got closer, I realized that he was with her and that they were Ike and Tina Turner. Good thing I didn't hit on her before he came around the corner. She was looking good, and she still looks good.

My second Sunday off, I decided to get up early and go to Hyde Park to hear the protesters and soapbox lecturers. They were all over the park, spouting off their grievances. There was a group of black West Indian men who were putting down the English people. They said that when one of them got hold of an Englishwoman, she never went back to an Englishman again. I thought, "Wow, let me get out of here, because there's gonna be a riot." But the English people were very tolerant. They just stood and listened. London is a very exciting city. I always enjoy going there.

I remember a tour I did for Norman Granz in Europe that included Muddy Waters. Muddy was doing a sound check, and his piano player, Otis Spann, hadn't shown up yet. They were in the midst of playing one of their blues numbers, and I was eager to sit in and get some of that groove. I sat down to play and discovered that they were in a key I had never played in before. It was either B-natural, E-natural, F-sharp, or A-natural. I don't remember which, but it was kickin' my ass.

In December 1962, the Horace Silver Quintet toured Japan. It was an experience I'll never forget. We were treated like royalty or superstars. Frank Sinatra couldn't have been treated any better. The red carpet was extended to us in those days. Japan was just beginning to import jazz artists. Today when we are touring Japan, we are treated well, but it's nothing like the treatment we received back in 1962. Japan has now become accustomed to visiting jazz artists, and the treatment is not as lavish as it used to be.

When we arrived in Tokyo the first time, the newsreel cameras were at the airport to film our arrival for Japanese television. Singer Chris Connor and her trio were also part of this tour. Chris and myself and all the members of our groups were presented with flowers. There was a press conference the day before the concert in Tokyo. After the concert, a group of beautiful Japanese ladies presented flowers to Chris, me, and each one of our musicians. This procedure was customary in each city where we performed. The treatment was so royal, I thought I had died and gone to heaven. The whole show was invited out to dinner by the promoters in all the cities we played. I learned how to use chopsticks.

Terry Isano, Japanese disc jockey, music critic, and master of ceremonies at jazz concerts, became a friend. When he visited New York, we hung out and went to all the jazz clubs, and I'd invite him to my home for dinner. I also met Japanese drummer Hideo Shiraki on this tour. He had a quintet consisting of trumpet, tenor sax, piano, bass, and drums. His tenor sax player was Sleepy Matsumoto, a real fine player whom I had heard about before we went to Japan. Shiraki was married to a famous, young, and beautiful movie star, whose mother was also a famous movie star. The band and I were invited to their home for dinner, along with Shiraki's band members. After dinner, his band and mine got together in the living room and had a jam session.

When Shiraki and his wife visited New York, I invited them to my house for dinner and then took them to Birdland. We were playing there, and I invited Shiraki to sit in and play with us. Shiraki was the Art Blakey of Japan at that time. Art was his idol, and he played like Art. Shiraki passed away at an early age. Before he died, he recorded an album called *Hideo Shiraki Plays Horace Silver.*

I had a Japanese girlfriend for a short time. Her name was Masako Idimitsu. She is one of the girls who appear on my *Tokyo Blues* album cover. Her father was an oil tycoon, and her family was very wealthy. I never met her father or mother, but I did meet several other members of her family when I was in Japan, and I liked them. I think they liked me, too. Masako was a very warm and beautiful person. I liked her very much, but I didn't love her. I was still married to Lady Music. I've had several one-night stands with Japanese women while touring, but Masako was my only Japanese girlfriend. I have fond memories of our association.

We had some days off between concerts, and friends would take me sightseeing. I saw Kabuki theater, which is very old, traditional Japanese theater. I visited rock gardens. I was taken to dinner at a Kobe steak house. The cattle these steaks come from are fed beer along with their feed and are hand-massaged to produce tender meat. The steaks were very tender and delicious.

Our concerts were all sellouts. It was the custom for fans to come backstage at the end of a concert to get autographs and to bring small gifts to the performers. I had so many gifts from fans that I couldn't take them all home with me—it would have been too expensive because of overweight charges on the airplane. I gave most of them away before we left to come back to the States. This Japanese tour was one of the most memorable events in my career.

Roy Brooks became ill just before we did the tour of Japan. I hired drummer John Harris Jr. from Bridgeport, Connecticut, to replace him. John remained with us until Roy recovered and rejoined us. John made the *Tokyo Blues* album with us.

ON SUNDAY EVENINGS, I used to enjoy a television show called *I've Got a Secret*, hosted by Gary Moore. A panel of well-known people would wear masks over their eyes while a famous person stepped to the mike and gave some information about his or her life and career. Then the panel had to guess who that person was. One Sunday when I was watching, Gary Moore happened to mention that he liked jazz and that he listened to it often for relaxation. He said that some of his favorite artists included Ella Fitzgerald, Miles Davis, and Horace Silver. I was thrilled when I heard this. This was a plug on CBS Channel 2 at prime time. You never know where the music reaches, and I was happy that it had reached him. Once, when the band was playing the Jazz Gallery in Greenwich Village, I met comedian Sam Levinson. He told me that Gary Moore had urged him to come down and check us out.

Louis Armstrong was a guest on Moore's show one Sunday evening, and the blindfolded panel had to try to guess who he was. Satch told a humorous little story that night. He said he had been to a hospital to visit a friend who was ill. He asked his friend what was wrong with him. His friend said, "Well, Satch, the doctor says I've got some very close veins."

Pianist Teddy Wilson told me a story about Satch and his great sense of humor. Satch told a certain joke on stage at Carnegie Hall, and Dorothy Kilgallen gave him a bad review in the paper the next day because of it. She said it was in bad taste. The joke goes like this: Satch said his favorite food was hamburgers. He would go into the same restaurant each day and order a hamburger. The waitress knew he loved hamburgers. One day they ran out of hamburgers, and the waitress scratched it off the menu. When Satch came in for lunch, the waitress told him that she had just scratched what he liked best. He said, "That's all right, baby. Wash your hands and bring me a hamburger."

Teddy Wilson has always been a role model and an inspiration to me. I met him at a club called Small's Paradise in New York, where we were performing. My dad and my brother, Gene, had come down to New York from Connecticut that night to hear the band. The place was packed, and Teddy shared a table with Dad and Gene. I was so proud to have him in the house sitting with them. We became good friends. He recorded two of my compositions, "Nica's Dream" and "Strollin'."

DURING THE MID-SIXTIES, there were race riots going on all over the country in the summers. In response, New York City started something called the Jazzmobile, a mobile unit that featured jazz musicians playing from the top of a float. Its director was jazz piano great Billy Taylor. The idea was to bring entertainment into the ghettos of New York in the hope of eliminating the threat of riots.

My quintet played many of these gigs, and I enjoyed them very much. We boarded the float at a certain location and were driven around for a few blocks while we played, with announcements that a concert would be held at a certain location at a certain time. We played in Harlem and Brooklyn and also went to Rochester and Buffalo in New York and to Washington, D.C., to perform on the Jazzmobile.

These concerts always had great attendance. They were free, and some of the best musicians in jazz played for them. In Harlem, we often played concerts in residential neighborhoods, and people would lean out of their apartment windows, looking and listening. We played at Grant's Tomb and in Central Park. The kids would follow us around like we were pied pipers. There were usually vendors around, selling food and other items.

I signed a lot of autographs and met some nice people on these Jazzmobile gigs. Once again, jazz was called upon to bring peace and harmony among people. I am grateful to have been a part of it.

SOME TIME IN THE MID-SIXTIES, I met Brazilian pianist Sergio Mendez in New York. Trumpeter Kenny Dorham introduced us. Sergio was playing on a State Department tour with some other Brazilian musicians. Kenny came to me one day and said that he had met this Brazilian pianist and that it was obvious to him that Sergio had been listening to me, because he played somewhat in my style.

Sergio and I became friends. He invited me to come to Brazil and witness Carnaval and stay at his home. Sergio and his wife lived in a little town called Niteroi, an island off the coast of Rio de Janeiro. You have to take a ferry boat to get back and forth from Rio to Niteroi, the same way you take a ferry from Staten Island to New York.

This Brazilian vacation was for two weeks. The first week, I stayed in Niteroi with Sergio and his wife. Sergio and his band were playing a gig in Rio that week, and I went with him every night to the gig and hung out with him and his musicians. Sergio's band had a trombone player who played quite well. He didn't speak any English, but every time I saw him, he smiled and said, "J.J. Johnson. J.J. Johnson." He loved J.J., and that was evident in his playing. Right next door to the club where Sergio was working was another club where some very fine musicians and singers were performing. It was there that I met drummer Dom Um Romão. I sat in and jammed on several occasions at that club.

Carnaval started on the second week of my vacation. Dom Um invited me to come to Rio and stay with him and his lady friend, Flora Purim, so that I could experience it. Sergio's wife was pregnant at that time and was almost ready to have her baby, so she and Sergio preferred to stay in Niteroi and avoid the excitement of Rio during Carnaval.

Believe me, Carnaval provided much excitement, most of it good, but some of it bad. Rio was a wide-open town during that week. There was singing and dancing in the streets twenty-four hours a day for the whole week. Masquerade dances were held in ballrooms throughout the city.

Prizes were given for best costumes. Several samba schools were competing for first prize. Dom Um and Flora took me to some of their rehearsals. One school was called Salgueiro, and the other was called Portelo. It was very exciting to watch them rehearse. I was told that some of the very poorest people in Rio, who lived in the mountainside shacks called *favelas*, would do without things to save their money so that they could buy the materials to make fabulous costumes for Carnaval.

For the most part, it was a very happy time, but there were some sad moments. Some of the young people were sniffing glue and getting high, and a few died from this. The Brazilian police tried to keep order in the streets, but they were very brutal in their approach. While the parade was going on, people were supposed to stay on the sidewalk to watch and were not allowed to step off the curb. One evening when Dom Um, Flora, and I were watching the parade from one side of the street, the people on the other side stepped off the curb. A motorcycle cop aimed his motorcycle directly at those people and drove right into the crowd at a fast rate of speed. If they hadn't gotten out of the way in time, many of them would have been injured.

Dom Um and Flora also took me to Copacabana Beach several times, where I saw all these fine ladies in bikinis. Brazil sure has some fine-looking women.

The people of Brazil are so laid-back. When I was staying with Sergio, he had a business appointment in Rio one day at one P.M. with an executive. He asked me to go with him. I looked at the clock, and it was twelve noon. I said, "Sergio, we're going to be late." He said, "Relax, take it easy. We'll get there." By the time we got there, it was two P.M., and the executive hadn't arrived yet.

Sergio's wife introduced me to her girlfriend, and we dated a couple of times while I was there. She worked as a secretary for a lawyer in Rio. She told me that on her lunch hour she would often go to the beach, which was not far from her office. She always kept a bikini in her purse. Sometimes she would enjoy the beach so much that she would call her boss and say that she wouldn't be back for the rest of the afternoon. I asked her if her boss was irritated by this—wouldn't he threaten to fire her? She said no. Sometimes he would say, "Have an enjoyable afternoon," and sometimes he would say, "I'll get my bathing suit and join you." Brazilian Airlines never seemed to run on time, either. There seemed to be no urgency to do anything.

Years later, I went back to Brazil on a tour with my band. Again, I experienced the laid-back attitude of the Brazilian people. That band featured Mike Brecker on tenor, Tom Harrell on trumpet, Anthony Jackson on Fender bass, and Alvin Queen on drums. One afternoon, we were doing a sound check before our evening performance, and Alvin Queen asked a stagehand to put a nail in the floor to keep his bass drum from sliding away from him. The stagehand went off and didn't return with the nail and hammer until the sound check was over.

We would wait in the lobby of our hotel to be picked up, to prepare for our concert, and they would invariably be one hour late picking us up. If the concert was to start at nine P.M., people wouldn't start to show up until ten or after. We had to wait around until the house filled up and then start the concert. We taped a couple of TV shows while there. The cameras and mikes were old and outdated. The camera kept breaking down, and we had to retape several times. It was quite exhausting. I don't mean to portray the Brazilian people as being lazy—they're just laid-back. Things eventually get done, but there is no rush about it. Maybe if they would rush a bit more and we Americans would rush a bit less, we'd all be better off.

After returning home to New York from my visit with Sergio and Dom Um, I was haunted by the bossa nova rhythm I had heard in Brazil. I said to myself, "I'm going to try to write a song using that rhythmic concept." I sat down at the piano for a few hours and came up with a new song using the bossa nova rhythm. However, the melody didn't sound Brazilian to me; it sounded more like some of the old Cape Verdean melodies my dad had played. Dad had always wanted me to take some of the old Cape Verdean songs and do jazz interpretations of them. This idea didn't appeal to me, but when I realized I had written a new song with a Brazilian rhythmic concept and a Cape Verdean melodic concept, I immediately thought about dedicating the song to Dad. So I titled it "Song for My Father." We had him pose for the cover of the LP, also titled *Song for My Father.*

We introduced "Song for My Father" at the It Club in Los Angeles. One night when owner John T. McLean was driving me to my motel, as he did every night after the gig, he said, "Horace, that new song you wrote is going to be a big hit. I can't get it out of my head. Every night when I go home and go to bed, it keeps running through my mind." Thank God, his prediction was right. When the record was released, it went on to become a great success. "Señor Blues" was my most successful selling record until "Song for My Father" came along. "Song for My Father" continues to sell well and has been recorded by many other jazz artists.

EVENTUALLY, I BROKE UP the Blue Mitchell–Junior Cook band. After all these years, I can't remember my specific reasons for breaking up the band. Maybe I just wanted a change. I immediately hired Carmell Jones as trumpeter for the new band. I had heard Joe Henderson playing with Kenny Dorham and was impressed with his talent, so I hired Joe on tenor. I had heard Teddy Smith playing around New York, and I liked the way he played, so I brought him on as our bassist. Different musicians had told me about a fine young drummer from Pittsburgh named Roger Humphries. I invited him to come to New York and audition. When I heard him play, I knew right away that he was the drummer for us.

When Carmell left the band in late 1965, a friend recommended trumpeter Woody Shaw. I had never heard Woody play, but I got hold of a couple of recordings he played on, and I liked what I heard. Woody was from Newark, New Jersey, but he was living and working in Paris at that time. I phoned him and offered him a job with our quintet. He accepted. The first gig he played with us was a two-week engagement at the Plugged Nickel in Chicago. I gave him the trumpet parts to take home with him and memorize. At the end of the first week, he had memorized all the parts and gave me back the music. Once again, I had another kick-ass band.

One night when I had Woody in the quintet, we were playing in Buffalo, New York. All of a sudden, he took the horn down out of his mouth and walked off the bandstand into the kitchen. I said to myself, "What's wrong with this motherfucker? That's very unprofessional, walking off the stage in the middle of a tune and leaving me and Joe Henderson and the rhythm up there." So when I got off, I went into the kitchen to chew him out.

But when I went in there, he said, "Man, I'm sorry, I ain't playin' shit"—and he was playin' his ass off! He was so hard on himself that he got disgusted with himself and walked off into the kitchen. So I didn't chew him out. I just said, "Man, what're you talking about? You sound great."

Years later, I had the same experience with Tom Harrell—not that Tom ever walked off a bandstand, but I would have to give him pep talks. He'd be playing his ass off and steadily saying he ain't playin' shit. And he's knocking everybody out.

When Joe Henderson left the band, Tyrone Washington came on board. At first, he was a very humble young man. He was glad to be there and was cookin' his ass off. But as people began to appreciate his playing and give him compliments, his head started to get big. He started taking solos in the avant-garde direction, which didn't fit what I was doing. I would talk to him and say, "Man, look, that ain't it, especially when we're playin' 'Filthy McNasty' or 'Señor Blues.' Don't take it out—play some funky stuff." He would do some funky stuff the next time, but the third time after that, he'd go back to playing that other shit, going way outside the chord changes.

And then there was his attitude—as I say, he was humble when he came into the band. But it was a time of racial conflict, riots and shit going on, and he was very anti-white. He was making anti-white comments out loud in the club, and that just tore the band apart.

The straw that broke the camel's back came when we were in Buffalo. The club owner came to me and said, "Horace, your band don't sound like it used to. What is all that stuff the guys are doing?" Tyrone was taking the music out, and Woody and the drums and bass players were following him. It didn't sound like the Horace Silver Quintet. I talked to them about it. They'd come back for a minute, but then Tyrone would go back out, the rest would follow him, and the shit was outside again.

I decided I'd fire all those motherfuckers. I finally said, "Shit, I'll fire the whole band and start all over again." Since then, I've had to do that two or three times, but it taught me a lesson. Now if I have a band and I have one guy in there causing dissension, I'm going to get rid of that guy and save the band. He might be one hell of a musician, like Tyrone, but Tyrone screwed up that whole band. If it wasn't for his attitude and his goin' outside, that band would have been together much longer, because it was a good band.

Throughout my career as a bandleader, I've found that one rotten apple can spoil the whole barrel. If one member of the quintet causes friction, he can spread that friction to the others, and pretty soon you have a big problem on your hands—things get out of control. I've had to fire a few good bands because of this and start all over again. I've learned a valuable lesson. If I have a good band and one member is causing friction, I get rid of him, no matter how great he plays, before he infects the whole band and I have to fire them all and start again.

A few years ago, I put a band together, and we went out on the road. Again, I had one musician who was causing dissension. He was a good player, and he wasn't playing out, but he instigated a lot of shit within the band, which was causing bad feelings directed against me among the musicians—"We ain't makin' enough money," or "We shoulda had this," or "We shoulda done that"—getting them all agitated, which would reflect on me and sometimes on the music. We got through that tour okay, so I didn't have to fire him, but I wouldn't hire him again. I don't need that kind of aggravation.

I FIRST HEARD PIANIST Phineas Newborn Jr. at the It Club in Los Angeles. John McLean had told me about him. Phineas came in one night to check us out, and John asked him to go up on stage and play a few numbers. Gene Taylor and Roy Brooks accompanied him. He broke it up. What a great talent he was.

I had the pleasure of knowing two great pianists who really had strong hands. One was Earl "Fatha" Hines, and the other was Erroll Garner. Their hands were like sledgehammers. The quintet and I played a Thanksgiving week in San Francisco, where Earl Hines was living with his wife and daughters. I met Earl's bass player, and he told Earl about me. Earl told the bass player to bring me by for Thanksgiving dinner. I enjoyed the meal and enjoyed meeting him and his family. After dinner, he asked me to play something for him. I went to the piano and played but had great difficulty getting my shit out because the piano had such stiff action. He played after me, and the stiff action didn't seem to bother him at all. Earl used to exercise his hands every day by squeezing a hard rubber ball.

I recall playing at the Newport Jazz Festival; we were playing "Filthy McNasty." I was taking my solo and was rolling some octaves at the top of the piano. Promoter George Wein yelled out from backstage, "Earl 'Fatha' Hines!" Later on, I realized that even though I've never been consciously or directly influenced by Earl Hines, I was influenced by him through Nat "King" Cole, who idolized Earl Hines and who in turn was one of my idols. So Earl's influence came to me secondhand, through Nat Cole.

I played a week at the Apollo Theater with Stan Getz when the Erroll Garner Trio was on the bill. The day before we opened, we rehearsed the show in the basement of the Apollo, where they had an old upright piano. After Erroll rehearsed his segment of the show, I had to rehearse with a juggling act. I sat down at the piano and found that four or five strings were broken. Another time, when I was working in Detroit with the Jazz Messengers, I complained to the club owner about the stiffness of the piano keys. I couldn't get my normal shit to come out right because the action was so stiff. The club owner said that a lot of pianists who played there complained about the same thing. Erroll Garner had picked out that piano for the club owner to purchase.

NEW YORK'S ENTERTAINMENT SCENE was flourishing during the 1950s and 1960s. Jazz abounded throughout the city and the surrounding area. In Manhattan, there were the Fifty-second Street basement clubs, one whole block of nothing but small jazz clubs, each with two bands alternating. There you would find the Onyx, the Three Deuces, the Downbeat, Ryan's, Kelly's Stables, the Hickory House, and others. Greenwich Village had the Cafe Bohemia, the Village Vanguard, the Village Gate, Basin Street West, and the Open Door. In Brooklyn, there was the Continental, the Blue Coronet, and Tony's. In Harlem, you found Small's Paradise (owned by basketball star Wilt Chamberlin), Count Basie's, the Baby Grand, Minton's Playhouse, Well's (known for good jazz and chicken and waffles), Club Baron, and the Paradise Bar. There were also three restaurant/bars where celebrities hung out: Sugar Ray Robinson's Bar (owned by Sugar Ray); the Bradock Bar, located just around the corner from the backstage door of the Apollo Theater; and the Palm Cafe on 125th Street, near the Apollo Theater. They had no live music, but they were very popular. All three had great food, and all the people performing at the Apollo ate there between shows.

Harlem had several ballrooms that featured jazz bands for dancing, including the Audubon Ballroom, the Renaissance Ballroom, and the Savoy Ballroom, which was known as the "Home of Happy Feet." Each ballroom featured two bands or sometimes three bands alternating. I played the Audubon and the Renaissance a couple of times with the Jazz Messengers and with my quintet. I never got to play the Savoy Ballroom. New York was a jazz boomtown in those days. I'll always cherish the memory of it all.

Tap dancing was associated with jazz in those days, and there were several very prominent tap dancers, including Baby Laurence and Bill Bailey (Pearl Bailey's brother, who later became a minister). Everyone used to talk about a guy from Baltimore named Groundhog, although he never came to New York. There was Teddy Hale, who was the boyfriend of Rose Hardaway, an exotic dancer and a very beautiful woman. She used to dance to my composition "Señor Blues." I caught Baby Laurence on an all-jazz show at the Apollo Theater, which was organized and hosted by jazz disc jockey Symphony Sid. Drummer Max Roach and Baby did a tap-drum duet together. That was something to see and hear.

Paterson and Jackson were a great tap dance comedy act. I caught them at the Apollo Theater several times. They were both very large men, but they were very agile and quick on their feet. I also saw the Nicholas Brothers at the Apollo. What a dynamite act! The great Bill Robinson died before I moved to New York, but I did see him perform once when I came down to New York from Connecticut to catch Jimmie Lunceford's band at the Paramount Theater on Broadway. There were also two other theaters on Broadway—the Strand and Loew's State—that featured big bands and acts.

Back in the 1950s, Atlantic City and Wildwood, both in New Jersey, were very popular summer resorts. Many jazz groups played weekly engagements there during the summer. I played a week in Wildwood with Stan Getz. It was very memorable because Redd Foxx and Slappy White were also working there, as a comedy team. The club where they appeared stayed open later than our club, so every night after our last show, I'd go catch their last show. I got to meet Redd and Slappy. I really enjoy comedy, and those two were among the best. Years later, when I got my own band, we worked two weeks at Redd's nightclub in Los Angeles, alternating sets with him. I laughed so much during those two weeks that my jawbones were aching. Dinah Washington also worked in Wildwood in the 1950s, and her drummer, Jimmy Cobb, introduced me to her. What a treat for a young piano player from Norwalk, Connecticut, to meet these great people. I was thrilled.

Later, I worked a week in Atlantic City with my own band. Organist Wild Bill Davis was also playing there that week. I got a chance to hear his group and to meet him. The Club Harlem in Atlantic City featured a Cotton Club–type revue with chorus girls and the whole bit. Tadd

Dameron wrote all the music and arrangements for the show, which I was able to see. I didn't meet Tadd that week but was introduced to him by mutual friends some time later in New York.

Duke Ellington came into the Atlantic City club we were working in to check us out. He had two beautiful white ladies with him. I can't remember if he was working in Atlantic City at the time or if he was just visiting, but I was happy that he chose to come and hear us. I might add that I was a bit nervous also. The great Duke Ellington came to check us out!

CLASSICAL AND JAZZ PIANIST Don Shirley called me one day in 1968 and asked me to come by his apartment in New York City to show him something about playing the blues. I was flattered because he is such a virtuoso pianist. He had a concert coming up at Carnegie Hall, which was to include a segment that featured the blues. I guess he wanted to make sure that the blues he played had some authenticity. I went by and played the blues for him. I showed him the old-fashioned turnaround on the blues. For example, in the key of B-flat, the last four bars of the twelve would be F7th, one bar; E-flat 7th, one bar; B-flat 7th, two bars. The beboppers used a slightly different turnaround when playing the blues. In fact, they had several different ones. But these were the old-fashioned chord changes that all the old blues singers and players used. Don invited me to come to his concert, which I enjoyed very much. He played the blues using those old-fashioned chord changes that I showed him.

At about the same time, I had the privilege of meeting Dr. Martin Luther King Jr. at a benefit concert given by baseball star Jackie Robinson at his estate in Stamford, Connecticut. The groups that performed were Gerry Mulligan and his band, the Billy Taylor Trio, the Erroll Garner Trio, and the Horace Silver Quintet. This concert was given to raise money for the Southern Christian Leadership Conference, which, under Dr. King's leadership, did so much to fight for civil rights for blacks in the South. NAACP leader Roy Wilkins spoke very eloquently at this concert, but it was Dr. King who touched the hearts and souls of the people when he spoke.

I've heard many orators in my day, but I've never heard anyone speak with the emotion of Dr. King. He could really capture an audience. Tears came to my eyes as he spoke. I was a bit embarrassed. I glanced around to see if anyone had noticed my tears. As I looked around, I observed many people dabbing their eyes with their handkerchiefs. Even the newspaper photographers who were taking his picture had their handkerchiefs out, dabbing their eyes. What a soulful person he was. He spoke with such feeling that you could not help but be moved by his words. What a blessing he has been to mankind. If my music can move the people and touch their hearts and souls like his words did, I'll be a very happy man.

LADY MUSIC WAS MY FIRST love and has remained my primary love throughout the years. I have placed no other woman before her. I remember seeing a man interviewed on TV whose life's dream was to sculpt a face out of the side of a rock mountain. This man met a woman, and they fell in love. He took her to the mountain and showed it to her and told her what his life's dream was. He said, "I love you and want to marry you. I'll be a faithful husband and a good provider, but you have to accept the idea that my life's dream, which is to carve a face in this mountain, comes first and you come second." She accepted this. They married and had a happy life together. The interviewer asked the wife how she could accept being second in his life. She said, "He fell in love with that mountain long before he ever met me. He has been and is a wonderful husband. I am willing to take second place to his dream." I presume he also took second place to her dream, if she had one.

Throughout my life, I've tried to adhere to the teachings that Dad and Mom and Aunt Maude taught me when I was a small boy. The things they taught me have helped me get through life. There are teachers all around us. Some are family, some are friends, some are strangers. We can learn a lot from each other if we so wish.

Some years ago, I read an interview with comedian Charlie Chaplin. In the interview, Chaplin said that he didn't buy his first Ford car until he could afford two of them. He didn't buy his first Cadillac until he could afford two of them. He didn't buy his first Rolls-Royce until he could afford two of them. I followed this pattern. The premise of this philosophy is to always have some money in reserve. Dad used to say, "Always save some money for a rainy day."

Henry David Thoreau's philosophy was to investigate as many religions as appealed to him and to use what he could from each of them to form his own religion. I also followed this pattern. One is never too old to learn and to grow. I will never be content to rest upon my laurels. I shall continue to seek and to grow.

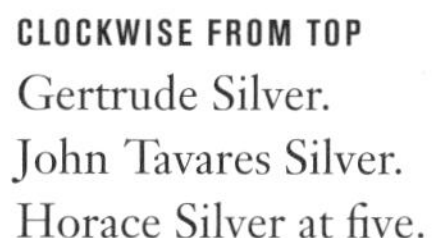

CLOCKWISE FROM TOP
Gertrude Silver.
John Tavares Silver.
Horace Silver at five.

Horace Silver at seven.

John O'Neil *(left)* and Horace Silver upon graduation from St. Mary's Grammar School, June 20, 1943.

Alan Burr (on drums) and the Music Makers. While in high school, Horace Silver *(far right)* played tenor saxophone with this dance band.

Eighteen-year-old Horace Silver playing tenor saxophone in 1946, with pianist Walter Radcliff, at the Monterey nightclub in New Haven, Connecticut.

Left to right: Horace Silver, piano; John Harris Jr., drums *(back)*; Gene Taylor, bass; Blue Mitchell, trumpet; and Junior Cook, tenor saxophone *(far right)*.

OPPOSITE

Top photo, left to right: The Jazz Messengers, ca. 1955—Hank Mobley, tenor saxophone; Art Blakey, drums; Donald Byrd, trumpet; Doug Watkins, bass; and Horace Silver, piano.

Bottom photo, left to right: Doug Watkins, bass; Hank Mobley, tenor saxophone; Art Farmer, trumpet; and Horace Silver, piano.

Photomontage by Gordon "Doc" Anderson, Apollo Theater, New York, ca. 1966. Anderson routinely made such photomontages to sell to the artists who worked at the Apollo.

OPPOSITE

Top photo, left to right: Louis Hayes *(standing);* Blue Mitchell, trumpet; Junior Cook, tenor saxophone. The man seated in the left foreground is not identified.

Bottom photo: Woody Shaw *(left)* and Tyrone Washington.

Horace Silver, Düsseldorf, Germany, ca. 1960. Photo by Hans Harzheim.

OPPOSITE

Horace Silver, Frankfurt, Germany, 1968. © Stephanie Wiesand. Courtesy Andreas Wiesand.

Gregory Silver *(left)* and Horace Silver, Westlake Recording Studios, Beverly Hills, March 29, 2005. Courtesy Gregory Silver and Ecaroh Music.

Chapter Five

WESTWARD BOUND
MIDDLE YEARS

The California immigrant, seeking to expand,
plants his feet on foreign soil
and starts to work his plan.
Time and application, with courage in the balance,
will bring forth new dimensions of the man and his talents.
The creative urge within him searching for brand-new channels,
that a new manifestation of love may be born
and recorded in history's annals.
His mind is dedicated, his soul is saturated, his body is activated
by the love that creates in and through him.
His plans are elongated, his growth is anticipated,
that the inventions of his mind
will bring forth in time
a larger degree of love.

THE HORACE SILVER QUINTET was booked back into the Showboat in Philly several times over the years after our debut performance there in 1956. We always drew crowds in Philadelphia. The people loved us. We also played Pep's Show Bar and the Blue Note in Philly. We worked a six-day week, Monday through Saturday, with a matinee on Saturday from four to seven o'clock and an evening performance at nine, with a two-hour break for dinner.

I first met comedian Bill Cosby in Philly. He has always been a big jazz fan, and he used to come into the Showboat to check us out. His cousin Dell Shields was a disc jockey, and I was usually invited to go on his show when I was in town. Bill often hung out with Dell at the studio. Sid Marks and Joel Dorn, who were also Philadelphia disc jockeys, invited me on their shows, too. Joel hung out at all the local jazz clubs, and we became good friends. He was always on the scene when we played in town.

It was at the Showboat in Philadelphia in 1968 that I met the lady who was to become one of the two major loves of my life. In fact, she was to become my wife.

That day, I arrived at the club about fifteen minutes before the four o'clock matinee and noticed a fine-looking, brown-skinned young lady wearing an Afro hairstyle, standing outside the club, looking like she was waiting for someone. Black women wearing Afro hairstyles always turned me on. I approached her and asked if she was coming in. She said she was waiting for her date. I said, "If he doesn't show up, come on in, and tell the doorman that you're my guest." Her date didn't show up, so she came in as my guest.

After the matinee, I invited her to have dinner with me. We went to Mom's soul food restaurant and ate, and then I walked her to the corner to get a bus. She lived in Camden, New Jersey. Her name was Barbara Jean Dove. She was a foxy-looking young lady with a beautiful butt. I don't know what came over me—I'd never done it before, and I haven't done it since—but something compelled me to reach out and pinch her on the ass. After I did it, I was embarrassed. I said to myself, "Aw, I blew it. I'll probably never see this chick again."

About a month later, she called me and said she had moved to Newark and was living with a girlfriend there. I invited her on a date. We were to go out to dinner and see a show. When she arrived at my apartment, I opened the door and said to myself, "Look at what the good Lord done sent me. The good Lord has sent me a care package. Thank you, Lord." She was really looking good.

That was the start of our romance. Barbara is an Aries, and I am a Virgo.

All the astrology books said that Aries and Virgo were not compatible, but we ignored them and fell in love anyway. We had several things in common. We both were vegetarians; we shared the same religious views; she liked music, and I loved music. After going together for two years, I asked her to marry me, and she accepted. I was forty-two, and she was twenty-four.

After we were married, my wife used to do secretarial work in an office in downtown Manhattan. One afternoon after work, she was waiting for a bus on Broadway to take her up to One Hundredth Street and Central Park West, where we lived at the Park West Village. Dizzy Gillespie and Teddy Reig spotted her. Teddy dared Dizzy to hit on her. Dizzy did not know that she was my wife. She told him that she was my wife and brought both him and Teddy home with her.

I was in the midst of writing some music for a series of three recordings called *The United States of Mind.* I played some of the music for Dizzy on my RMI electric piano, and he played a few things of his for me. Dizzy was a member of the Baha'i faith (pronounced "Ba-*high*"). When he and Teddy were leaving, my wife said jokingly, "Dizzy, what does the Baha'i say about gettin' high?" We all laughed. I had a great time that afternoon. It was an honor having Dizzy Gillespie in my home. He's always been one of my inspirations.

I have a test for you males to find out which of your male friends are your real true friends. Get yourself a real pretty girlfriend or wife, and introduce her to your male friends. The ones that don't try to hit on her behind your back are your real true friends. Hold on to them and cancel the others.

My wife was a very attractive woman. When I would come home from a few weeks on the road, she would tell me about some of my so-called best friends calling her up when I was away and inviting her out. I quickly canceled my friendship with these guys. They are the kind of guys that would smile in your face and stab you in the back. There's a saying that the old folks used to have: "A stiff dick has no conscience." But a true friend does not abide by this saying. He loves you and has respect for you and all that is yours. Choose your friends wisely. You don't need any bullshit friends. True friendship is about love and respect for each other. I'd rather have a few true friends than a whole lot of bullshit friends. I can't stand hypocrisy. It turns me off.

I made out with a lot of women of all races when I was single and on the road. Once I got married, I canceled all of that and was true to my wife. I took my marriage vows seriously and did my best to live up to them. A lot of fine chicks were hittin' on me, but I respectfully declined. It wasn't easy to refuse, but I did. In the five years that we were married, I never cheated on my wife. That's a statement that I'm very proud to make.

WHEN I FIRST MET BARBARA, I was living in Park West Village. After we were married, our son was born, and we continued to live there for several years. Drummer Sonny Greer and his wife, Mill, who also lived in Park West Village, used to babysit my son when my wife and I wanted to go out to dinner and see a show. But eventually the rent increased to the point that we couldn't afford it. We then moved to an old brownstone apartment at 83 West Eighty-second Street.

Of all the places I've lived, this was the only one where I never felt comfortable. Even though I encountered a somewhat prejudiced air during my stay at 23 West Seventy-sixth Street, I enjoyed living there. At 83 West Eighty-second Street, the tenants were interracial and there was no prejudice, but the environment was loud and noisy. I could never sleep well there. It was a three-flight walk-up. No elevator. A vocal coach who lived in the apartment below us gave lessons at nine A.M., not long after I went to bed at six, after coming home from a gig. There were some gay guys who lived above us who were very nice, but they played their stereo so loud that the walls would vibrate. Bassist Jimmy Garrison and his wife lived in another apartment above us. They didn't get along very well and often had screaming arguments that could be heard throughout the building because the walls were so thin. I don't think I ever got a good night's sleep while living at that address.

We were burglarized while living there. The band and I were booked to do a European tour. I decided to bring my wife and son to London, where our tour ended, and send the band back to New York while the family and I stayed in Europe for a two-week vacation. Two days after my family arrived in London, we received a phone call from my wife's girlfriend, saying that our apartment had been burglarized. We had to cancel our vacation and go back to New York to investigate the situation. The burglars did a good job—they nearly cleaned out the apartment. The police never found out who did the job, and they were never able to retrieve any of the things that were stolen.

At one point, I had played a gig with the quintet at Concerts by the Sea, in Redondo Beach, California. On our closing day, Howard Rumsey, the owner, invited me to have dinner with him at a nice restaurant a couple of doors down the pier from Concerts by the Sea. As we finished eating, it was the time of day when the sun was setting, and we could see it from the restaurant, which faced the ocean. In the distance, we could see the Palos Verdes peninsula. I said, "Dog, Howard, I sure would like to live in a place like that." Lo and behold, I eventually wound up living in Rancho Palos Verdes.

The band and I had played in California several times, and I had fallen in love with the climate and the people. I thought of living there at some point in the future. After the burglary, which happened around 1974, I said to myself, "California, here we come." I discussed it with my wife, and she agreed. I've never regretted making that decision. I enjoy my life in California. I'll most likely spend the rest of my earth life here. In my opinion, it's the most progressive state in the Union.

ABOUT SIX MONTHS AFTER my family and I moved to California, I got a call from drummer Frank Butler, who wanted to work with my band. Musically speaking, having Frank Butler with my band would have been like being in heaven, but Frank was a drug addict. He was always in and out of jail. I knew if I hired him, he would bring the heat down on us.

We would be followed by the vice squad. I didn't want to return to the police scrutiny of those old Jazz Messenger days, so I politely declined.

AS FOR BARBARA AND ME, the first two years of our marriage were great. I divided my energies between my music, my wife, and my son. But then it started to go sour, and the next three years were all downhill. We could never seem to agree on anything, especially about how to raise our son. She had one concept, and I had another. I began to realize that the astrology books were right. After five years of marriage, we divorced. She is a wonderful woman and a wonderful mother to our son, which I am very grateful for.

A certain amount of heartache usually follows any divorce, and it took me several years to heal. I had taken my marriage vows with the intent to stay together until death do us part. I had lost a wife I deeply loved, but I still had music and my son. I decided to give my all to them. I don't think either one of us was to blame for our separation. Barbara and I just weren't compatible from the beginning, but it took us a few years to find that out. We parted friends and are still friends today. After we parted, she legally changed her name to Jemela Mwelu and got married and divorced a second time.

My son's name is Gregory Paul Silver. We had some wonderful times together when he was growing up. He lived with his mother, but I had him on weekends. We went to Disneyland, Knott's Berry Farm, Universal Studios, the movies, nice restaurants, and concerts. We had so much fun just being together. He came to live with me at two different periods of his teenage life, and each time he returned to his mother because he didn't like my discipline. As long as everything went his way, we got along well; but when he couldn't have his way and I enacted some sort of discipline, we had friction. I was not a tyrant, but I believed in tough love. I didn't want him to grow up to be an asshole. I wrestled with myself many times in choosing directions in which to rear him.

Between his mother's direction and my direction, Gregory has grown up to be a fine, responsible young man. I am very proud of him. He's a rap music composer and lives in New York City. He goes under the stage name of G. Wise. Although I live in Malibu, I see him once or twice a year, and we talk on the phone often. Thank God for helping us through the friction of those teenage years. Our relationship now is one of peace, love, and harmony.

I recall an incident that happened when my son was a small boy. His mother and I were divorced by then, and he was staying with me for the summer. I had taken the summer off from touring so we could spend it together. I had to discipline him for something that he had done, and he became very resentful because of it. I had been nurturing an aloe vera plant in a pot in the dining room, and it was growing very slowly. I caught him pissin' on my aloe vera plant to spite me. I gave him a good spanking. There must be something in urine that's good for plants, though, because that aloe vera plant really started growing after he pissed on it. I always get a kick out of telling this story to my friends. Those preteenage days I spent with Gregory were some of the happiest days of my life.

TENOR SAXOPHONIST BENNIE MAUPIN turned me on to the study of metaphysics when he was working with my band, around 1969 or 1970. He introduced me to an author named Yogi Ramacharaka, and I bought a whole series of Ramacharaka books. They really opened my mind to a greater spiritual concept of God and how we relate to each other.

I was brought up in the Catholic religion, but in my mid-twenties I became dissatisfied with it because it didn't answer some of the questions I was asking. Catholicism was all right as far as it went, but it didn't go far enough to satisfy my spiritual hunger. It embodies a lot of truth, but not all of it. I was interested in communicating with the spirit world and read a lot about it but had never had any personal experience in that field.

One evening in the late 1960s, when I was visiting my father in Connecticut, I was thinking about my brother, John, who died of pneumonia when he was six months old. If he had lived, he would have been about five years older than me. When I was a little boy, I always yearned to have a big brother, one who would look after me and keep the big boys from picking on me. He was on my mind all that evening.

When I woke up the next morning, I went to the refrigerator to take out some leftovers for my breakfast. The leftovers were in a bowl, with a saucer covering it. I set the bowl down on the kitchen countertop, removed the saucer, and laid it down. As I did so, the saucer began to spin counterclockwise and move forward. I recognized this as some sort of psychic experience. I said aloud, "Is that you, John?" The saucer kept spinning counterclockwise and moving forward until half of it was hanging off the edge of the countertop. It stopped spinning and remained stationary, balancing without falling to the floor.

I said to myself, "Which one of my friends or relatives can I share this experience with? If I tell them, they're going to think I'm crazy." Then I thought of Doc Hamilton. Around this time, my dad had left the Norwalk Tire Company and had a job at Mel's Diner in Norwalk as a dishwasher and cleanup man. Some of the people who ate at Mel's would read the newspaper while they ate and then leave the newspaper behind. Dad would pick up all these papers—New York, New Haven, Bridgeport, Stamford, and Norwalk—and bring them home for us to read. One day, I came across an ad in a New Haven newspaper from a chiropractor and physiotherapist named Dr. Dwight Hamilton. I was having problems with my back, so I made an appointment, and he helped me greatly. In the years to follow, we became almost like father and son. He was a wonderful person and a great doctor. God truly blessed him with the gift of healing. We were both born on September 2, both Virgos.

I called Doc Hamilton and told him what had happened with my psychic experience. He said, "Horace, I think someone from the spirit world is trying to make contact with you." He and his wife had been on a vacation boat cruise, and he had become friendly with one of the waiters on the boat. They spoke about psychic matters, and the waiter gave him the name and phone number of a psychic medium who lived in New York. Her name was Reverend Beaulah Brown. Doc had never gone to her, but he suggested that I call her and arrange for a reading. I did just that.

She told me that it was my brother, John, who had performed this feat, to attract my attention to things beyond the physical. She also told me that my brother and my mother were looking after me. Another time when I was thinking about my brother while eating dinner, I saw my fork levitate from my plate. Now that I firmly believe in life beyond the physical, John doesn't perform these tricks for me anymore. I have made contact with my sister, Maria, through Reverend Ena Twigg of London. Maria is also looking after me. Both brother John and sister Maria made their transition before I was born. I look forward to meeting them and getting to know them when I make my transition.

I became interested in Spiritualism and attended services at the Spiritualist church where Reverend Beaulah Brown was the minister. I also received private readings from her. There are many phony psychic mediums out there, but if you are lucky enough to find a genuine one, he or she can be very helpful in guiding you to make right decisions in your life's planning. It is not the medium who advises you, but the spirit of the so-called dead: your loved ones, your teachers, your friends.

Finding a good medium is like trying to find a good musician. Some are geniuses; some are very good; some are good; some are fair; some are mediocre; and some are phonies with no talent at all, just trying to fake their way through for the buck. This last type of medium can be very dangerous, giving you wrong information that might be detrimental to your progress. If, after a reading with a medium, you've received only trivia, don't go back. If you receive in-depth information, something positive that you can take home and work on, something that helps you make the right decisions that will propel your life forward, then you've found a good medium. Of course, God has given us all free will, and we don't have to follow the guidance that comes to us through a medium. That is our choice. But our dearly departed loved ones are still concerned about us and want to help us, if only they can reach us through a dream, through mental telepathy, or through a psychic medium.

Reverend Brown's readings were always very helpful to me and my family. When Gregory was an infant, his pediatrician outlined a diet for him that was making him obese. Reverend Brown told my wife that this doctor was slowly killing our child with this diet. I remember Barbara crying when Reverend Brown told her this. We changed pediatricians, and Gregory eventually trimmed down to a normal weight.

At one time, I couldn't seem to get rid of a rash on my penis. I had been faithful to my wife, so I didn't think it could be any venereal disease. My doctor gave me ointment, but the rash would not go away. He then sent me to a skin specialist, who had me put my penis under an ultraviolet lamp and gave me another ointment. The rash persisted. I was afraid to have sex with my wife for fear of infecting her with something—I knew not what. I went to Reverend Brown for a reading and told her my problem. She said to sit still for a moment and not to speak, because she was calling on Dr. Stevens from the spirit world to come and examine me. We both sat still and didn't talk for a few minutes. When she finally spoke, she said that Dr. Stevens had examined me and that I could stop spending so much money on the skin specialist. All I needed to do was to get some white petroleum jelly and rub it sparingly on my penis, and that would take care of the problem. I did just that, and the rash went away, along with my worries.

Although I've received guidance through several other mediums throughout my life, Reverend Brown was the first and the greatest. After Reverend Brown passed away, I got readings from her friend Reverend Rose Ann Erickson. All this took place while I was living in New York. When I performed in London, I got a reading from the well-known psychic Reverend Ena Twigg. When I moved to California, I got readings from Reverend Elizabeth Long. All were good, but Reverend Brown was the greatest. My wife and I were married by Reverend Brown, and she became my son's godmother.

YEARS LATER, I WAS LIVING in Rancho Palos Verdes, at the Porto Verde Apartments. One Sunday afternoon, I fell asleep on the couch in the living room. When I woke up, I heard a voice in my head. I can't remember the exact words, but it was something about using a pendulum and "dowsing" over a photo of myself in order to contact my Spirit Teachers. I bought a pendulum and started using it for this purpose. To dowse over the photo, I was told to face in a northerly direction, hold the pendulum over my forehead where the pituitary gland is located, and ask a question. If the pendulum swings in a circle to the right, it's a *yes* answer. If the pendulum swings in a circle to the left, it's a *no* answer. If the pendulum swings straight up and down, it's a we-don't-know answer. Between recording and analyzing my dreams and dowsing, I have received much guidance from my Teachers. I know my Teachers by name and commune with them every day, several times a day.

I've been dowsing for more than twenty years, since about 1984. I have found it to be a great help, especially when making important decisions. Before I dowse, I say a little prayer to God and thank Him for my many blessings. Then I ask to contact my Teachers. I always stand slightly left of the photo and ask God to help me keep myself out of the way so that I do not influence the pendulum, so that I may receive my Teachers' impressions and not my own. I use a silver pendulum and an eight-by-ten photo of myself. I usually dowse at home or in my hotel room when I'm traveling. At times when I've been out and about and had to make an important decision, I've used the photo on my driver's license. Although even our Teachers sometimes make mistakes and give inaccurate information, I have found my Teachers to be accurate most of the time. I look forward to meeting them when I make my transition.

I am fortunate to know my Spirit Teachers by name. Names are usually impressed on my mind just before I awake in the morning. As I awake, I write them down on a pad, and then when I get up, I dowse to find out exactly who they are and their connection with me. I arrive at answers by a process of elimination. Some are new Teachers, coming in to help me. Some are replacing old Teachers who are moving on to a higher form of existence. Sometimes family members and friends who have passed on come in just to say hi and to wish me well.

First thing after my morning prayer, I dowse and ask the Teachers what foods that I have on hand would be best for my body that day. I get their reply, and I eat accordingly. If I have to make decisions that day, I ask them to guide me. When I'm writing my music and I'm indecisive about which direction to take it, I ask their advice. Most times I've taken their advice and used it, but on occasion I've thought that my way was the better way and remained with my concept. They never try to force their will on me. They come to advise and guide, but I have free will to accept or reject their help. I am very grateful for their help. Their guidance has been right on and has helped me work through many problems.

THE STUDY OF METAPHYSICS has changed my life for the better. Beginning in 1970, the study of metaphysics led me to write and record *The United States of Mind*, a musical work in three parts. A lot of my fans were turned off when I recorded this music because they thought I was trying to preach to them. I wrote this music not as a teacher or preacher but as a student who wished to share the beauty of these teachings with others, hoping that they, too, would benefit, as I have, from these teachings.

With religion as well as with my music, I like to dabble in more than one concept. I still consider myself a Christian, although I don't belong to any one religion because I don't think any one religion has all the answers or all the truth. That's why I'm a dabbler. I got that idea from reading Henry David Thoreau's *Walden.* As I mentioned before, he took concepts from here and there and made his own religion, and that's what I try to do. I study the religious teachings of Ernest Holmes and Science of Mind, the Church of Religious Science, Paramahansa Yogananda and the Self-Realization Fellowship, Charles and Myrtle Fillmore and Silent Unity, Brother Mandus and the World Healing Crusade. I do the same thing with music. Although I'm a jazz musician, my musical influences include the blues, black gospel music, Latin music, symphonic music, Broadway show music, and folk music. In short, whatever appeals to me. I gather influences from all those sources and combine them in various ways in my own music. It's important to me to keep an investigative mind as far as religion and music are concerned. There is always something new to discover in both areas.

One afternoon, I had a business appointment at United Artist/Blue Note Records. The executive I was meeting with excused himself for a moment and went into an adjacent office. When he came back, he said that he had been talking to John Lennon of the Beatles in the next office. John said that he had a great idea for a new recording called *The United States of Mind.* The executive told John that Horace Silver had already done that. Composers often do come up with the same or similar ideas without knowing what their colleagues are working on. This is not thievery, but merely coincidence. It then becomes a matter of who gets it out there to the public first.

Some years ago—I can't remember just exactly when—the phone rang, and it was Sherman Helmsley, who played George Jefferson on the TV comedy *The Jeffersons,* which, along with *Sanford and Son,* was one of my favorite shows. To my delight, he expressed his admiration for *The United States of Mind.* He said he had all three LPs in the series, liked them, and played them a lot. It was great to get that compliment from him. Then he said he had written some lyrics, and he wanted to know if I would be interested in putting some music to his lyrics. It was an honor to be asked to work with such a great performer and entertainer. I never saw his lyrics, but I wasn't into and still am not into collaborating with anybody when I write music. I like to write my own melodies and my own lyrics.

In my formative years, before I became interested in writing lyrics, I would get Jon Hendricks and a few other people to write for me here and there. Hendricks did "Doodlin'," "Come on Home," and "Home Cookin'" and was supposed to do several others that he never got around to. But then I discovered that I had the gift of lyric writing. I never knew that I could do it—I had never thought about it. I wrote lyrics to "Señor Blues" out of necessity, because I couldn't find anyone else to do it at the time. I thought, "Well, hell, I can do that. It's only a blues. It's not a beautiful ballad that has a lot of curves to it. It's just a twelve-bar blues. I can write something humorous to that." Same thing with "Sister Sadie"—I couldn't find anyone else to do it at the time.

But *The United States of Mind* was more serious music: pretty ballads,

Latin stuff—it was a mixture of different things. It was evident from listening to the melodies that the lyrics had to be heavy. I couldn't do the light stuff I had done before, and I didn't know if I could do that kind of writing. I tried it, and it came out well. In fact, after I got done writing that stuff, I sat down and went through it all and said, "Damn! Did that come from me?" Well, I knew it came from the Man Upstairs *through* me, but after I did *The United States of Mind*, I decided that I would do my own lyrics from then on. I didn't want anyone else to write lyrics for me anymore.

I used the RMI electric keyboard for *The United States of Mind* because I just wanted to do something different. I was tired of hearing everyone play the Fender-Rhodes. Not that I didn't like the Fender-Rhodes—it was a good instrument. But I didn't feel that piano players could show off their identity with it. I heard some records by Ahmad Jamal where he played the Fender-Rhodes and an acoustic piano. On the acoustic parts, I could identify him—"Oh, that's Ahmad Jamal"—but when he played the Fender-Rhodes, it could have been anybody, as far as my ears were concerned. I couldn't detect his style. And with some other pianists, too, piano stylists, when they got on the Fender-Rhodes, I couldn't detect their style. They all sounded the same. So that's why I didn't use the Fender-Rhodes. I was searching for some kind of electric keyboard that would allow my identity to come through, and the RMI does that.

It's kind of a difficult instrument to play because the action is so slow. If you want to sustain a note, there's a sustain pedal, but it doesn't sustain very long. You have to hold the key down *and* use the pedal to get a note to hang out, and you've got to play real simple because the keys don't come back fast. If you try to play fast, it gets all jumbled. But I liked the sound. They had stops on that keyboard, too. You could get a simulated sound between a piano and an organ, or you could get the plain organ. The only sound I never used was the string sound; I didn't like it. But they had a guitar stop, an organ stop, a piano stop. Sometimes, I'd use the piano and organ, or the guitar and the piano, or I'd mix all three. I'd change it around. And I used the wah-wah pedal on a couple of tracks.

I played the RMI for about three years. I took it on the road with me, too, but it was a pain in the ass to carry, even though I enjoyed playing it. I had a big case built for it, lined with foam rubber. I'd get the other guys in the band to help me lift it, put it in the box, close the box, and lock it up. Then I'd have to get somebody to help me carry it to a taxi, lift it into the taxi, and lift it out.

Physically, it was a hassle, but it served my purpose well, for what I wanted it to do. I wanted something different with the spiritual stuff—I wanted a different sound. I used it for a specific purpose, and when that purpose was finished, I put it away.

Ain't nothin' like the acoustic piano, as far as I'm concerned.

After I recorded the first LP of *The United States of Mind*, which was called *Phase I: That Healin' Feelin'*, I was called into the Blue Note office for a meeting with one of the executives. He said, "Horace, this new album you did is not selling as well as your usual releases. I understand you have two more of these albums to record. Why don't you go back to your original concept and finish this project another time?" I said, "My contract gives me free rein, so I would like to finish this project before going back to my usual thing. After I finish the project, if it doesn't sell well, you can can me."

I did finish it, but the records did not sell well. They didn't can me, though. They kept me on, and I went back to doing my usual Horace Silver thing. Because *The United States of Mind* didn't sell, it went out of print rather quickly, and for many years it was hard to get, even in secondhand record shops. But recently, in 2004, Blue Note reissued the complete series in a two-CD set. Needless to say, I'm happy it's available once again. There is a lot of fine music there and a lot of great philosophy.

One aspect of the project I found especially rewarding was working with some very fine vocalists. I first met Andy Bey when he was singing with his sisters, Salome and Geraldine, in a group called Andy and the Bey Sisters, which was managed by promoter George Wein. I've always enjoyed Andy's singing, and he's quite a good piano player, too. We've been friends and on-and-off working associates for more than thirty-five years, including work on *The United States of Mind.* I admire him both as a person and as a singer. He has tremendous range and intonation and always sings with feeling. Throughout all the years that Andy recorded with us and traveled on tour with us, I've never had to change the key of any of my songs to fit his range; he always sang them in the original key. He always sang my music to my satisfaction.

When I was looking for singers for *The United States of Mind,* I auditioned a black male singer whose name I can't remember. He didn't have the sound I wanted, so I didn't use him, but I remember that he sounded a lot like Elvis Presley. I mentioned this to him. He told me he used to do demo tapes for Elvis of songs his manager and recording company wanted him to learn and possibly record. According to this man, Elvis took on *his* style of singing. I do not know if this is true or not, but this man certainly sounded like Elvis—or Elvis sounded like him.

Some of the singers I recorded with over the years, in addition to Bill Henderson and Andy Bey, were Salome Bey, Gail Nelson, Chapman Roberts, Jackie Verell, Brenda Alfred, Carol Lynn Maillard, and Gregory Hines. I met Gregory some years ago when he lived in Venice Beach, California. He was fairly well known at that time but not as world-famous as he became. He was one hell of a talent. He could sing, dance, act, and play a little drums and guitar. He was also a good songwriter—I heard some of his compositions and was impressed. I engaged him to sing on a recording called *Silver 'n Strings Play the Music of the Spheres,* which I did for Blue Note Records. I wanted him to sing on more than one track, but his availability was limited because he was also filming the movie *Wolfen.* The song he recorded with us was "We All Have a Part to Play." He did a wonderful job, and trumpeter Tom Harrell played a great solo on it.

After I finished *The United States of Mind,* I signed a contract for five LPs. I did the first one using a brass section. Charlie Lorie was at Blue Note at that time. I had planned to name the album after one of the tunes, but Charlie said to me, "Man, why don't you call it *Silver 'n Brass?*" When I thought about it, I said, "Hey, yeah, that's a good title. I'll use that." Then

I got to thinking, and all of a sudden it hit me: "Why don't I dissect an orchestra? I've got five albums to do. The first is *Silver 'n Brass;* the second will be *Silver 'n Wood*, and then *Silver 'n Percussion*, *Silver 'n Voices*, and *Silver 'n Strings*. That's five LPs, so it covers my whole contract."

Several years back, jazz writer, producer, and archivist Michael Cuscuna called me and said, "Horace, we're thinking of rereleasing the *Silver 'n* series, but I think it could have been mixed better. Would you consider coming into the city with me to remix some of that stuff?" I said, "Yeah, I'd love to." But that's the last I heard about it. He never got back to me.

TRUMPETER RANDY BRECKER left Blood, Sweat, and Tears to join my quintet in 1969. When he left them, the band was not doing well, although later they became very popular. I don't know if he ever regretted leaving, but I know I was happy to have him with me. He's a fine musician and a beautiful person. The quintet he played in also included Bennie Maupin on tenor, John Williams on bass, and Billy Cobham on drums (who was later replaced by Alvin Queen). A kick-ass group.

Later on, Randy joined another one of my quintets, along with his brother Michael on tenor, Will Lee on Fender bass, and Alvin Queen on drums—another kick-ass group. We stayed together for about a year and a half. I regret that I didn't get a chance to record this band. My contract with Blue Note Records had expired at that time, and we were at odds on agreeing to terms for a new contract.

Once, at the Jazz Workshop in Boston, that band was cookin'—so much so that on the first set of opening night, when I walked off the bandstand, I said to myself, "I don't care if the people liked us or not. I know we played our ass off." As I walked to the bar, a young black gentleman approached me. He said, "Mr. Silver, I've been a fan of yours for years. When I walked in here tonight, I looked up on the bandstand and said to myself, 'Why has Horace got all those whiteys with him? I've seen him before when he had one, but now he's got three. He and the drummer are the only blacks in the quintet.' I started not to come in, but I decided I would. I sat at the bar and listened to the whole set. Shit, dem niggers is cookin'!"

Great musicians and performances transcend prejudice and break down racial barriers on both the black and white sides of the fence. Music (and in particular jazz music) helps to bring people of all races together.

Bandleader Woody Herman had told me about Tom Harrell, a young trumpet player in his band who loved my music and wanted to play with my group. I heard Tom play and was very impressed. I got his name and phone number for future reference. When Randy left the band in 1975, I called and hired Tom, who turned out to be a great guy and a great musician. The group then included Tom on trumpet, Michael Brecker on tenor, and Alvin Queen on drums. At one point, we had Chip Jackson on bass; and at another time, we had Mike Richmond on bass.

When Michael Brecker left the group, he recommended Bob Berg to take his place. I heard Bob and liked his playing and hired him. We were still kickin' ass. Eventually, Larry Schneider took Bob's place. When Larry left, Ralph Moore replaced him on tenor. Then Brian Lynch took Tom Harrell's place on trumpet. That band also included Bob Maize on bass and Carl Burnett on drums. God has blessed me throughout my career with some fine young musicians. I am grateful.

FOUR SMALL JAZZ RECORD LABELS were prevalent in the 1950s: Blue Note Records, owned by Alfred Lion and Francis Wolff; Prestige Records, owned by Bob Weinstock; Savoy Records, owned by Herman Lubinsky; and Riverside Records, owned by Bill Grauer and Orrin Keepnews. All of these labels produced many great jazz recordings. I was signed with Blue Note Records and stayed with them for twenty-eight years. They let me do my thing and gave me an increase in salary at the signing of every new three-year contract.

On two occasions when my contract expired, I was approached by Riverside Records, who wanted to sign me up and offered me more money. I considered it, but I said to myself, "I'm happy with Blue Note. They let me do my thing without any interference. Will Riverside do the same? The increase in money won't make much difference to me if I don't have the freedom to do my thing the way I want to do it." I went to Alfred Lion each time and told him about Riverside's offer. I let him know that I was happy with Blue Note and didn't want to leave, but business is business. When I told him what Riverside had offered me, he matched it both times, and I stayed on.

In the late 1960s, Alfred Lion sold Blue Note to United Artists Records; and he and his wife, Ruth, retired to Cuernavaca, Mexico. I vacationed there with them for a couple of weeks one summer and had a great time. United Artists Records was later bought by Capitol Records. I remained signed on throughout these changes. I noticed, though, that Capitol was giving less and less attention to their jazz artists and concentrating on their pop artists such as Kenny Rogers and Dotty West. Capitol was dropping jazz artists when their contracts expired and not picking up their options. I didn't think they were going to pick up my option when my contract expired, and I was right.

George Butler had been my producer when Blue Note was owned by United Artists. He had left to go with Columbia Records and wanted me to contact him and join him at Columbia when my contract ran out with Blue Note/United Artists Records. I did call him, but it was bad timing—Columbia was then in the process of letting many of their artists go and was not taking on any new ones. I decided that I was going to start my own record label because I wanted to continue my metaphysical approach to my music. In 1980, I formed a production company called Silveto Productions Inc., of which Silveto Records and Emerald Records were a part.

One summer day back in 1981, I received a call from Bill Cosby's secretary, and a series of events began that led to my first Silveto album, *Guides to Growing Up*. She said Cos had a song that he had made up, but he didn't know how to write it down on paper, since he was not a musician. He was to be the master of ceremonies at the Newport Jazz Festival, and he wanted his song to be played by one of the groups on the program. He was performing in Reno at the time and wanted to fly me there and put me up in a hotel, food and expenses included, so that I could write and arrange his song for a small combo. I don't remember what the instrumentation was.

I told his secretary that I would love to go to Reno and do this writing and arranging for him, but I had my son staying with me for the summer. She said, "I'm sure Mr. Cosby wouldn't mind if you brought your son with you." I agreed to go.

Gregory and I had a ball while we were there. We were flown first class. A limo met us at the airport and took us to our hotel. We ate delicious meals in our room and at the hotel restaurant. We rode around with Cos in one of his Rolls-Royces. I was impressed by his friendly response to fans who would wave to him or yell out some comment from the sidewalk as we drove by.

Cos was working at Harrah's in Reno at that time and had his family with him. They were living in a big house that had a swimming pool inside and a tennis court in the backyard. He went to bed late after his show and slept late the next day. I called each morning to see if he had woken up yet. His wife, Camille, would tell me if he was up or when he would be getting up. Then Greg and I would take a taxi to his house and have breakfast or brunch with him and his family.

After the meal, Cos and I would go into the living room to the piano and work on putting his song down on paper and arranging it for a small combo. We'd work for a couple of hours, and then Cos would go out to the tennis court and practice. I didn't know how to play tennis, so I would just watch. Greg and Bill's son, Ennis, who was about the same age as Greg, would go swimming in the in-house pool. Greg was seven years old at the time. We stayed in Reno for about four or five days.

When the work was finished, Bill asked me how much he owed me. I said, "Bill, you've treated my son and me so royally while we were here. It's been like a mini-vacation. You don't owe me anything." He said, "Well, that's not the way to conduct business, but I'll accept that." The arrangement I wrote for him was never used in the Newport Jazz Festival. Someone told me that a couple of the musicians in the group that agreed to play the song couldn't read music; therefore, the arrangement couldn't be used.

At about the same time, I was producing the first Silveto album, *Guides to Growing Up*, which was directed at small children. It expressed some of the principles children should adhere to in the process of growing up. When I conceived this idea, I thought to myself, "Why not try to get Bill Cosby to do some recitations on this LP? He has such a way with children." I was in New York and went to his show at Carnegie Hall. I went backstage afterward to say hello and ask him to be part of my project. He agreed to do it.

When it came time to do the project, he was out of town shooting a Jell-O commercial for TV. He told me to send him the recitations. He went into a local recording studio, put them down on tape, and mailed me the tape. I proceeded to write some background music to go under his recitations. I went into Sage and Sound Studios in Los Angeles with engineer Jim Mooney and my quintet and recorded the music, adding Bill's recitations. The quintet consisted of Eddie Harris on tenor, Joe Diorio on guitar, Bob Magnusson on bass, Roy McCurdy on drums, and myself on piano.

I added the vocal duo called Feather, the husband-and-wife team of Weaver Copeland and Mahmu Pearl, who have been my dear friends for many years. (Their names were originally Alan and Joyce Copeland.) They both sang on my Blue Note LP *Silver 'n Voices*. Weaver is a fine pianist, composer, lyricist, arranger, and orchestrator, and they are both fine singers. I could always rely on them to give me a good performance and their full cooperation on a project. Weaver used to sing with the Modernaires and still does on occasion.

After the project was completed, I asked Bill how much I owed him. He said, "Nothing." I had done him a favor, and now he was doing me one. I wanted to use Bill and myself on the cover, with an interracial group of kids. Bill said that his wife, Camille, was studying photography and that she would take the pictures for the LP. She did a wonderful job. I asked her how much I owed her. She said, "Nothing." Bill's brother ran an interracial private school in Los Angeles at that time, which my son attended. I asked Bill if he could get his brother to round up a small interracial group of kids for the cover photo with him and me. We included his son, Ennis, and my son, Gregory, in this shoot.

Bill and Camille both were instrumental in helping me do a successful job in producing the LP *Guides to Growing Up*. They are wonderful, down-to-earth people. I am grateful for the help they extended to me.

Many musicians, actors, and comedians who have become superstars become unapproachable by the man in the street. Because of ego, they place themselves above the common folk. I'm happy to say that my friends Bill Cosby and George Benson are not of that opinion. They are both superstars but free of ego and approachable by all people.

The biggest problem I had with Silveto Records was distribution. The large distributors didn't want to be bothered with me because I was a small operation. I had to deal with the small distributors, who were not all completely honest. Hardly any of them paid COD for the records. They ordered, you mailed, and they had three months in which to pay you. Most of them didn't pay you until your next record release. They wanted the new release, so they would finally pay you for the previous release. This is the way they operated, leaving you with very little, if any, cash coming in.

We recorded five albums of new music, including *Guides to Growing Up*, *Spiritualizing the Senses*, *There's No Need to Struggle*, *Continuity of Spirit*, and *Music to Ease Your Disease*. The musicians included the rhythm team of Bob Maize on bass and Carl Burnette on drums, trumpeters Clark Terry and Bobby Shew, and tenor saxophonists Eddie Harris and Ralph Moore. These records sold very well at our nightclub performances, but things did not go well with our distributors and our mail-order sales. Other musicians had started their own record companies and failed, but I had always thought that they failed because they didn't hang in there long enough. I hung in there for ten years, and I still couldn't get the company off the ground. I finally decided to throw in the towel and look for a record contract with a major label.

In 1992, I approached George Butler once again at Columbia Records. This time they had an opening, and I signed on. I made two albums for them: *It's Got to Be Funky* and *Pencil Packin' Papa*. Then I signed with GRP/Impulse! Records and did two albums on the Impulse! label: *The Hardbop Grandpop* and *A Prescription for the Blues*. Then Verve Records merged with GRP, and they switched me to the Verve label. My first and only album on Verve is *Jazz Has a Sense of Humor*.

Even though I didn't have great success with Silveto and Emerald Records, I still kept Silveto Productions Inc. When I signed up with GRP/Impulse!, I signed as Silveto Productions to produce Horace Silver. All the recordings I've done for GRP/Impulse! and Verve were produced by Horace Silver and Silveto Productions Inc. My executive producer was Tommy LiPuma. We have great rapport, and I always enjoy working with him. He's a very experienced producer and really knows his stuff. I also enjoy working with recording engineer Al Schmitt. Art director Hollis King and photographer Rocky Schenck and I work well together. Compatibility is so important in this business.

Everything I know about producing a record I learned from observing Alfred Lion. Most musicians in those old days concentrated on making a great record but were not interested in getting involved in the other aspects of producing, such as photography, graphics, and liner notes. I wanted to be involved in all of it, and Alfred was kind enough to allow me to do so. Recording engineer Rudy Van Gelder gave us some great-sounding records. The fidelity on those old records we made at his studio years ago still sounds good today. He's a fine engineer. I had the pleasure of doing two CDs for Sony/Columbia with Donny Hahn, who also is a great engineer.

There is so much work that goes into making a record, from composing to arranging, orchestrating, writing lyrics, rehearsing, recording, editing, mixing, mastering, taking photographs, creating graphic design, writing liner notes. Then comes distribution and promotion and, hopefully, big sales and success. I always hope each recording will bring pleasure and entertainment to people all over the world.

AROUND 1983, I WAS STILL living in my apartment in Rancho Palos Verdes when I decided to get a house in that area. They had some nice houses down there, but they were quite expensive. A realtor suggested I look up here in Malibu. Then I found this house, which wasn't quite as expensive as houses down in Palos Verdes. When I first saw it, even with its great view of the ocean, I started not to buy it because I had my heart set on living in the Palos Verdes area. But after I considered it, I said, "Well, gee, this is a nice house, the price is fairly reasonable, and it has a great view." So I decided to take it.

Years earlier, when I first moved to Los Angeles, I had met drummer Osie Johnson's daughter. I had worked several gigs in New York City with Osie, who was a fine drummer, composer, and arranger. He always had a smile on his face and a good joke to tell you. Unfortunately, he died at an early age. Some years later, after I bought my house in Malibu, Osie's daughter informed me that her mother (a Caucasian lady) was coming out from New York for a few weeks and that she would like to see me. They both came out to Malibu to visit me, and I gave them a tour around my house. I have a lovely home with a beautiful view of the ocean. I live in a nice, quiet neighborhood. My neighbors are nice people, and I'm very happy here. When we finished the tour, Osie's wife said, "Horace, you're shittin' in high cotton." This is an old expression that black people from the South used. It means that you are enjoying a successful life, that you are doing well. I was so surprised to hear this come out of a white lady's mouth. We all had a good laugh and an enjoyable time together.

My neighbors are friendly. They say hello when I'm out walking, and sometimes we stop and talk. Occasionally, one might knock on my door to see if I'm okay. There's another family named Silver down the street, Paulette and Rick Silver, and they have several sons. Sometimes they get my mail or I get theirs, and we have to make an exchange.

One day several years ago, one of their sons, Alex, rang my doorbell. When I went to the door, he said, "Mister Silver, would you like to have Thanksgiving dinner with my family? We'd like to invite you."

I said, "Tell your mom and dad thank you very much, but I always have Thanksgiving dinner with my goddaughter and her mother."

The next time I saw Alex's mother, I thanked her personally, but she said, "Don't thank me—thank Alex. He came to me and my husband one day and said, 'You know, Mister Silver is down there all by himself, and he's an old man. Maybe we should invite him for Thanksgiving dinner.'" I thought that was very nice of him and his family.

Another time, I was out taking my after-dinner walk and Alex was out there in the street playing ball with some of the kids. When they hit the ball, it just missed my head. He yelled out to his playmates, "Hey, hey, watch out there! That's a famous man, and besides, he's an *OLD* man."

THERE WAS A PERIOD BETWEEN 1980 and 1985 in which it became increasingly difficult to get young jazz musicians for my quintet who were of the caliber that I was used to. Most of them read well but were not well schooled harmonically. They were lacking in improvisational skills. They couldn't get down with the chord changes. They played too many notes, and some of them were wrong. They played too long and didn't have much to say. They weren't consistently good soloists. It's not how many notes you play but the value of the notes you play that counts. If you can play a lot of notes and make a valid statement, fine. But just a display of technique doesn't mean you're saying something. There should be some space in the music. Music has to breathe, just like we do.

I was seriously thinking of taking a leave of absence from the music business at that time, because I was disappointed in the young musicians who were available to me. I hung in there, though, and stuck it out, even though I wasn't satisfied with some of the groups that I put together. Around 1986, conditions improved, and I was able to put together the kind of band I was happy with. The musicians I hired during that period shall remain nameless, because I don't wish to hurt anybody's feelings or offend anyone.

I do have a pet peeve I would like to address. It concerns the young jazz students who are attending the various jazz schools throughout the country. The majority of them can't improvise worth a shit, and their teachers don't seem to be concerned about helping them in this area. I've been invited to many of these schools and have heard their bands play. Their arrangements and ensemble playing were fine, but when one of the students stood up to take a solo, there wasn't shit happenin'. It was obvious to me that they didn't know the chord changes to the tune and were fumbling around in the dark, trying to improvise by ear. Either that, or they did know the chord changes to the tune but lacked the ability to improvise on them. They had what I call tin ears—they couldn't hear the relationship of one chord to another. Those who have tin ears will never become great, or even good, improvisers.

Jazz is basically improvisation. For those who would like to become great jazz improvisers, a good knowledge of harmony is absolutely essential. The music schools concentrate on reading, section playing, arranging, orchestration, and many other valid aspects of music, but they do not stress the need for good harmonic knowledge in order to improvise well. Young musicians have to get this on their own, but it's well worth the effort. Without it, they're groping in the dark.

I don't mean to condemn these young people or their teachers. I would just like to bring attention to the matter in the hope that something positive can be done about it. When I was a teenager, the guys I hung out with who played jazz were all into chord changes. We practiced improvising on standard tunes every day. We could read music, although we weren't good sight readers. Our emphasis was on chord changes and improvising. Let's face it, jazz is about ten percent arrangement and ninety percent improvisation. These schools are supposed to be jazz schools. Why aren't they putting the emphasis on improvisation? All their emphasis seems to be on ensemble playing and arrangements rather than trying to cultivate improvisational skills. This is very good, but not good enough. There should be a balance maintained in all three of these areas. Without good solos within the context of the arrangement, the total performance is sadly lacking.

SOME YEARS EARLIER, when I lived in New York City, I had met Brazilian musician Moacir Santos. He was a singer, composer, arranger, and orchestrator. He and his wife became great friends with my wife and me. I introduced him to George Butler, who was the producer at Blue Note Records at that time. Blue Note signed him up, and he made several recordings for them. Moacir later moved to California and signed with Discovery Records, which was owned and operated by Albert Marx. Moacir is one hell of a talent, and I have great respect for him and his talent.

Originally a New York–based label, Albert Marx's Discovery Records had a reputation for recording new talent from the late 1940s through the 1950s, when business started to steadily decline. Marx revived the label in Los Angeles during the 1980s. I introduced Don and Alicia Cunningham, a very fine husband-and-wife singing team and good friends of mine, to Albert; and they wound up making three albums for Discovery Records. Don wrote a lyric for my song "Quicksilver" and recorded it on Discovery. Don had worked with Harry Belafonte's group before he and his wife started doing their own thing.

Blue Note Records, owned by Alfred Lion, and Discovery Records, owned by Albert Marx, were the only two labels I knew of where an unknown talent might hope to get a shot. Albert Marx didn't have to be in the recording business to make money; he was already rich. His father was the Marx of the famous Hart, Schaffner, and Marx men's clothing stores, and Albert inherited a fortune when his father died. He was in the business because he loved the music. Alfred Lion was not rich when he started Blue Note Records, but he also was in the business because he loved the music.

Before starting the Discovery label, Albert had two others labels: Guild Records and Musicraft Records. Diz and Bird recorded the original "Salt

Peanuts" on the Guild Record label. Guild Records had their records pressed at a plant in Norwalk, Connecticut, my hometown.

I once interviewed Albert Marx for a radio show I had in Los Angeles, and he told me some interesting stories. Back in the 1930s, someone had brought a piano player to him in the hope that Albert would record him. The piano player happened to be Art Tatum, who was unknown at that time. Albert asked the man how much money he wanted. The man said ten dollars per tune. Albert said no problem.

About ten years later, Albert was about to record Stuff Smith and his combo. The day before the session, Albert attended one of Stuff's rehearsals. Stuff wanted Albert to hear the songs he had written for the date. Albert listened and liked them all. Stuff had written a ballad, and he said that there was a girl in the back room who he'd like to bring out to sing this ballad for Albert. He wanted to use her on the session. The girl came out and sang, and Albert liked her and gave the okay for her to be on the session.

Stuff said, "You know you have to pay her." Albert said, "How much does she want? Stuff said, "Ten dollars." The girl was Sarah Vaughan. She was unknown at that time.

Can you imagine recording Art Tatum and Sarah Vaughan for ten dollars per tune? Thanks to the popularity of Art Tatum and Sarah Vaughan, these recordings through the years must have accumulated an income of at least ten thousand dollars. Not a bad investment. Alfred Lion and Albert Marx knew how to pick talent.

Speaking of Sarah, I remember a young black man named Johnny Gary who used to be her road manager. He later worked with the Jazzmobile and then became a bartender at Birdland. He told me that once when he was out on tour with Sarah, she was to hook up with Ella Fitzgerald to do a concert together. All through the tour, up until the day before she was to sing with Ella, he was teasing her, saying, "Ella's gonna kick your ass." He said when they got together and sang, they were really cookin', and they knocked the audience out.

On their final song, they proceeded to scat sing. After scatting for some time and exchanging eight-bar phrases, Sarah said to Ella, "Well, Ella, I think we better take this song out because I'm running out of ideas."

Ella replied, "I don't know about you, Sarah, but I'm just gettin' started."

Next day, Johnny said to Sarah, "I told you Ella was gonna kick your ass." Sarah's reply was, "Yeah, that's a bad lady."

We all know how great both Sarah and Ella are, but when it comes to scat singing, no one can compete with Ella, in my opinion. She is king and queen of that realm. My second favorite scat singer is Mel Torme. I've always enjoyed Carmen McRae and Jon Hendricks when they scatted, but Ella is the master scatter.

IN 1986, MY FATHER DIED. He had been a member of St. Mary's Catholic Church in Norwalk, so when he died, I went to St. Mary's rectory to meet Father John Sanders and arrange for Dad's funeral service.

I had heard that Father Sanders was a black priest. Norwalk had made considerable progress in race relations since I was a child growing up there. St. Mary's Church had a black priest, and Norwalk High School had a black principal.

I met with Father Sanders, and we made the funeral arrangements. Father Sanders said the funeral mass and also spoke at the cemetery. After Dad's coffin was lowered into the ground, I approached Father Sanders and thanked him for arranging everything. I handed him an envelope with some money in it as a contribution to the church. He said that it wasn't necessary for me to give money; Dad had been a member of the church and the church did not charge for this service. I asked him to please accept the money for the church because I knew that Dad would have wanted me to do this. He accepted.

As I was about to leave, he asked if I was Horace Silver, the well-known jazz pianist, composer, and bandleader. I said yes. He then told me that he was a trombonist and that he had taken Juan Tizol's place in the Duke Ellington Orchestra. He had worked with Duke for five years before entering the priesthood. When I think of Dad's funeral being conducted by a black priest who used to play trombone in Duke Ellington's band, I feel very proud of Norwalk's racial progress. May Norwalk continue to move forward in this area. May we all continue to move forward in this area.

Chapter Six

OFF THE MERRY-GO-ROUND
LATER YEARS

I am a cell in the organ of the Earth in the body of the universe,
and my body is a universe to my organs and my cells.
I am a thought that is music in the mind of the spirit of the universe,
and within me lives a universe fed by music of my thought.
I am, I always was, I always will be.

BY THE END OF THE 1980S, I had come to feel that keeping a working band together and living on the road had become a merry-go-round, and I wanted to get off. But I didn't know how. For many years, I had been successful with the quintet; people still liked my group, and I still liked it, too. It's not that I didn't like what we were doing, but I just wanted to expand and grow. I wanted to get off the merry-go-round of the quintet and the same tours every year, every year, around and around.

Finally, I decided I just had to quit—that was the only way. If you're still on the go, how can you put your attention into a new direction while you're still going in the old direction? I had to just say, "Fuck it. Whether or not I get into what I want to do right away, I don't want to do this old stuff anymore. I've got to expand and do something else." It's like I've been raising sheep for several years and I'm successful at it, but I get tired of it. I want to change and be a vegetable farmer. Now, if I keep on raising sheep, I ain't gonna have time to put into doing what I want. I just have to give up the sheep and take a chance.

I'm grateful to God that my many fans like my music, that they like me and want me out there. It's an honor to be wanted, but I've got to fulfill myself, too. I just can't do the same thing over and over; I get bored with it and feel I'm not growing. When a plant pops through from out of the ground, you have the shoot first, and then a little bud, and then the flower. I don't want to do the same shit all the time; I want to add. It's like you're building a structure, and you've got the framework and what you want to put on top of the framework. But then you want to add to it—a kitchen, a bedroom, or a second level. You want to keep growing.

When I was in London, playing at Ronnie Scott's, I often went to Reverend Ena Twigg for a psychic reading. During the many times I've been there, my brother, John, or my mother, or Bud Powell would come to me and speak to me through her. One time Satchmo came, and Reverend Twigg related his message to me. He said, "When you have enough, have enough"—meaning, when you're through, when you're tired of the road, cut it loose. He also said, "I left my work half done. Will you help me?" I said, "I'd be delighted to help you."

Since that incident, I've written a couple of tunes for him. "Red Beans and Rice" is dedicated to Satchmo. And one time he gave me a tune. It happened when I was playing a gig up in Milwaukee. One night, it was very quiet in my room, and a melody came into my mind. I heard the whole thing in my head, and I could hear his voice singing this thing—not with a lyric, but singing it with the harmonies. I sang it into my little tape recorder, and when I got home, I figured out the changes and wrote it down. The tune wound up titled "Out of the Night Came You." I have also written a tune called "Satchmo's Song," which is part of my musical work *Rockin' with Rachmaninoff.*

But at the time of Reverend Twigg's reading, when Satchmo said he left his work half done, I couldn't figure how in the hell he meant that. The man did so many things: he was on radio and television and in the movies, he recorded, he was considered the jazz ambassador to the world—

what did he not do that he was supposed to do, that God had put him here to do? Evidently, it was something, so he was trying to work through me—and I'm sure through other people, too—to complete what he had not done on earth. That's the way it works. When you come here, you have a destiny to perform, to fulfill. And if you die leaving some things undone, you have two choices: you can be reincarnated and come back here to fulfill your destiny, or you can work through someone else who's still in the body to complete what you should have done when you were here.

I DON'T REMEMBER EXACTLY how soon after that experience *Rockin' with Rachmaninoff* came along, but that certainly was an early part of my expansion. I had to do something other than just play nightclubs and a few jazz concerts here and there, in Europe and the United States. Once, pianist Jimmy Jones told me what Duke Ellington had said to him: "Man, music is vast. Do some of it all. Don't just get hung up in one little area of it." I always thought about that, and I still do. That's one of the reasons I wrote *Rockin' with Rachmaninoff*.

One night back in 1990, I had a dream about Duke Ellington and Serge Rachmaninoff. I dreamt they met in the spirit world. They were both enamored of each other's talents and had great respect for each other. Duke appreciated classical music, and Rachmaninoff appreciated jazz. Duke took Rachmaninoff on a tour of the spirit world to meet all the jazz greats who had made their transition, people such as Louis Armstrong, Coleman Hawkins, Thelonious Monk. When I awoke, I thought to myself, "This dream would make a good storyline for a stage production," and I got to work developing the idea. I'd never done anything for the theater before, and that was a real expansion: an eight-piece band, five dancers, two singers, and a narrator.

After completing it, I wondered how I would get the backing to put it on stage. I read in the paper that pianist Billy Taylor and his trio would be performing in Los Angeles at the Biltmore Hotel, with Mayor Tom Bradley in attendance. He and Billy Taylor were friends and had attended the same college. I decided to put a package of my recordings together to give to Mayor Bradley at the concert. In the package, I included a note saying that I had written a musical work for the stage called *Rockin' with Rachmaninoff*, and if he could help me put it on here in Los Angeles, I would donate my services free to his favorite charity. Only the musicians, singers, dancers, narrator, and choreographer had to be paid.

About two weeks later, I received a phone call from Mayor Bradley's secretary saying that the mayor wanted to meet with me and Valerie Fields from the Los Angeles Cultural Affairs Department. It took about a year to work out all the details, but we finally got it on stage for a weekend in June 1991. We did a Friday and Saturday night performance and a Sunday afternoon matinee.

Our choreographer and director was Donald McKayle. Our singers were Andy Bey and Dawn Burnett. Our musicians were Michael Mossman on trumpet, Andy Martin and Bob McChesney on trombones, Ralph Bowen and Ricky Woodard on tenors, Bob Maize on bass, Carl Burnett on drums, and myself on piano. Our narrator was Chuck Niles. Chuck wouldn't accept any pay; all he wanted was twenty-five dollars for gas for his car. Our dancers were Atalya Bates, Maisha Brown, Victor Butler, Larry Sousa, and Tamica Washington.

I'll always be grateful to Mayor Tom Bradley and his assistants for helping me to get *Rockin' with Rachmaninoff* on the stage. The proceeds went to his favorite charity, the Challengers Boys and Girls Club of Los Angeles, of which Lou Dantzler is the president. I always thought Tom Bradley was a great mayor and a great guy. And, of course, he was a big jazz fan. The show got good reviews in the newspapers, but nothing ever happened with it after that. Many composers write extended musical works and never get to see them on stage. I at least had the joy of seeing my work performed for a weekend.

After that weekend, I decided to take the band and the singers into the studio and record the music for release on my Silveto Records label. I recorded it but never got to release it because things got so bad with the label that I had to throw in the towel and go out of business.

When I did two albums with Columbia, I approached George Butler and the people there. I said, "I've got a tape of music from my show *Rockin' with Rachmaninoff.* Would you like to hear it and maybe put it out?" They didn't even express an interest in hearing it. When I left them and went with GRP/Impulse!, same thing: Tommy LiPuma and the folks expressed no interest, no desire to hear it. It's almost as if they wanted to produce only their own records. I had produced this one through Silveto Productions, so their producer would not receive any producer's money. That could be one reason they didn't even want to listen to it. I couldn't put it out myself because I was under exclusive contract, so it just sat.

Then they switched me from Impulse! to Verve, and I did the album *Jazz Has a Sense of Humor* in 1999. When my contract expired after that album and they didn't pick up the option, I was free. So I said, "Now's the time to get *Rockin' with Rachmaninoff* out of the closet." Actually, the companies did me a favor by not picking up my option, because if they had, I'd still be doing stuff for them, and *Rockin' with Rachmaninoff* would still be lying in the closet. I found a record label willing to put it out, Bop City Records, and the CD was released in 2000. I leased the recording to the label; I didn't want to sell it. (For all the stuff I've done in the past, I don't own any masters. I own the copyrights to the compositions but not the master recordings themselves—"the masters," as we say in the business. The recording companies paid me for the recording sessions, they paid me composer's royalties through my publishing company and artist's royalties, but they own the masters.) I didn't care if the label leased this project for three years or seven years, so long as they gave me a fair deal. I wanted them to make a profit, because, if they didn't, they wouldn't have wanted to take my next album.

The first thing I did was get together with engineer Donny Hahn in the studio to mix each tune and get the levels right. Luckily, we didn't have to do any editing, but the sound had never been mixed. When that was done, I wrote a letter to Fantasy Records, who had just put out the album *Horace Silver: Paris Blues*, recorded by Norman Granz at a concert in 1962. But Fantasy wasn't interested. Concord wasn't interested—I got no reply at all from them.

Then I got in touch with Bop City—a new company just starting up a jazz label—and they liked it. The guy who negotiated the contract said, "How much do you want for it?" I said, "I don't know. This is the first time I ever did this. Why don't you get together with your partners and your lawyer and make me an offer? Then I'll take it to my lawyer, and if it's cool, we can sign up. If not, maybe we can make a few adjustments. I want you guys to make a profit, and I want to make a little myself. I spent a lot of time not only writing the music but arranging it, orchestrating it, rehearsing it, recording it, and mixing it, so I hope to make a little profit myself—not a million dollars, but let's share in the profit."

I'M VERY FORTUNATE that I was able to get off the road and do all that, and more. I don't have to worry about my income because God has been kind to me. Jazz musicians are still recording my tunes—things that have become standards, like "Doodlin'," "The Preacher," "Filthy McNasty," "Song for My Father," "Señor Blues," "Nica's Dream," and "Strollin' "—so I have a steady income from royalties. If I didn't have that, I'd be forced to go out on that road to pay off my house notes, property taxes, bills, and expenses. Instead, I can allow myself to do what I really want, in an extension of my career. I don't want to come back like Satch and say, "I left my work half done, because I didn't do what I wanted before I died." If I had to come back like that, I would, but I'd prefer to get my work done before I go.

To tell the truth, I hope I don't have to come back—and it's not because I don't love this earth. I do love it, and I love this country, and I love California. But I'm tired of living in a world where people are killing each other and fighting. When I die, whatever the next world is like, I hope there's no war there. I hope people there can get along with each other, love and help each other, and live in peace and harmony.

I'm sick of every time I turn around there's another war, and another war. The leaders say, "Now that we got that war over with, there's not going to be any more war." And then five, six, ten years later, here's another war—and it keeps going on and on and on, and it will keep going on until people learn to love one another. Love conquers war, but we've got all those greedy people who are after oil or gold or silver or diamonds, or whatever the resources of another country are, and they plot to dominate those other countries. I'm sick of living in a world like that; I want to live where there's peace and harmony.

AT ABOUT THE SAME TIME I was working on *Rockin' with Rachmaninoff*, about 1990, Art Blakey and I reconciled our differences over the recording sessions we had done for Columbia for the album *The Jazz Messengers* in 1956. When we did the sessions, somehow they gave all the money to Art, who took it and never paid anybody. I guess he went out and got high with the money, but I know I never got mine. I had rehearsed with the group, contributed two tunes to the album, and felt I should get paid for what I had done, so I took Art to the union. The other guys in the band didn't do that, and maybe I shouldn't have done it either. I don't know. It didn't detract from my love for Art—I knew he was a drug addict, so I didn't hate him or have any animosity toward him.

The union didn't do shit. The only thing that happened was a series of letters that transpired between me and the union, and the union and Art, and Art back to the union. Finally, the union wrote me a letter congratulating me that I had won the case and saying that Art Blakey was obligated to pay me when he got the money—which was never. Meanwhile, these events made Art fall out with me for several years.

Then, around 1989 or 1990, a friend of mine in New York, a public relations guy, put me on the Joe Franklin show on WOR, Channel 9. He'd arrange to do this whenever I had a new record out. Sometimes, even if I didn't have a new record out, they'd be short of talent and would call me to be on the show. It was an all-night interview program that came on at midnight and went on until about four in the morning, five or six nights a week. One morning when I was on, I said, "Thank God for Art Blakey, because through him I got a lot of my tunes recorded in the early days—like on *A Night at Birdland*, we did 'Quicksilver,' 'Split Kick,' and 'Mayreh.' I love Art Blakey."

It just so happened that Art was watching the show that night, and that turned his whole thing around. Where maybe before he had a little animosity toward me because I had taken him to the union, now he forgave me, because he knew I loved him.

Not long after, my group played opposite his at the John Anson Ford Theater, near the Hollywood Bowl. We went on first. When he came on, I went backstage and changed my clothes. Then I went to stand in the wings and listen to his band. He saw me and called me out to sit in with them. When I sat down at the piano, he said to the people, "I was watching Joe Franklin one night, and Horace came out and said, 'Thank God for Art Blakey, 'cause he gave me a big break, and I love him.'" The tune we played was my "Mayreh," from *A Night at Birdland.*

Art was very sick at the time. His face was all sunken in, he had lost a lot of weight, and he was obviously in the last stages of cancer. But he played as well as ever—that man, we used to call him the "Little Dynamo," because he had so much energy, so much will power and strength. In spite of his illness, he hadn't changed a bit. He played his ass off no matter where he was at—healthy or sick, he gave one hundred percent, one hundred and fifty percent of himself, all the time.

I'VE HAD FOUR NEAR-DEATH experiences in my life, the most recent in 1993, just a few years after I last saw Art Blakey. The first was when my wife and I went on vacation in North Africa around 1971. We spent two weeks there through the Club Med vacation program, one week in Marrakech, and one week in Agadir. I got a very bad throat infection while I was there. My tongue swelled up as big as an orange, and it pained me to swallow. I presume it was brought on by something I ate or drank. There was no doctor in the Club Med complex, only a nurse. She gave me a throat spray, which did no good. I was afraid to go outside the complex and see a Moroccan doctor.

When I returned to New York, I called my doctor as soon as I got off the plane. He told me to come right over. When he examined me, he said that I had picked up some kind of bug over there and that he would give me a shot of penicillin to get rid of it. I pulled down my pants, and he shot me in the rear. All of a sudden, I started to get dizzy, and I heard a loud ringing in my ears. I felt like I was going to faint. The doctor grabbed me by the arm and sat me down. He then reached for a big syringe filled with red liquid and shot it into my arm. I remember saying to myself, "You've got to keep talking, even though what you say may not make sense. You've got to stay conscious, because if you allow yourself to pass out, you may not wake up." I felt a burning sensation as this red liquid he injected into my arm went through my blood vessels like a tornado. Its final destination was my rectum.

I had taken penicillin before for various reasons without any ill effects, but now I had apparently become allergic to it. If my doctor hadn't had the antidote handy to inject me with, I could have died. He told me a story about a doctor friend of his who, after finishing up with his patients one day, gave himself a shot of penicillin for a cold. The doctor had taken penicillin many times before without any ill effects, but now he had become allergic to the drug. He dropped dead on his office floor. His wife kept calling the office and finally sent someone there to investigate. They found him dead. He had not had the antidote prepared and handy. My doctor told me that, after what happened to his friend, he always kept the antidote prepared and handy in case he had to deal with a similar experience.

This bug was extremely difficult to get rid of. I took antibiotics for about a month and thought I had gotten rid of it, but in two weeks it came back. I had to resume the antibiotics for another month until I finally got rid of it. All through these two months, I had a constant itching in the palms of both hands, which was driving me nuts. They sure have some weird bugs over there in North Africa.

My second near-death experience happened when I lived in Rancho Palos Verdes. I was divorced by that time and had my son with me on weekends. He was about five years old. I took him to the YMCA every week for a swimming lesson. I usually brought a book and read while he was taking his lesson. This particular day, I decided to drop him off at the YMCA and go apartment hunting in San Pedro and then pick him up later. They kept raising the rent every six months at the Porto Verde Apartments, where I lived. I thought I might be able to do better in San Pedro. I drove through a few very nice residential districts and spotted a nice-looking apartment building that had an "APARTMENT FOR RENT" sign. I got out of the car and walked around the grounds, trying to locate the superintendent's office.

All of a sudden, a car pulled up to the curb, and a Caucasian man motioned for me to come over to the car. I went over, thinking that he was about to give me some information about finding the building superintendent. He asked me what I was doing there. I said I was looking for an apartment to rent. He said, "Not in this neighborhood," and pulled a gun and pointed it at my chest. At first, I thought he might have been a fan playing a joke on me, and I almost started to laugh. But as I looked into his eyes, I realized that he was serious. I didn't laugh or smile. I remained motionless. He drove off with gun in hand.

After he drove off, I thought to myself, "What if he had pulled the trigger and left me dead on the sidewalk?" My son, Gregory, would have been waiting for me to pick him up at the YMCA—and no daddy. Prejudice is a terrible thing. It drives people to insanity.

My third near-death experience also happened in Rancho Palos Verdes. While on vacation in Hawaii, I met Heidi Chang, a young American-born Chinese lady who was a jazz disc jockey. She invited me to come on her program and be interviewed, and I accepted. After the program, we had dinner together. She mentioned that jazz trombonist Trummy Young lived in Hawaii and that he was having a birthday that day. We decided to call him and wish him a happy birthday. Trummy used to play with the Jimmie Lunceford band. I never got to meet Trummy in person, but we talked for quite a while on the phone that day. I told him how much I loved the Lunceford band and all its members. He said that he was familiar with my music and that he knew that I dug Lunceford, because he could hear the Lunceford influence in my music.

Several months later, Heidi Chang came to Los Angeles, and she called me. I invited her out to dinner, and after dinner we went to the Parisian

Room to catch Eddie "Lockjaw" Davis. We stayed through two shows. I dropped her off at her motel and proceeded to drive home to Rancho Palos Verdes. On the freeway, I became very sleepy. I could hardly keep my eyes open. I rolled down the window to get some air, but it was a fight to stay awake. I should have pulled over and taken a nap, but I kept thinking I could make it.

About three blocks from my apartment building, I fell asleep at the wheel. The car went out of control, and the next thing I knew, I felt a jolt that woke me up. The car had jumped the sidewalk and was in an empty lot. The brakes were jammed, the gas pedal was stuck, and the steering wheel wouldn't work. The car was moving fast, and I had no control over it. I finally got the steering wheel to work and steered the car toward the street. In doing so, I sideswiped a telephone pole and caved in the whole right side of my car.

I began to pray, "Dear God, if it's my time to go, so be it. I'm not afraid to die. But I would like to live long enough to see my son raised to adulthood and to see the realization of some of my musical goals." I didn't have an up-to-date will made out at that time.

Once I got the car into the street, I saw that I was headed toward a row of parked cars. The gas pedal was stuck, the brakes wouldn't work, and my steering wheel once again became inoperative. I prayed and put myself completely in God's hands. All of a sudden, the brakes became operative, and I was able to stop the car about five feet away from the row of parked cars that I would have crashed into. The car was totaled, but I walked away without a scratch.

My fourth and most recent near-death experience happened in Malibu in 1993. I went into the hospital on a Thursday for same-day hernia surgery. On Friday, I was feeling a little soreness but in general was feeling pretty good. On Saturday, I noticed I was having trouble breathing. My dear friend Don Williams came by the house to visit and noted my difficulty. He rushed me to the emergency ward, where they examined me and admitted me.

I was in the hospital for three weeks. The first two weeks, they couldn't find out the cause of my problem. The third week, I got worse and had to be put into intensive care. They found out I had blood clots in my legs and in my lungs. They then started to give me a medication called Coumadin, which is a blood thinner to help dissolve clots.

One night in intensive care, I almost died. I have no recollection of the incident, but my family told me about it later. They received a call from the hospital at about three A.M., saying that they should come to the hospital because I had stopped breathing and the doctors had put me on a respirator to try to get me breathing again. It all happened while I was asleep.

Coming so close to death gives one a greater appreciation of life. When I got out of the hospital, I started taking notice of and giving thanks for all the things I usually took for granted—the moon, the stars, the blue sky, the ocean, the flowers, the trees, my family, my friends, and a host of other blessings that I took for granted. I took time to stop and smell the roses. I began to realize what a great blessing life is and how wonderful it is to be alive and living in this paradise called earth! I am blessed with a talent and a purpose or destiny given by God that is part of His master plan for the uplift of mankind.

WHEN SHE WAS SINGING with the Thad Jones/Mel Lewis orchestra, singer Dee Dee Bridgewater was married to Cecil Bridgewater, who played trumpet in my band. She later appeared in the Broadway production of *The Wiz* and also had a small part in the movie *The Brother from Another Planet.* She and Cecil eventually divorced, and she later moved to Paris and married a Frenchman. I remember performing at Ronnie Scott's club in London with singer Andy Bey. Dee Dee came in one night to hear us. She was doing a one-woman show in London at that time, based on the life of Billie Holiday. She invited Andy and me to see her show on our off night. We went and enjoyed it immensely. She gave a great performance.

Dee Dee called me from Paris one day and said she wanted to do a tribute album dedicated to me and my music. She gave me a list of tunes she wanted to do. I already had lyrics to some of these songs, but not to others. I was leaving to go on tour with the band then, so I spent a lot of time in hotel rooms and on plane flights writing lyrics to the songs she wanted.

Dee Dee flew me to Paris in 1994 to perform on a couple of tracks on the album. She also brought organist Jimmy Smith to Paris to play. I enjoyed every minute of the experience. The CD, which was released in 1995, is called *Love and Peace: A Tribute to Horace Silver*. I am very proud of that album. She and her musicians did a great job. Dee Dee is a fine singer and a wonderful person.

At about the same time, I had the privilege of having O. C. Smith do some recording with me on the Columbia album *Pencil Packin' Papa*, on which he sang four tunes: "I Got the Dancin' Blues," "Soul Mates," "Red Beans and Rice," and "Let It All Hang Out." I could always rely on him to do a great job and give me his full cooperation. I had met O. C. earlier, when he was singing with Count Basie's band at the Apollo Theater in New York. Like Bill Henderson and Andy Bey, O. C. had style and feeling. Some years ago, he had a hit record called "Little Green Apples." He continued to record, but, until his death, most of his time was spent as a minister at his Religious Science Church, where he sang at every service.

THE LAST JAZZ FESTIVAL TOUR I did in Europe and Japan was very disappointing. Out of thirteen festivals that we played in Europe, we had good sound on only three. We would do a sound check for about an hour in the afternoon and get the sound right. But when we came back in the evening to perform, it would be all screwed up. It was frustrating. How can you give a good performance when you can't hear your fellow musicians properly and blend in with them? You travel halfway across the world to perform and then feel that you haven't given as good a performance as you could have if the sound system had been right. All these festivals pay good money and the hotel accommodations are first class, but who needs it if you have to be frustrated and feel that you and your band haven't performed up to your standard because of a screwed-up sound system? I'd rather stay home and practice and write some new tunes for my next recording session.

We played the Mount Fuji Jazz Festival in Japan, and the sound was horrible. We weren't even given any time for a sound check—we went on cold. The Japanese have always been noted for good sound, but they didn't give us any that time. They taped the performance for TV and sent me a copy, and the sound was terrible. J. J. Johnson and his group were on the program, but his performance was deleted from the tape that was shown on TV. What an insult this was to J. J. and the whole jazz world—inexcusable. I would gladly have relinquished some of our playing time, had they asked me, so J. J. could have been on the TV program. I think they exercised poor planning and poor judgment. They had other, more commercially constructed groups on the show, which they chose not to delete from the program. Commercialism won out over pure art once again.

ANOTHER GROWING PROBLEM over the last twenty or thirty years has been bootlegging—the pirating of albums and live music. Italy is famous for that. Italian bootleggers have put out several Horace Silver albums, and albums by other people, too. And you can't do a thing about it. They have a law over in Italy that after so many years everything becomes public domain. Not so here in the USA. In this country, it takes seventy-five years for something to become public domain, and even then you can renew your rights. But Italy doesn't honor that; they go by their own law. They've got together a lot of my old stuff that was on Blue Note, and they're releasing it over there on their bootleg records—*Baghdad Blues* is one of them. I ain't getting a penny on it.

When I called Michael Cuscuna to ask him what Blue Note could do, he said, "There's not much you can do. You'd have to get an Italian lawyer to sue them, and he'd bleed you to death. And by the time you were through, you still wouldn't get any results." If the tune is played on the radio, the only thing you can collect on is performance; you'll get some money on it, but you don't get artist royalties. It's a damn shame something can't be done about that. And then the bootlegs find their way into this country. It's bad enough they do it in Italy, but then they ship it out, and you go to Tower Records here in L.A. and find *Baghdad Blues,* which is a compilation of some of the old Blue Note stuff that they've stolen.

And then there are the bootlegs of live performances. Some years ago, I played a concert somewhere in Europe, where we went on just before vibraphonist Gary Burton. After my set, I went to my dressing room to change my clothes because, as usual, I was sweaty. When I came out into the lobby, Gary had finished his show, and I heard this music playing that sounded like the same shit we had just played at our concert. They just put a mike or something in front of the speakers and recorded the whole damn thing. But I was in a crowd of people, and I couldn't tell where it was coming from.

Another time, I was playing the Jazz Workshop in Boston, and this young man came in who had some kind of contract with somebody in Europe to get tapes of concerts, all the American groups that went to play there. Somebody had taped them at the concert halls direct from the speakers, and this young man was selling the cassettes right there in front of us, in the club. Lots of people out to rip you off.

IT IS INTERESTING TO NOTE that several great artists who excelled in their particular or main pursuit also had another talent they dabbled in on the side. Miles Davis, Tony Bennett, Anthony Quinn, and Red Skelton chose painting. Paul Newman chose auto racing. Artie Shaw gave up music and became an author. I don't consider myself an author per se, but I do feel qualified to write books on the subject of music as it pertains to jazz. I have written one such book so far, *The Art of Small Combo Jazz Playing, Composing, and Arranging,* which was published by the Hal Leonard Corporation. I also consider myself a good poet and lyricist. I enjoy these endeavors almost as much as I enjoy the pursuit of music. Lady Music still holds first place with me, however. I am married to music and always will be.

In writing my music, I find that the so-called hard shit is easy to write. It's the easy shit that be kickin' my ass—kickin' my ass in terms of concept, harmony, phrasing, lyrics, song titles, and so forth. The hard shit might be a bit difficult to play, but it's easy to write. The easy shit might be easy to play, but a bit difficult to write. For example, after employing so much sophisticated harmony, it becomes difficult to scale down to thirds and triads and make them sound hip and not corny. There are times when it becomes difficult to improvise on an easy song because of the simplicity of the harmony. It's rather paradoxical, I would say, but that's part of the challenge that Lady Music presents to the musician, composer, arranger, orchestrator, lyricist. It's very gratifying when one can meet the challenge and overcome it.

I don't know what triggers the minds of other composers and prompts them to write their music, but I look for inspiration all around me. I'm inspired by nature and by some of the people I meet and some of the events that take place in my life. I'm inspired by my mentors. I'm inspired by various religious doctrines. These are just some of the ways that inspiration comes to me from outer sources.

Many of my songs are impressed on my mind just before I wake up. Others I get from just doodlin' around on the piano until I luck up on something. This was the case when I wrote the song "Peace." I was doodlin' around on the piano, and it just came to me, but I also had the impression that there was an angel standing over me, impressing my mind with this beautiful melody and harmony. This angelic melody seemed to me to be something beyond Horace Silver's comprehension.

One night here in Malibu, when I had the sliding panels of my back door open, I heard a cricket. I noticed that a cricket sings only one note, but he has a rhythm pattern, which goes crick-*et*-crick-*et*-crick-*et*. I took that pattern and the one note and wrote "Philley Millie," on the *Jazz Has a Sense of Humor* album. And then there was a blue jay singing in my backyard one day, and I got a little melody from that. I haven't recorded it yet—I don't even have a title for it, but a blue jay suggested it to me.

And then there's "Serenade to a Tea Kettle," which is on *The Hardbop*

Grandpop. I was heating water for a cup of tea, and it came to a boil and started whistling. As I lifted the kettle from the flame, I noticed that the tone of the whistle slid from a higher to a lower note. I said, "I wonder what those notes are?" So I went to the piano, found those notes, and made a tune out of them. "The African Queen," from the *Cape Verdean Blues* album, was inspired by a tune sung by a tribal group on some African folk music records I bought at Tower Records one day when I was searching for inspiration to do something different.

My inner source of inspiration is quite fascinating to me. I wake up some mornings with an eight-bar melodic phrase in my head. A couple of times, a whole tune came to me that way, but usually it's just an eight-bar phrase. It goes through you. It doesn't come *from* you. It comes from the spirit and goes into you and goes through you, as opposed to those times when you sit down and conjure up something in your own head, go to the piano, fool around, hit a chord, and then say, "Wait a minute—what was that?" And then you work it out, and you've got a tune. But the other way—when I wake up in the morning with an eight-bar phrase in my head—that comes from spirit. Of course, I have my own involvement in it. I harmonize it, put a bridge to it, and maybe sometimes a shout chorus or an interlude. But when it starts, I'm taking dictation. The main theme comes from out there somewhere. If I allow myself to go back to sleep, I lose it.

Once, when I was on vacation in Hawaii with my son when he was little, I had a dream about Count Basie, and he was playing a very beautiful tune. When I woke up, I said to myself, "Oh, that's so simple. I can remember that." I had my tape recorder with me, but I didn't record it. I went back to sleep, woke up, and it was gone. I could kick myself in the ass a thousand times about that.

Anyhow, when I wake up with a melody in my head, I jump right out of bed before I forget it and run to the piano and my tape recorder. I play the melody with my right hand and then harmonize it with my left. I put it down on my tape recorder, and then I work on getting a bridge or eight-bar release for the tune. I might spend anywhere from one to two hours working on the tune. I might write an introduction, or a background part behind the singer or horn player, or a shout chorus, or a tag ending—if I think the tune needs it. I don't just throw things in there. Every tune doesn't need a shout chorus, or a tag ending, or a written interlude between solos, but if I feel a particular tune should have one, I'll write it. The shout chorus to "The Walk Around—Look Up and Down Song" from the 1993 album *It's Got to Be Funky* came to me in my sleep. The tune itself is based on the chord changes to "In a Little Spanish Town." I took a nap one afternoon, and when I woke up, the whole shout chorus came into my head. I only had to go to the piano and figure it out and write it down.

On the same album, I did a new version of "Song for My Father," which uses the longest tag ending on any of my tunes since "In Pursuit of the 27th Man." On "In Pursuit," recorded back in the early 1970s, the vamp is longer than the tune. For that one, I got to stretching out on the vamp along with David Friedman, the vibes player, and we got into some interesting shit and didn't want to stop. I was just experimenting, trying to fit the polyharmonics that would sound right there. I've done that before, but not as long as on those two tunes.

I also wrote a lyric for the 1993 version of "Song for My Father." I don't want to offend anybody, but the woman who wrote the first lyric for "Song for My Father" gave it to Leon Thomas, who recorded it without even consulting me about whether I liked it or whether I wanted him to record it with that lyric. He just recorded it. So I had two alternatives: either sue him or the record company, or just sign a contract with the girl and let that be the lyric. Well, I figured that I wouldn't get anywhere suing anybody, so I had the girl sign a contract stating that she was the lyric writer.

Her lyric was okay, but it didn't please me that much. I didn't dislike it or hate it, but I thought it could have been better. It didn't express the way I felt personally about my dad—maybe it expressed how people in general feel about their dads, but it didn't say something personal. So when I worked with the Silver Brass Ensemble for *It's Got to Be Funky*, I decided to rerecord "Song for My Father" and have it done vocally with an entirely new lyric. I got Andy Bey to sing it.

Although I call it my inner source of inspiration, sometimes I believe that the eight-bar phrase is a telepathic impression given to me by an out-of-body composer from another level, from the spirit world, who still would like his or her music to reach and bless the earth and its people. It's like being a co-author with an unseen and unknown composer. Not all of my compositions are written this way, but many of them are. God gives us the talent and helps us to continually cultivate it. Songs used to come to me that way even before I became interested in Spiritualism. When I wrote "Split Kick," I was a teenager in Norwalk. I woke up one morning with the melody in my mind, and I went to the piano and wrote it out.

Most of us leave something undone when we die. It's a lucky man or woman who can say, after they die, "Well, I accomplished all that I wanted to accomplish in life." When you die leaving some things undone, you can try to come back and get them done through somebody else. The main thing is giving that accomplishment to the world, in order to bring joy to the people. It ain't always the money. While you're here in the body, the money helps, naturally, but when you're in the spirit, you don't need anything because you've got everything, or so they say. If you've got tunes that you missed getting out to the world, you pass them on to someone else.

We're all divine, because God's spirit is in everybody. The Jesus Christ spirit is in everybody. The yoga people say the Christ center is in the pituitary gland, in the forehead—what they call the "third eye." And the pineal gland on the top of your head, that's the God center. So the spirit of God and Jesus is in every man, woman, and child. That's why we're all one big family, because everything is spirit—that lamp over there, the couch, the coffee table—it's all spirit. Just variations on a theme.

I often call a friend on the phone and play a new song I have just written. When you write a new song and it's good, you just want to share it with someone. Sometimes it's a musician, and sometimes it's not. One day, Miles Davis called and played a test pressing of "So What" over the phone for me, before it was released. Tadd Dameron called me and played an arrangement of "Round About Midnight" that he had written and recorded for Milt Jackson. Gil Evans played his recording of "Sister Sadie" for me on the phone before it was released to the public. I was honored to think that all these great musicians wanted to share their new unreleased music with me.

Back in the days when I recorded the *Silver 'n* series for Blue Note, I got Wade Marcus to do the arrangements, because I didn't have confidence in myself to do them. I had never written for anything bigger than a quintet or a sextet, and some of the *Silver 'n* albums called for twelve, thirteen musicians. But then after a while, I got more confidence, and I tried it. The local musicians here in Los Angeles were very kind to me. I would call them up and say, "I've got some new music, and I'd like to hear it. Could you come in and run it down for me?" They'd come in and run it down, and I'd put it on my little tape recorder and take it home and listen to it. Where it didn't sound right, I'd try to make corrections. A lot of times, everything was cool, except for maybe a little part here or there. And I learned that way, just trying it out with the guys—Oscar Brasheer, Ron Stout, Ricky Woodard, Bob Maize, Carl Burnett, and others.

The Silver Brass Ensemble was a perk-up for me. It was a nine-piece ensemble, six brass and three rhythm—actually, sax player Red Holloway, whose role was strictly soloist, made it ten. I got enthused about writing for this band because the musicians played the arrangements very well. But also it was just nice to be in a different setting for a change and to hear all that harmony come back at you—five-, six-point harmony. It was fun writing for them, so I wrote a lot of arrangements we haven't even played yet. It was once my hope to go back into the studio with that group and do some of that stuff, but with my back problems, I doubt it will happen. We did just two albums, *It's Got to Be Funky* and *Pencil Packin' Papa.*

As much as I enjoyed that experience at the time, I couldn't see myself continually out there on the road or doing the Silver Brass Ensemble. It was expensive: ten guys, ten air fares, ten hotel reservations, ten salaries to pay. So it was not always feasible. With the quintet, it was easier; and, from what I gather, people loved the quintet—it was their favorite thing. I could have gone out there with a trio, and I'm sure they would have liked it, but they would still have wanted the quintet. That's the way they heard me, and I'm glad they liked it; I liked the quintet, too. But I didn't want be limited to doing that, and that alone.

My latest album, *Jazz Has a Sense of Humor*, features my most recent and probably my last quintet, with Ryan Kisor on trumpet, Jimmy Greene on tenor and soprano sax, John Webber on bass, and Willie Jones III on drums. The album is dedicated to the memory of the late, great Thomas "Fats" Waller, master pianist, composer, vocalist, entertainer, and humorist. When I was a teenager, I saw Fats at a theater in Bridgeport, Connecticut. Bridgeport is only a half hour by bus from Norwalk, so I went over one afternoon to catch the show. Ivie Anderson was singing with the band—the big band, not the combo—and she was singing "I've Got It Bad and That Ain't Good." She sang the bridge: "And when the weekend's over, and Sunday rolls around, my man and I we gin some, embrace some and sin some," and Fats yelled out from the piano: "Yeah, but I don't never get in on the sinnin' part."

On PBS one day, they were showing some of those old "soundies," and I recorded some of them. Soundies were films shown on a little box, almost like a TV; they had them in bars and restaurants years ago, before television. You could put a quarter in there, and here comes Cab Calloway, or Fats Waller, or Jimmie Lunceford, or Count Basie, and they'd do one number. My dad and I used to go to a black restaurant in my hometown that had a soundie machine

One of the soundies I recorded from PBS featured Fats Waller. He was singing with his small combo and two fine-lookin' young ladies sittin' on the baby grand piano with their pretty legs crossed. I recognized one of them as the mother of Eddie Henderson, the trumpet player, and the other was her twin sister. Fats is singing "Ain't Misbehavin'" and rolling his eyes and muggin'. He looks up at these chicks as he's playin' and says, "My, my! Look at those fine dinners!"

Fats was Count Basie's idol. He was one hell of a musician.

Someone asked Duke Ellington in an interview if music should have a sense of humor. He said, "Oh, definitely. All the music I've heard without it is nothing."

WHEN I WORKED WITH the Jazz Messengers, we were booked by Shaw Artists Corporation and their booking agent Jack Whittemore. Former tenor sax man Walter "Foots" Thomas, who used to play with the Cab Calloway orchestra, also worked at Shaw Artists as a booking agent. When I formed my own group, I stayed with Shaw Artists and Jack Whittemore. When Jack left Shaw Artists and went on his own, I went with him, and he booked us for many years.

Some of my friends thought I could do better being booked by the Joe Glaser Agency. Joe had died, and Oscar Cohen was running the operation at that time. I decided to try them and signed a one-year contract. They did practically nothing for us. They sat on their asses, waiting for the phone to ring. They got us a few gigs, but for the most part, I had to book myself—and they expected ten percent commission on the gigs I booked. They finally settled for five percent on the gigs I booked. I was so glad when that year was up. I went rushing back to Jack, and he got us plenty of work.

When Jack died, his protégé, Joanne Jimenez, took over his operation. She is a good booking agent and kept us working when we wanted to work, before my retirement. Because of my scoliosis and related back problems, I didn't care to participate in the grueling schedules I used to adhere to when I was a young man. I only took on as much work as I felt I could handle at my age. Joanne was very understanding of this and booked us accordingly. It's extremely important to have a good booking agent in this business of music.

One composes music, arranges it, and orchestrates it and then rehearses and records it. You hope that your recorded effort then goes forth to bring some happiness and joy into the lives of people all over the world. One seldom knows just how far the music reaches. I am continually being delightfully surprised by some of the uses of my music that I wouldn't have expected. I know that my music has reached the homes and automobiles of many jazz fans. Some of my prerecorded music has been heard in movies. Music of mine has been used on Muzak, which pipes in music to shopping malls, department stores, elevators, and offices. I am aware of my music being played and sold on the Internet. Much of my music is available in print.

I recently learned that my music is sometimes used in the medical profession. While touring with the quintet, I met two doctors, one a brain surgeon, who told me they play my music in the operating room while doing surgery. I was also introduced to a chiropractor and to a dentist from Norway who both play my music in their offices to relax their patients. It brings joy to my heart to know that my music is being used in this manner. It is my hope that my music will reach every country and every city and every town or village throughout the world. God has made me and all composers and musicians a channel of His love to the people of the world through music. I intend to do everything I can to keep that channel open.

The mind and the brain are fascinating channels. Through our brains, we can reach the minds of others. Through their brains, they can reach our minds. We are both sending and receiving channels, just like a telegraph station. That's why it's so important to listen inwardly, to hear what's going on in your mind. Pay attention to your dreams and your intuition and your inner voices. Much valuable information may be attained if we will only listen and not ignore our inner voices.

Part 1 of "Message from the Maestro," the three-part suite for string orchestra I wrote in honor of Duke Ellington, is called "My Spirit's with You." I am including the lyric to this song here because it expresses the premise of mental telepathy, which I firmly believe in. There are many so-called dead people, including family, friends, teachers, and guardian angels, trying to impress our minds each day with positive thoughts and directions that will propel our lives forward if we will only listen and implement what is given.

My Spirit's with You
Music and Lyrics by Horace Silver

1.
Composer, composer, the melody's closer now.
Look over your shoulder, don't worry I'll show you how.
My spirit's with you, leading you on.
My spirit's with you, so go ahead and write your song.

2.
If you will take sight of humanity's plight right now,
And structure your music to bless and uplift somehow.
My spirit's with you, leading you on.
My spirit's with you, so go ahead and write your song.

TAG:
So go ahead and write
It might just take all night,
But go ahead and write your song.

(Rubato) MY SPIRIT'S WITH YOU.

Several musicians have told me that my music sounds easy to play when they listen to it. But when they try to play it, they find that much of it is challenging and a bit difficult—some of the forms are different, and some of the harmonies a bit complex. A few weeks after trumpeter Woody Shaw joined our band, he told me that he had started to play avant garde because he thought he had learned all there was to learn about harmony. After joining the band and playing our music for a few weeks, he realized that he needed to put in some more time on the study of harmony. In my opinion, there's no end to the study of harmony. There are harmonies that have not been discovered yet. Although Duke Ellington and Thelonious Monk were masters of harmony, there are harmonies that are even beyond their comprehension. For the time being, I'll be happy if I can reach the harmonic level of Duke and Monk.

I seek new directions in my career. I seek to serve God and humanity on a broader and more worldwide scale. I am not content to do the same old thing over and over. I wish to grow and expand. My health, both mental and physical, is good, and I intend to pursue new and different approaches to my music and my career. I will search for hidden talents that I didn't know I had and do my best to cultivate them. Each day presents an opportunity for me to grow and move forward. I am grateful for each day, and I will try to use each day as a stepping-stone to greater achievements.

As I finish writing this chapter, it is May 2005. I will have my seventy-seventh birthday on September 2 and am reflecting on some of the goals I aspire to fulfill before I make my transition from this earth to the spirit world. If the good Lord will spare me a few more years on earth, I would like to have a documentary film done about my life. I would also like to get my music choreographed by a well-known dance troupe, who would do a world tour featuring my music. I would like to write a movie score—not just any movie score, but something I could sink my teeth into, a movie that my music would enhance and be compatible with, a movie that would become a classic.

I would like to have someone write a musical comedy for Broadway theater using all my music and lyrics and utilizing all the characters portrayed in my song titles. I would like to see this musical comedy have a long run on Broadway and eventually be made into a successful motion picture. I would like to write, perform, and record a musical work for full symphony. I would like to get more of my music recorded by vocalists, both jazz and pop. I would like to continue to record as long as I am mentally and physically capable of doing so.

The next project I had planned to do with Verve, which unfortunately was dropped, was to be with the Silver Brass Ensemble. I still plan to do my next recording with the Ensemble. This time, I'll be producing it myself, but I don't know exactly when. I've got a lot of shit going on right now, so everything is up in the air: this autobiography, the Horace Silver Foundation. And I have also downloaded all of my own Silveto catalog onto a hard drive—if I hadn't, I could have lost the whole catalog, because the original tapes were deteriorating. I've gotten just about all the two-inch, twenty-four-track master tapes onto the hard drive, along with all my quarter-inch master tapes. (I do own these masters because Silveto was my own label.) The engineer I'm working with advises me to make another copy as a backup, to be stored in my safety deposit box. Once I do that, my catalog will be secure.

Also, I've got a lot of tunes that I haven't recorded. I have a couple of cardboard cartons of cassettes with tunes on them. I've used some of them, but there's a lot of stuff in there I haven't used. Sometimes, I pull those boxes out and play the cassettes. None of them are bad, but some are stronger than others. My hope is that before I die I can record some of the stronger ones and get them to the public.

I HAVE ESTABLISHED the Horace Silver Foundation to give scholarships to deserving young jazz pianists and composers. As the Horace Silver Foundation grows with its work, we hope to eventually give scholarships to players of other instruments also. In my youth, jazz scholarships were not available to us. If you wished to pursue a classical career, you might be able to get a scholarship. But there was no such thing as a jazz scholarship, because there were no schools teaching jazz. We had to learn from association with older musicians and by listening to and analyzing records. The jazz schools of today are great, and aspiring musicians should attend them if possible. There is no substitute for hands-on experience, however. The same holds true for any career choice. You can and should study as much as possible, but until you get out there and do your thing, it's not going to all come together for you. God has been good to me through the years, and I would like to pass on some of that good to the young musicians who need assistance. May jazz music stay alive and continue to move forward through the talents of these young men and women.

EPILOGUE

It is my desire, before I expire
to be lifted higher, so that I may acquire
and start to sire, that burning fire that ignites the wire
of my mind to inspire the minds of other people
and to give their thoughts a shove,
so when I'm gone, I will have left
a legacy of love.

I ALWAYS KEEP IN MIND my conversation with pianist Jimmy Jones, who passed along to me Duke Ellington's observation that music is vast and that we who have been blessed with talent should utilize it in ever-expanding ways—that we should not get hung up on one approach. Life is all about the growth of our talents; we must not allow them to wither and die. We should water the flower of our talents with enthusiasm, so that they can grow in many different directions. This is not always easy for me to do, especially when adversity stands in my pathway. But the thought of getting involved in a brand-new, exciting musical project gives me the incentive to overcome adversity and get on with the work that God has put me here to do.

I have been blessed to walk among and perform with some of the great geniuses of this music we so lovingly call jazz, blessed to have been born at a time when I could be inspired by their genius. I hope that I may inspire some of the youth of today, as these musicians inspired and still do inspire me.

I took a vow and married Lady Music when I was eleven years old. That's when I first heard the Jimmie Lunceford band. They turned me on, and I've been turned on ever since. I may have the body of a seventy-seven-year-old, but my mind is young, and I believe that it is my love for Lady Music that keeps it that way. I'm always my happiest when I'm involved in a new musical pursuit. I'm always reaching and searching for something new and different to do musically. Music is so much fun. Not everybody is happy with the work they do, but I'm happy with mine. I suggest that anybody who is not happy with their work stop what they are doing and pursue a new type of work, one they enjoy.

In interviews, I am often asked what I think about the state of jazz music today, compared to what it was like when I was young. That was a time when so many great jazz musicians were on earth, and most of them resided in New York City. New York was jazz heaven in those days. I have been concerned about the state of jazz today, mainly because most all of the older masters of the music have died. We still have a few of them left, but not very many. We need to ensure that musicians such as Louis Armstrong and Duke Ellington and many others who gave their lives to this music did not do so in vain. We need to ensure that jazz music will live on through eternity—not only live on but maintain its purity.

I am happy to say that I am no longer worried about the situation. There are some fine young musicians out there, playin' their asses off and helping to ensure the future of jazz. It does my heart good when I hear them cookin'. Keep on cookin', youngsters, and keep the music pure. Do your thing with it. Keep the music alive, pure, and progressive. You have inherited a great legacy from all those who preceded you. Study it and add your thing to it. We old-timers can't live forever, but I'm gonna be writing and playin' 'til the good Lord says it's time for me to split from this earth. I thank you for helping to ensure the future of this music called jazz, which we all love so dearly.

I feel that if the general population only knew how many prominent people from all walks of life were jazz lovers, they would stop and take a closer listen and embrace jazz music. Clint Eastwood, Mel Brooks, and Burt Reynolds are lovers of jazz music, as were Jack Lemmon and Dudley Moore. Former president Bill Clinton digs jazz music and plays the tenor saxophone. Mayor Tom Bradley of Los Angeles loved jazz. Diana Barrymore was also a great fan of jazz music.

Another supporter of jazz was Hank Ketchum, the creator of the cartoon strip *Dennis the Menace*. Hank, who passed away recently, was a painter as well as a cartoonist. He painted portraits of famous jazz musicians. He had a showing in Los Angeles a couple of years ago, and bandleader Gerald Wilson and myself were invited. He had paintings of Louis Armstrong, Coleman Hawkins, Art Tatum, and many other jazz greats. To my surprise, he handed me a cartoon sketch of myself and Dennis the Menace and autographed it to me. He dug my music. I had the sketch framed and proudly hung it in my music room.

I met Sophia Loren backstage at a jazz concert a few years ago. She is a friend of jazz pianist Michael Camillo, who introduced us. Sophia's son and Michael are also close friends. I shook her hand, and I didn't wash that hand for about a week after that. I wanted the vibes to remain. I had a crush on her when I was a teenager, as most teenage boys at that time did. She was still lookin' good. One never knows who's listening out there.

I REMEMBER THE DAY when jazz was considered a part of pop music, but that's no longer true. The most dominant style in pop music today seems to be rap, which is fine for young folks, and maybe some older folks like it, too, but it's not my cup of tea. I don't hate it—different strokes for different folks. As long as it's satisfying young people and keeping them out of trouble, or keeping them interested in something, I say, "Hallelujah! God bless them, and God bless the music." But I can't get into the rap thing. It doesn't satisfy my soul—it doesn't reach me inwardly whenever I hear it. But if it reaches young people and gives them pleasure as they dance or sing to it or go to rap concerts, I say, "Fine. Nothing wrong with that." Everything can't be the same. As Duke said, music is vast—classical, gospel, country and western, Broadway show music, jazz, blues, folk music, rap, whatever turns you on.

As for today's pop music in general, the caliber of talent is not up to the standard set years ago by people such as Ray Charles, Aretha Franklin, Stevie Wonder, even the Beatles. That's not to say they don't have good talent out there, but those people were and are giants.

ALL THE ARTS ARE MEDIA through which people may be uplifted. Realizing this statement to be true, it is then criminal not to use the arts for this divine purpose. Music has been accepted as the highest art form because it not only reaches the bodies and minds of people but also can reach straight through to the soul. Music should be used to promote the highest ideals. To conceive music that keeps the consciousness of people at the status quo, music that devalues all the principles of good living, music that lowers and demoralizes the consciousness of people shows ignorance and lack of growth on the part of the conceiver, or possibly a deliberate attempt by the conceiver to hamper the growth of people's minds so that they continue to be manipulated and used. If people's minds are so involved with mundane matters, they will not have the time or desire to learn the principles that will free them from a life of confusion and problems and open up a life of happiness and fulfillment.

How long will the people of the world be content to be brainwashed with mundane music? Do we not have the will to grow and stretch our minds and expand our consciousness? It doesn't matter what form music takes; what does matter is the content and intent of the music. The music should be entertaining as well as uplifting. God has blessed the composer with a precious gift that can be used to uplift the minds of people or help them stagnate. The composer first must uplift his or her own mind, with all sincerity, before it is possible to uplift the minds of other people. The composers of the world have the potential for expanding the consciousness of the people of the world—and in so doing bring about a greater civilization than that which exists at present. Will the composers accept this responsibility? With a little effort on their part, composers will be rewarded with greater service to God and humanity and greater fulfillment for themselves. Greater fulfillment also includes greater financial stability.

Let us demand not to be treated like children when it comes to listening to music. We want music with depth, beauty, and uplift. We will not be satisfied with mundane music. We refuse to listen to it or support it. Composers, open your minds and give us something of lasting value.

AFTERWORD

PHIL PASTRAS

FOR MORE THAN A YEAR, I regularly made the glorious drive south on the Pacific Coast Highway from my apartment in Ventura to Horace Silver's home in Malibu: to the left, the Santa Monica Mountains, vertical cliffs that border the highway; or, around the next bend in the road, rolling hills baked in the sun, lush gardens, or the green, manicured lawns of the Pepperdine College campus; to the right, the surf in all its many moods, from fog to brilliant sunlight, from calm to storm. Quite naturally, from now on, whenever I think about that stretch of Southern California coast, I'll also think of Horace Silver.

Horace speaks about his adopted home state with great warmth and affection. With its warm, sunny climate, its multiplicity of cultures, and the paradoxical pace of its rhythms, at once both laid-back and intense, Southern California seems a perfect fit for Horace's personality. Clearly, after the thirty years he has lived here, he shows no trace of second thoughts about the move, even though it removed him from what many still consider the hub of the jazz world, New York. From time to time, like many Southern Californians, he wonders, tongue in cheek, why anyone would want to live anywhere else. Of course, Malibu is a quintessential Southern California destination, with Horace's house in a dream location in the hills overlooking the Pacific. He sums it all up musically in one of the most engaging pieces of his later years, "Sunrise in Malibu" (1997), a deceptively simple melody with a soaring lyricism that perfectly evokes the beauty of the place. Perhaps it is no accident that, although the full quintet plays the melody, Horace has the only solo, in effect turning the entire composition into a kind of personal homage to the setting.

Soon after we met and agreed to work together on the manuscript of his autobiography, Horace and I quickly and easily fell into a friendly and productive mode of work, meeting at his house every other Sunday to edit and expand his text—and enjoying the work, to boot. My wife, Elaine, has the last word on the subject. One Sunday, she came along and sat on the patio working on her latest jewelry project while Horace and I did our thing in the living room. As we pulled away from his house after the session, she said, with a smile, "You guys don't sound like you're working in there—you're laughing too much."

When we began, I remembered mostly the Horace Silver of the late 1950s to the late 1960s. Back then, I was living in the New York/New Jersey area and went to hear the Blue Mitchell–Junior Cook version of the quintet as often as possible. Many still regard that as the archetypal Horace Silver Quintet; it certainly was the longest-lived version, and, until recently, it was the group that came to mind whenever I heard the words "Horace Silver Quintet." Certainly, it was one of the greatest small groups of all time.

The music Silver recorded just before, during, and after the time when that group was a regular working unit played a large role in the Golden Age of jazz, then centered in New York. That music also encompassed the Jazz Messengers, which Silver co-founded with Art Blakey and which took on a life of its own under Blakey's leadership for many decades afterward; Silver's early quintets, with either Kenny Dorham or Donald Byrd on trumpet and Hank Mobley on tenor sax; and the groups that followed the Blue Mitchell–Junior Cook quintet, especially the one with Woody Shaw on trumpet and Joe Henderson on tenor sax, which recorded Silver's most popular composition, by far, "Song for My Father." Between 1955 and 1970, as composer, pianist, and bandleader, Horace Silver created a body of work for which he has few peers. But the same could be said of his work since then, though not enough critics, scholars, and fans seem to have noticed.

After 1970 or thereabouts, I myself lost contact with Horace's music, for a variety of reasons having nothing to do with the music itself. A very nice fringe benefit of editing this autobiography was listening to all of his music, much of which I had never heard before, most of it from the post-1970 period. Before that process began, I thought I knew the Horace Silver oeuvre as well as anyone. But, because he is such a prolific composer and recording artist, I discovered, to my surprise and delight, hours and hours of music that I would hear for the first time. Of all the surprises and revelations that lay in wait for me, the most astonishing was the realization that I didn't know Silver's work anywhere near as fully as I had thought.

But the more I listened to the post-1970 music, the more I wondered: how could such an impressive body of work be so neglected? One obvious answer is that, on most jazz radio stations, the year 1970 marks a dividing line, defining the Horace Silver music one is more likely to hear. One reason for that situation has to do with the economics of radio stations. Although most of the NPR-type stations that play jazz are classified as "noncommercial" and "independent," in reality they are neither when it comes to music; as a result, they tend to play it safe with their play lists, staying with the time-tested "oldies" rather than taking a chance on newer, untested material. For Silver's music, that means most jazz radio stations seldom, to this day, play anything recorded outside the 1955–1970 period.

The average jazz fan depends on those stations to keep up with current developments. Consequently, because the music has been little heard, anything Silver has recorded after 1970 is too often hard to find or simply out of print, especially the music he put out on his own independent label, Silveto. Also, one seldom hears much nowadays of his last series of albums for Blue Note Records, made during the late 1960s and 1970s: *You Gotta Take a Little Love* (1969); the three-LP set *The United States of*

Mind (1970, 1971, and 1972); *In Pursuit of the 27th* Man (1972); and the five-LP *Silver 'n* series, including *Silver 'n Brass* (1975), *Silver 'n Wood* (1975), *Silver 'n Voices* (1976), *Silver 'n Percussion* (1977), and *Silver 'n Strings Play the Music of the Spheres* (1979)—all out of print, except *In Pursuit.*

Even some of his 1990s recordings for major labels are hard to come by, including what is, to my ear, one of his best albums—the semi–big band Columbia album *It's Got to Be Funky* (1993), which is now out of print, though it occasionally becomes available through Internet retail sources. Among many fine performances, the album includes a new version of "Song for My Father" that rivals or at least complements the very popular original. The new version includes a powerful vocal by Andy Bey and ends with a lengthy, polyphonic, "free-form" coda that bears witness to Silver's ability to place himself "beyond category," as Duke Ellington put it. But that version of "Song" seldom gets any airplay on jazz radio stations, where most deejays go with the tried-and-true original, which has almost literally been played to death over the last forty years.

It's Got to Be Funky also includes a number of previously unrecorded originals that bear witness to a composer, pianist, and bandleader whose creative energy is still at its highest level, in compositions such as "The Lunceford Legacy" and "The Walk Around—Look Up and Down Song." In the Lunceford piece, Silver makes no attempt to imitate the style of his musical hero—he simply writes a lyrical, melodically rich tribute to the man and the band who inspired him to become a jazz musician. The "Walk Around" piece, in contrast, is as playful as its title, a neat foreshadowing of Silver's most recent album, 1999's *Jazz Has a Sense of Humor,* dedicated to—who else?—Thomas "Fats" Waller.

UNTIL 1970, THE VEHICLE through which Silver expressed himself was the Horace Silver Quintet, which made its recording debut under that title in early 1956, first with the Columbia album *Silver's Blue* and then, later the same year, with *Six Pieces of Silver,* this time on the Blue Note label. The second album featured "Señor Blues," still one of Silver's most popular tunes.

Although Silver did not invent the quintet format, one might say that he reinvented it. Before the Silver group, quintets were most often vehicles for "head" arrangements that, stereotypically, fell into the following pattern: statement of theme, trumpet solo, sax solo, piano solo, and restatement of theme. Sometimes the order of solos would be reshuffled, and at other times a bass or drum solo might be included, usually before the restatement of the theme.

But, from the beginning, Silver's approach to the quintet was far more complex and orchestral than most, making greater use of breaks, shout choruses, countermelodies, melodic interludes, and background riffs—an approach no doubt inspired by his first great passion in jazz music, the Jimmie Lunceford Orchestra. The effect of that approach was to firmly establish the quintet composed of trumpet, sax, piano, bass, and drums as a sub-genre in jazz, on a par with the piano trio. This kind of quintet was well on its way to attaining that status when Horace came along; his work in that format was a definitive confirmation of a trend already at work in this tradition. The quartet format, led by one horn, most often a tenor sax, lends itself far less readily to the orchestral approach; the combination of the two horns up front gives the quintet something like the "punch" of a big band, while still allowing it to remain a small group. For the next fourteen years, the quality and quantity of Silver's work set a standard by which quintets are still being measured today.

His work of that period is often credited with having created a new style in jazz, which some have called "hard bop" and others "funky jazz," the style that supposedly defines the music of the "post-bebop" generation on the East Coast. For those who place great importance on such terminology, Horace Silver's place in jazz history rests heavily on his status as an innovator, a "pioneer of hard bop," a phrase that often crops up in discussions of his early work in the quintet format. For instance, in the original edition of *The New Grove Dictionary of Jazz* (1988), now one of the most authoritative reference works in the field, Bill Dobbins's entry on Horace Silver states the conventional view of Silver's career, a view that has become a critical commonplace: "[His] music was a major force in modern jazz on at least four counts," first and foremost of which was his role as "the first important pioneer of the style known as HARD BOP, which combined elements of rhythm-and-blues and gospel music with jazz."

As for Silver's career after 1970, the only recordings Dobbins mentions by name are those in the *United States of Mind* series; the others, some ten albums if we include one that came out in 1988, are simply lumped together as "a number of albums featuring the quintet with ensembles of brass, woodwind, percussion, voices, and strings." The select discography does list Silver's last five albums on the Blue Note label (1975–1979) but says nothing of the five that came out under his own Silveto label (1981–1988). This neglect of such a significant body of work is symptomatic of the treatment Silver's later recordings have received at the hands of most jazz historians and critics, the implication being that his most "influential" recordings were those he made as a "pioneer of hard bop" and that, ipso facto, they are his most important as well.

That assumption is only made more explicit by the revised article that appears in the second edition of the *New Grove Dictionary* (2002). The revision, which lists editor Barry Kernfeld as co-author, does devote much more space to Silver's later life but dismissively declares that his later work "had little impact on developments in jazz." Oddly, however, the same article adds that Silver "continued to serve as a mentor to emerging musicians" and provides an impressive list, including Tom Harrell, Ralph Moore, Brian Lynch, and Carl Burnett, among others. Evidently, such mentoring has "little impact." Again, the article fails to discuss any of Silver's later work by name, and the discography lists only one album from the period after 1979 *(Hardbop Grandpop)*. That sad neglect might be understandable if the music Silver recorded from roughly 1970 to 1999 (the year of his latest album) represented a decline in the quality of his work, but such is not the case. In fact, he made some of his best recordings during that period.

What's going on here? The answer is simple: the culprit lurks in the faulty assumption that equates influence with importance and even, at times, with quality. It is all too easy to fall prey to that confusion, especially for the historian who needs to fashion a narrative about the development of an art form, something along the lines of the "begats" in the Bible that create a chronological framework: Louis Armstrong begat Roy Eldridge, who begat Dizzy Gillespie, and so forth.

That approach does have some merit, but the nature of artistic influence is notoriously elusive and difficult to trace with any precision. The idea that Horace Silver had his greatest impact on jazz as the pioneer of a new style rests on at least two faulty assumptions. The first assumes that the innovators are necessarily the most influential and therefore the most important artists in any field. In fact, as Ezra Pound pointed out many years ago about the art of poetry, the innovators sometimes turn out to be minor artists who make discoveries that others realize more fully. And sometimes the "influence" of a great artist amounts to creating a body of work that consistently, from beginning to end, sets high standards and challenges fellow artists to do the same. Such is the case with Horace Silver, though, thank God, we've yet to see the end.

The second faulty assumption has to do with the style itself. The existence of a clearly definable style defined as hard bop has been called into question by some historians and critics, especially those who see the style as a natural development and extension of the innovations that had been introduced to the tradition by beboppers such as Dizzy Gillespie, Charlie Parker, Bud Powell and Thelonious Monk.

In fact, Horace made exactly that objection when I asked him whether he thought the term "hard bop" was at all useful in discussing his music and that of the post-bop generation in general. He emphatically expressed his doubts about whether what the writers call "hard bop" could be accurately described as a "new" style and clearly stated that "we" (referring to his generation) were simply exploring, extending, and developing the innovations of the previous generation. Like most creative people, he is not comfortable with the labels writers and fans want to pin on his work. And he has every right to be suspicious of such terms, given that the fuss over the term "hard bop" and that particular period of his work has had the effect of casting his subsequent thirty years of music into the shadows.

It should be evident that the scholarly and critical community has a duty to consider the entire career of a major artist such as Horace Silver—including not only his relation to emerging trends like hard bop but also the quality and range of his entire oeuvre, his mentoring of younger musicians, and his courage in taking chances with his career in the name of maintaining the integrity of his artistic vision, as Silver obviously did in his determination to complete the *United States of Mind* project and in his ten-year venture with his independent Silveto label. As he makes abundantly clear in this autobiography, Silver was eager to try something different by the end of the 1960s, even though Blue Note Records and at least a segment of his fan base would have been happy to rally 'round the flag of "the Horace Silver Quintet forever."

But his restlessness did not stem only from the quintet format—indeed, he has returned to that format more than once over the past two decades, most recently in the albums *A Prescription for the Blues* (1997) and *Jazz Has a Sense of Humor* (1999). Beginning in 1970, the release of the first of the three-album set with the general title *The United States of Mind* (1970–1972) gave some indication of at least three new territories Silver wanted to explore: first, instrumentation (electric keyboard, electric guitar à la rock, wah-wah pedals and all); second, vocal music featuring one or more vocalists singing Silver's own lyrics; and, third, his determination to express his newly found spiritual and religious quest through his music. The first of the three albums, interestingly enough, is still a quintet (plus vocalist Andy Bey), but Silver's use of an electric keyboard changes the traditional quintet sound dramatically; the addition of the electric guitar on the last two albums of the project heightens the contrast.

In addition, by the end of the 1970s, Silver had grown weary of constantly being on the road and wanted time to continue to explore new avenues. Despite protests from management and fans, he decided not to keep a working band on the road continually; instead, he would tour from time to time, usually to promote the release of a new recording. Silver had wisely and effectively tended to the business aspects of his career so that he no longer had to do tour full time to pay his bills. Unfortunately, that also meant that his music was heard less frequently in nightclubs and concert halls.

Another aspect of the neglect of Silver's post-1970 recordings is that, historically, the jazz world—especially a large segment of the jazz press—has been notoriously reluctant to accept change of any kind, from Duke Ellington's ambitions to write extended works for Carnegie Hall concerts during the 1940s, to the post–World War II innovations of bebop, to Miles Davis's move into electronic music in the 1970s. All art forms have their purists, but the jazz world has always had more than its fair share, and any change of direction by a major artist such as Horace Silver was bound to meet resistance. Many critics described the lyrics of *The United States of Mind* as too "preachy," for example. The first album of the series didn't sell, and Blue Note asked him to postpone the other two and go back to his usual thing. Silver had to stand his ground to finish the project.

He did just that, to his credit, but at a price. Suddenly, an artist who had been one of the most successful in the jazz field, both artistically and commercially, had to fight to make his next album with the recording company that had always given him carte blanche in the past. Additionally, some of the more purist elements among Silver's critics began to turn his past against his present efforts, a pattern of behavior that would repeat itself more than once in the post-1970 period.

The *United States of Mind* series is a departure from his previous work in many ways. Silver's reliance on vocalists in the new music is a measure of this departure, though it must be said that he has always been open to turning his compositions into vocal showcases—witness "Señor Blues," "Doodlin'," and "Peace." "Peace," especially, is a pivotal work. It began as an instrumental ballad on the 1959 album *Blowin' the Blues Away* and reappeared some ten years later on the first album of *The United States of Mind*, this time with lyrics sung by Andy Bey, who would prove to be Silver's chief collaborator in his efforts to expand his range to include vocals and vocalists.

Bey's roots in gospel music served Silver well in his foray into the kind of jazz/gospel fusion music attempted in *The United States of Mind* and on most of his Silveto recordings. And Bey's contributions to more "secular" tunes like those on the album *It's Got to Be Funky* are an indication of just how important Andy Bey has become in the world of Horace Silver's music. The best analogy would be Duke Ellington's long collaboration with Ivie Anderson: Andy Bey is uniquely suited to express Horace Silver's vocal music in the same way that Ivie Anderson was uniquely suited for the Ellington idiom.

When Silver finished *The United States of Mind*, he did not return immediately to the quintet format in his recorded work, although the Horace Silver Quintet continued to tour as a working unit. Instead, he embarked on a new series of five albums, the *Silver 'n* series mentioned earlier. On the first two, he composed and arranged for larger ensembles (thirteen pieces); the last three featured his regular quintet, augmented by voices, percussion, and strings, in that order. And when he had fulfilled the terms of his contract with Blue Note, in 1979, he spent most of the next decade trying to get his own Silveto label off the ground. He did not return to another major label until he signed with Columbia for the two almost-big-band albums in 1993.

Like most jazz musicians who have attempted to create an independent label, Silver had problems with advertising and distribution. To this day, the five Silveto albums are extremely rare, even in the few stores that cater to collectors of 33⅓ rpm LPs; they have never been reissued on CDs. In other words, from 1979 to 1993, all of Silver's work appeared on a small independent label and thus got nowhere near the attention it deserved. That fourteen-year period includes the five years that separate the last of the Silveto albums (1988) and the first Columbia album (1993). In short, if we go back to 1970 and the poor showing, both critically and commercially, of *The United States of Mind*, Silver's various attempts to turn in new directions had the effect of moving him away from centerstage—one of the main reasons the post-1970 recordings are still so hard to find.

When he discusses this experience, Horace expresses a good deal of frustration, as might be expected, but no bitterness, anger, or regret. In fact, when he was negotiating with the University of California Press over the title of this autobiography, he sternly rejected the suggestion of one reader that the book be named after one of his most popular albums, *Blowin' the Blues Away,* because of the possible implication that his life has been a hard or sad one. "I've had a good life," he said to me, "and I don't want people to get the impression that the story of my life has to do with getting rid of the blues."

Horace comes closest to expressing anger when he discusses the reception of *The United States of Mind* and the gospel/fusion work that followed, especially the criticism that his lyrics are too "preachy." In his own defense, he explains in this autobiography that he had experienced a genuine spiritual revelation and simply wanted to share the benefits with his public. But moving in that direction was bound to alienate at least some of his fans and critics. The issue is an old one and often has little to do with the quality of the lyrics themselves. Whenever artists use their art as a vehicle to express their religious or political beliefs, they risk having those works automatically rejected by certain segments of the audience, especially those who do not share the beliefs or find them somehow objectionable—and especially the purists who subscribe to the "art for art's sake" aesthetic. Perhaps the most notable example of that conflict is the Italian poet Dante. Even though he is ranked among the greatest of all poets, many readers of the *Divine Comedy* reject the idea that a loving God could forever impose horrible tortures on those souls condemned to Hell in the *Inferno.* It takes an effort to put aside one's own beliefs in order to appreciate the greatness of Dante's poetry, and some readers cannot do that.

The issue of genre comes into play as well. When Silver decided to use his art as a vehicle to express his spiritualism, he was attempting to create a fusion of jazz and gospel music, in effect embracing a tradition inaugurated by Duke Ellington in his three spiritual concerts, all performed in churches and cathedrals. It is no coincidence that Ellington faced the same kinds of criticism as Silver has with his spiritual works: superficial or naive lyrics, preachiness, music not up to the usual standards. The last of these criticisms is patently untrue: those works contain some of the finest writing by both Ellington and Silver. And when one listens to gospel, spiritual, or other religious music, criticizing the lyrics as "preachy" is to disregard the issue of genre. It is one thing to criticize lyrics as ineffective or as failing to do the job, but spiritual and religious lyrics were certainly appropriate for the genres in which both Silver and Ellington were working. In addition, the question of what makes a "good lyric" is complex. On paper, a lyric might seem trite or superficial, whereas in performance it might work quite well, as in the song "How Much Does Matter Really Matter" from the second *United States of Mind* album. This recording, with just Silver on electric piano accompanying Gail Nelson's vocal, is one of the highlights of the three albums.

The recent reissue on CD of *The United States of Mind,* in its entirety, has vindicated Silver's faith in the quality of his spiritual works. Michael Cuscuna's liner notes point out that although the recordings were not a commercial success, musicians and singers soon began to welcome compositions from the series of albums into their repertoires—and have continued to do so over the years. Organist Charles Earland recorded "The Happy Medium" soon after its release; singer Marlena Shaw recorded "Wipe Away the Evil" and "The Show Has Begun"; both Dee Dee Bridgewater and Chet Baker covered "Love Vibrations"; and on Bridgewater's 1995 tribute to Silver, *Love and Peace,* the first track is "Permit Me to Introduce You to Yourself."

Cuscuna adds:

> In 2001, a 21-year-old singer/pianist called Norah Jones cut a demo for Blue Note that included a riveting rendition of "Peace." Norah sold it at gigs and Blue Note circulated it to select radio stations, writers, and musicians. When the tragedy of September 11, 2001, struck, KCRW in Los Angeles began playing Norah's version of "Peace," and other stations followed suit. During an especially difficult time, it had an enormously soothing and healing effect on those who heard it. Horace's intent for his music had finally connected on a large scale when it was needed most.

I remember the impression "Peace" made on me when I first heard it as an instrumental on the 1959 album *Blowin' the Blues Away.* It was a stunning reminder that, for all of Silver's reputation for writing hard-driving, funk-driven cookers, he could always turn out ballads marked by a strong and pure vein of lyricism.

More than ten years later, in 1970, "Peace" reappeared on the first installment of *The United States of Mind,* this time with Silver's lyrics, certainly one of his finest moments as a lyricist, and a soulful vocal by Andy Bey, accompanied by Silver alone, on electric keyboard—beyond a doubt, one of their finest collaborations. Perhaps the most masterful touch comes at the end, as Bey's final note fades and Silver plays a quiet figure that is almost angelic in its beauty. Whenever I hear it, I remember asking Horace whether he could remember what inspired him to write "Peace." He paused for a few seconds, smiled, and said, "I was doodlin' around on the piano, and it just came to me, but I also had the impression that there was an angel standing over me, impressing my mind with this beautiful melody and harmony."

I HAVE COME TO KNOW Horace Silver as a compassionate, spiritual presence, who helped me get through one of the worst years of my personal life, and as a restless artist, always eager to try something new, never content to stay within the happy confines of the style and format that brought him great success, both commercially and artistically. In the face of resistance from record company executives, critics, and fans, he has always been willing to take musical chances, even when it meant straying from the quintet format and the focus on "funky" hard bop. He never completely abandoned that format, however. In fact, he still expresses great fondness for it and has returned to it regularly and with great success over the last thirty years or so, refreshed, one suspects, by his willingness to try something different, by his steadfast refusal to let a groove become a rut.

DISCOGRAPHY

COMPILED BY ERIC B. OLSEN

Note from the compiler: This discography presents, to the best of my knowledge, a complete list of all of Horace Silver's commercially recorded performances, along with the single most familiar format on which the session was available. It includes live sessions that were released by any record company, however small, and sessions that were recorded but never released. Video soundtracks are excluded. To avoid repetition, the list does not contain compilation albums on which Silver's recordings appear, unless a compilation is the only available source for a unique recording (e.g., Europa Jazz*). The reader should also bear in mind that additional live and studio sessions are always becoming available. As in conventional use on albums and discographies, symbols like asterisks and daggers are used when a musician does not appear on all tracks: if a name in a personnel list has one asterisk next to it, that musician appears only on the tracks marked by one asterisk; a name with a dagger means that musician plays on those tracks with a dagger, and so forth.*

SESSION NO. 1: STAN GETZ QUARTET
DECEMBER 10, 1950: NEW YORK CITY

Stan Getz, tenor sax; Horace Silver, piano; Joe Calloway, bass; Walter Bolden, drums.

1. Tootsie Roll (Getz)
2. Strike Up the Band (Gershwin)
3. Imagination (Van Heusen-Burke) [two takes]
4. For Stompers Only (Getz)
5. Navy Blue (Getz) [alternate take, For Stompers Only retitled]

6. Out of Nowhere (Green-Heyman)
7. 'S Wonderful (Gershwin)

Stan Getz: The Complete Roost Recordings (Blue Note)

SESSION NO. 2: STAN GETZ QUARTET
MARCH 1, 1951: NEW YORK CITY

Stan Getz, tenor sax; Horace Silver, piano; Joe Calloway, bass; Walter Bolden, drums.

1. Penny (Silver)
2. Split Kick (Silver) [two takes]
3. It Might as Well Be Spring (Rodgers-Hammerstein) [two takes]
4. The Best Thing for You (Berlin)

Stan Getz: The Complete Roost Recordings (Blue Note)

SESSION NO. 3: STAN GETZ QUINTET
AUGUST 15, 1951: NEW YORK CITY

Stan Getz, tenor sax; Jimmy Raney, guitar; Horace Silver, piano; Tommy Potter, bass; Roy Haynes, drums.

1. Melody Express (Gryce)
2. Yvette (Gryce)
3. Potter's Luck (Silver)
4. The Song Is You (Hammerstein-Kern)
5. Wildwood (Gryce)

Stan Getz: The Complete Roost Recordings (Blue Note)

SESSION NO. 4: STAN GETZ QUINTET
APRIL 15, 1952: RADIO BROADCAST FROM BIRDLAND, NEW YORK CITY

Stan Getz, tenor sax; Jimmy Raney, guitar; Horace Silver, piano; Tommy Potter, bass; Connie Kay, drums.

1. Potter's Luck (Silver)
2. I Can't Get Started (Duke-Gershwin)
3. Parker 51 (Getz)

Stan Getz, *Birdland Sessions 1952* (Fresh Sound)

SESSION NO. 5: LOU DONALDSON QUARTET
JUNE 20, 1952: WOR STUDIOS, NEW YORK CITY

Lou Donaldson, alto sax; Horace Silver, piano; Gene Ramey, bass; Art Taylor, drums.

1. Roccus (Silver) [two takes]
2. Cheek to Cheek (Berlin) [two takes]
3. Lou's Blues (Donaldson) [two takes]
4. Things We Did Last Summer (Styne-Cahn)

Lou Donaldson Quartet/Quintet/Sextet (Blue Note)

SESSION NO. 6: TERRY GIBBS SEXTET
JULY 11, 1952: PYTHIAN TEMPLE STUDIOS, NEW YORK CITY

Terry Gibbs, vibes; Don Elliott, mellophone; Horace Silver, piano; Chuck Wayne, guitar; George Duvivier, bass; Sid Bulkin, drums.

1. T and S (Gibbs)
2. You Don't Know What Love Is (Reye-DePaul)

Terry Gibbs, *Jazz USA* (Brunswick)

SESSION NO. 7: COLEMAN HAWKINS QUINTET
SEPTEMBER 6, 1952: RADIO BROADCAST FROM BIRDLAND, NEW YORK CITY

Coleman Hawkins, tenor sax; Howard McGhee, trumpet; Horace Silver, piano; Curly Russell, bass; Arthur Taylor, drums.

1. Rifftide (Hawkins)
2. I Can't Get Started (Gershwin-Duke)
3. Disorder at the Border (Hawkins)

Coleman Hawkins, *Disorder at the Border* (Spotlite-LP)

SESSION NO. 8: COLEMAN HAWKINS QUINTET
SEPTEMBER 13, 1952: RADIO BROADCAST FROM BIRDLAND, NEW YORK CITY

Coleman Hawkins, tenor sax; Roy Eldridge, trumpet; Horace Silver, piano; Curly Russell, bass; Art Blakey, drums.

1. Disorder at the Border (Hawkins)
2. Blue Room (Rodgers-Hart)
3. Stuffy (Hawkins)

Coleman Hawkins, *Disorder at the Border* (Spotlite-LP)

SESSION NO. 9: HORACE SILVER TRIO
OCTOBER 9, 1952: WOR STUDIOS, NEW YORK CITY

Horace Silver, piano; Gene Ramey, bass; Art Blakey, drums.

1. Horoscope (Silver)
2. Safari (Silver)
3. Thou Swell (Rodgers-Hart)
4. Yeah! (Silver) [unreleased]

Horace Silver Trio (Blue Note)

SESSION NO. 10: HORACE SILVER TRIO
OCTOBER 20, 1952: WOR STUDIOS, NEW YORK CITY

Horace Silver, piano; Curly Russell, bass; Art Blakey, drums.

1. Quicksilver (Silver)
2. Ecaroh (Silver)
3. Yeah! (Silver)
4. Knowledge Box (Silver)
5. Prelude to a Kiss (Ellington)

Horace Silver Trio (Blue Note)

SESSION NO. 11: LOU DONALDSON QUINTET
NOVEMBER 19, 1952: WOR STUDIOS, NEW YORK CITY

Lou Donaldson, alto sax; Blue Mitchell, * *trumpet; Horace Silver, piano; Gene Ramey, bass; Art Taylor, drums.*

1. Sweet Juice (Silver)
2. Down Home* (Donaldson)
3. The Best Things in Life Are Free* (DeSylva-Brown)
4. If I Love Again* (Murray-Oakland)

Lou Donaldson Quartet/Quintet/Sextet (Blue Note)

SESSION NO. 12: LESTER YOUNG QUINTET
JANUARY 3, 1953: RADIO BROADCAST FROM BIRDLAND, NEW YORK CITY

Lester Young, tenor sax; Jesse Drakes, trumpet; Horace Silver, piano; Franklin Skeete, bass; Lee Abrams, drums.

1. Up 'n Adam (Young)
2. Blue and Sentimental (Basie)
3. After You've Gone (Creamer-Layton)

4. In a Little Spanish Town (Lewis-Young)
5. Jumpin' with Symphony Sid (Young)

Lester Young, *The Pres Box, Vol. 10–12* (JazzUp)

SESSION NO. 13: LESTER YOUNG QUINTET
JANUARY 10, 1953: RADIO BROADCAST FROM BIRDLAND, NEW YORK CITY

Lester Young, tenor sax; Jesse Drakes, trumpet; Horace Silver, piano; Franklin Skeete, bass; Lee Abrams, drums.

1. Lullaby of Birdland (Shearing)
2. Indiana (MacDonald-Hanley)
3. Almost like Being in Love (Lerner-Loewe)
4. Neenah (Young)
5. D.B. Blues (Young)

Lester Young, *The Pres Box, Vol. 10–12* (JazzUp)

SESSION NO. 14: LESTER YOUNG QUINTET
JANUARY 15, 1953: RADIO BROADCAST FROM BIRDLAND, NEW YORK CITY

Lester Young, tenor sax; Jesse Drakes, trumpet; Horace Silver, piano; Franklin Skeete, bass; Connie Kay, drums.

1. Lullaby of Birdland (Shearing)
2. Up 'n Adam (Young)
3. Too Marvelous for Words (Mercer-Whiting)

Lester Young, *The Pres Box, Vol. 10–12* (JazzUp)

SESSION NO. 15: LESTER YOUNG QUINTET
JANUARY 17, 1953: RADIO BROADCAST FROM BIRDLAND, NEW YORK CITY

Lester Young, tenor sax; Jesse Drakes, trumpet; Horace Silver, piano; Franklin Skeete, bass; Lee Abrams, drums.

1. Oh, Lady Be Good (Gershwin)
2. A Foggy Day (Gershwin)
3. In a Little Spanish Town (Lewis-Young)
4. Lester Leaps In (Young)

Lester Young, *The Pres Box, Vol. 10–12* (JazzUp)

SESSION NO. 16: SONNY STITT WITH THE JOHNNY RICHARDS ORCHESTRA
MARCH 18, 1953: COASTAL RECORDING, NEW YORK CITY

Sonny Stitt, alto/tenor sax; Don Elliott, mellophone; Kai Winding, trombone; Sid Cooper, woodwinds; George Berga, bari sax; Horace Silver, piano; Charles Mingus, bass; Don Lamond, drums.

1. Sancho Panza (Richards)
2. Sweet and Lovely (Arnheim)
3. If I Could Be with You (Johnson)
4. Hooke's Tours (Richards)

Sonny Stitt, *Arrangements by Richards* (Roost-LP)

Sonny Stitt, *The Complete Roost Sonny Stitt Studio Sessions* (Mosaic)

SESSION NO. 17: HOWARD MCGHEE SEXTET
MAY 20, 1953: WOR STUDIOS, NEW YORK CITY

Howard McGhee, trumpet; Gigi Gryce, alto sax/flute; Tal Farlow, guitar; Horace Silver, piano; Percy Heath, bass; Walter Bolden, drums.

1. Shabozz (Gryce)
2. Tranquility (McGhee)
3. Futurity (Gryce)
4. Jarm (McGhee) [two takes]
5. Ittapanna (Bolden)
6. Goodbye (Jenkins)

Howard McGhee, *Howard McGhee, Volume 2* (Blue Note)

SESSION NO. 18: AL COHN QUINTET
JUNE 23, 1953: NEW YORK CITY

Al Cohn, tenor sax; Nick Travis, trumpet; Horace Silver, piano; Curly Russell, bass; Max Roach, drums.

1. I'm Tellin' Ya (Cohn)
2. Jane Street (Cohn)
3. That's What You Think (Cohn)
4. Ah Moore (Cohn)

Al Cohn, *Al Cohn's Tones* (Savoy)

SESSION NO. 19: ART BLAKEY QUINTET
OCTOBER 31, 1953: RADIO BROADCAST FROM BIRDLAND, NEW YORK CITY

Kenny Dorham, trumpet; Lou Donaldson, alto sax; Horace Silver, piano; Gene Ramey, bass; Art Blakey, drums.

1. An Oscar for Oscar*† (Dorham)
2. If I Love Again* (Murray-Oakland)
3. Split Kick† (Silver)
4. Get Happy† (Koehler-Arlen)
5. Lullaby of Birdland† (Shearing)

*Hurray for Milt Jackson, John Lewis, Art Blakey, Kenny Dorham** (Sessions-LP)
Kenny Dorham, *New York 1953–56, Oslo 1964†* (Landscape)

SESSION NO. 20: HORACE SILVER TRIO
NOVEMBER 23, 1953: WOR STUDIOS, NEW YORK CITY

Horace Silver, piano; Percy Heath, bass; Art Blakey, drums.

1. I Remember You (Mercer-Schertzinger)
2. Opus de Funk (Silver)
3. Day In, Day Out (Bloom-Mercer)
4. Silverware (Silver)
5. How about You (Freed-Lane)
6. Buhaina (Silver)

Horace Silver Trio (Blue Note)

SESSION NO. 21: ART FARMER QUINTET
JANUARY 20, 1954: NEW YORK CITY

Art Farmer, trumpet; Sonny Rollins, tenor sax; Horace Silver, piano; Percy Heath, bass; Kenny Clarke, drums.

1. Soft Shoe (Farmer)
2. Confab in Tempo (Farmer)
3. I'll Take Romance (Hammerstein-Oakland)
4. Wisteria (Farmer)

Art Farmer, *Early Art* (Prestige)

SESSION NO. 22: ART BLAKEY QUINTET
FEBRUARY 21, 1954: LIVE RECORDING FROM BIRDLAND, NEW YORK CITY

Clifford Brown, trumpet; Lou Donaldson, alto sax; Horace Silver, piano; Curly Russell, bass; Art Blakey, drums.

1. Split Kick (Silver)
2. Once in a While (Green-Edwards)
3. Quicksilver (Silver) [two takes]
4. Wee-Dot (Johnson-Parker) [two takes]
5. Blues (traditional)
6. A Night in Tunisia (Gillespie)
7. Mayreh (Silver)
8. If I Had You (Shapiro-Campbell)
9. The Way You Look Tonight (Kern-Fields)
10. Lou's Blues (Donaldson)
11. Now's the Time (Parker)
12. Confirmation (Parker)

Art Blakey Quintet, *A Night at Birdland, Volume 1 & 2* (Blue Note)

SESSION NO. 23: MILES DAVIS QUARTET
MARCH 6, 1954: VAN GELDER STUDIOS, HACKENSACK, N.J.

Miles Davis, trumpet; Horace Silver, piano; Percy Heath, bass; Art Blakey, drums.

1. Take Off (Davis)
2. Lazy Susan (Davis)
3. The Leap (Davis)
4. Well, You Needn't (Monk)
5. Weirdo (Davis)
6. It Never Entered My Mind (Rodgers-Hart)

Miles Davis, Volume 1 (Blue Note)

SESSION NO. 24: MILES DAVIS QUARTET
MARCH 15, 1954: BELTONE STUDIOS, NEW YORK CITY

Miles Davis, trumpet; Horace Silver, piano; Percy Heath, bass; Art Blakey, drums.

1. Four (Davis)
2. That Old Devil Moon (Harburg-Lane)
3. Blue Haze (Davis)

Miles Davis, *Blue Haze* (Prestige)

SESSION NO. 25: MILES DAVIS QUINTET
APRIL 3, 1954: NEW YORK CITY

Miles Davis, trumpet; Dave Schildkraut, alto sax; Horace Silver, piano; Percy Heath, bass; Kenny Clarke, drums.

1. Solar (Davis)
2. You Don't Know What Love Is (Raye-DePaul)
3. Love Me or Leave Me (Donaldson-Kahn)
4. I'll Remember April* (Raye-DePaul-Johnston)

Miles Davis, *Walkin'* (Prestige)

Miles Davis, *Blue Haze** (Prestige)

SESSION NO. 26: MILES DAVIS SEXTET
APRIL 29, 1954: VAN GELDER STUDIOS, HACKENSACK, N.J.

Miles Davis, trumpet; J. J. Johnson, trombone; Lucky Thompson, tenor sax; Horace Silver, piano; Percy Heath, bass; Kenny Clarke, drums.

1. Blue 'n' Boogie (Gillespie)
2. Walkin' (Carpenter)

Miles Davis, *Walkin'* (Prestige)

SESSION NO. 27: PHIL URSO–BOB BROOKMEYER QUINTET
APRIL 30, 1954: NEW YORK CITY

Phil Urso, tenor sax; Bob Brookmeyer, valve trombone; Horace Silver, piano; Percy Heath, bass; Kenny Clarke, drums.

1. Chiketa (Urso)
2. Wizzard Gizzard (Urso)
3. Stop Watch (Urso)
4. Ozzie's Ode (Herman)

Phil Urso, *The Philosophy of Urso* (Savoy-LP)

SESSION NO. 28: ART FARMER–GIGI GRYCE QUINTET
MAY 19, 1954: VAN GELDER STUDIOS, HACKENSACK, N.J.

Art Farmer, trumpet; Gigi Gryce, alto sax; Horace Silver, piano; Percy Heath, bass; Kenny Clarke, drums.

1. A Night at Tony's (Gryce)
2. Blue Concept (Gryce)

3. Deltitnu (Gryce)
4. Stupendous-Lee (Gryce)

Art Farmer and Gigi Gryce, *When Farmer Met Gryce* (Prestige)

SESSION NO. 29: HENRY DURANT QUARTET
MAY 20, 1954: NEW YORK CITY

Henry Durant, tenor sax; Horace Silver, piano; Percy Heath, bass; Art Blakey, drums.

1. In the Basement (Blakey-Durant)
2. Try a Little Tenderness (Campbell-Woods)
3. Little Girl Blue (Rodgers-Hart)
4. On the Roof (Blakey-Durant)

Art Blakey, *The Complete Art Blakey on EmArcy* (EmArcy)

SESSION NO. 30: LEONARD FEATHER PRESENTS
JUNE 2, 1954: NEW YORK CITY

Clark Terry, Norma Carson,† trumpet; Urbie Green, trombone; Lucky Thompson, tenor sax; Tal Farlow, Mary Osborne,† guitar; Horace Silver, Terry Pollard,† piano; Oscar Pettiford, Percy Heath, bass; Kenny Clarke, drums.*

1. Cat Meets Chick (Feather)
2. Mamblues (Terry)
3. The Man I Love* (Gershwin)
4. Anything You Can Do*† (Berlin-Balin)

Leonard Feather Presents Cats vs. Chicks (MGM-LP)

Clark Terry, *Clark Terry* (EmArcy)

SESSION NO. 31: ART FARMER SEPTET
JUNE 7, 1954: NEW YORK CITY

Art Farmer, trumpet; Jimmy Cleveland, trombone; Charlie Rouse, tenor sax; Danny Bank, bari sax; Horace Silver, piano; Percy Heath, bass; Kenny Clarke, drums; Quincy Jones, arr.

1. Evening in Paris (Jones)
2. Wildwood (Gryce)
3. Elephant Walk (Jones)
4. Tia Juana (Gryce)

Art Farmer Septet (Prestige)

SESSION NO. 32: MILT JACKSON QUINTET
JUNE 16, 1954: VAN GELDER STUDIOS, HACKENSACK, N.J.

Milt Jackson, vibes; Henry Boozier, trumpet; Horace Silver, piano; Percy Heath, bass; Kenny Clarke, drums.

1. Opus de Funk (Silver)
2. I've Lost Your Love (Jackson)
3. Buhaina (Silver)
4. Soma (Jackson)

Milt Jackson Quartet/Quintet (Prestige)

SESSION NO. 33: MILES DAVIS QUINTET
JUNE 29, 1954: VAN GELDER STUDIOS, HACKENSACK, N.J.

Miles Davis, trumpet; Sonny Rollins, tenor sax; Horace Silver, piano; Percy Heath, bass; Kenny Clarke, drums.

1. Airegin (Rollins)
2. Oleo (Rollins)
3. But Not for Me (Gershwin)
4. Doxy (Rollins)

Miles Davis, *Bag's Groove* (Prestige)

SESSION NO. 34: HORACE SILVER QUINTET
NOVEMBER 13, 1954: VAN GELDER STUDIOS, HACKENSACK, N.J.

Kenny Dorham, trumpet; Hank Mobley, tenor sax; Horace Silver, piano; Doug Watkins, bass; Art Blakey, drums.

1. Room 608 (Silver)
2. Creepin' In (Silver)
3. Doodlin' (Silver)
4. Stop Time (Silver)

Horace Silver and the Jazz Messengers (Blue Note)

SESSION NO. 35: CLARK TERRY SEPTET
JANUARY 3, 1955: FINE RECORDING STUDIO, NEW YORK CITY

Clark Terry, trumpet; Cecil Payne, bari sax; Jimmy Cleveland, trombone; Horace Silver, piano; Oscar Pettiford, cello, bass; Wendell Marshall, bass; Art Blakey, drums; Quincy Jones, arr.*

1. Double Play* (Jones)
2. Slow Boat (Terry)

3. Swahili (Jones)
4. Co-Op* (Henderson-Terry)

Clark Terry, *Clark Terry* (EmArcy)

SESSION NO. 36: CLARK TERRY SEPTET
JANUARY 4, 1955: FINE RECORDING STUDIO, NEW YORK CITY

Clark Terry, trumpet; Cecil Payne, bari sax; Jimmy Cleveland, trombone; Horace Silver, piano; Oscar Pettiford, cello, bass; Wendell Marshall, bass; Art Blakey, drums; Quincy Jones, arr.*

1. The Countless (Green-Terry)
2. Chuckles* (Terry)
3. Tuma* (Jones)
4. Kitten* (Terry)

Clark Terry, *Clark Terry* (EmArcy)

SESSION NO. 37: KENNY DORHAM SEXTET
JANUARY 30, 1955: VAN GELDER STUDIOS, HACKENSACK, N.J.

Kenny Dorham, trumpet; Hank Mobley, tenor sax; Cecil Payne, bari sax; Horace Silver, piano; Percy Heath, bass; Art Blakey, drums.

1. Venita's Dance (Dorham)
2. K.D.'s Motion (Dorham)
3. Echo of Spring (Dorham)
4. La Villa (Dorham)

Kenny Dorham, *Afro-Cuban* (Blue Note)

SESSION NO. 38: HORACE SILVER QUINTET
FEBRUARY 6, 1955: VAN GELDER STUDIOS, HACKENSACK, N.J.

Kenny Dorham, trumpet; Hank Mobley, tenor sax; Horace Silver, piano; Doug Watkins, bass; Art Blakey, drums.

1. Hippy (Silver)
2. To Whom It May Concern (Silver)
3. Hankerin' (Mobley)
4. The Preacher (Silver) [two takes]

Horace Silver and the Jazz Messengers (Blue Note)

SESSION NO. 39: QUINCY JONES BIG BAND
FEBRUARY 25, 1955: COLUMBIA STUDIOS, NEW YORK

Ernie Royal, Bernie Glow, Al Porcino, Jimmy Nottingham, trumpet; J. J. Johnson, Kai Winding, Urbie Green, Jimmy Cleveland, trombone; Herbie Mann, flute; Davey Schildkraut, alto sax; Sonny Stitt, Al Cohn, tenor sax; Jack Nimitz, bari sax; Horace Silver, piano; Oscar Pettiford, bass; Art Blakey, drums; Quincy Jones, arr./cond.

1. Grasshopper (Jones)

Various artists, *Giants of Jazz* (Columbia LP)

SESSION NO. 40: HANK MOBLEY QUARTET
MARCH 27, 1955: VAN GELDER STUDIOS, HACKENSACK, N.J.

Hank Mobley, tenor sax; Horace Silver, piano; Doug Watkins, bass; Art Blakey, drums.

1. Walkin' the Fence (Mobley) [two takes]
2. Avila and Tequila (Mobley)
3. Hank's Prank (Mobley) [two takes]
4. Just Coolin' (Mobley)
5. My Sin (Mobley)
6. Love for Sale (Porter)

Hank Mobley Quartet (Blue Note)

SESSION NO. 41: KENNY DORHAM OCTET
MARCH 29, 1955: VAN GELDER STUDIOS, HACKENSACK, N.J.

Kenny Dorham, trumpet; J. J. Johnson, trombone; Hank Mobley, tenor sax; Cecil Payne, bari sax; Horace Silver, piano; Oscar Pettiford, bass; Art Blakey, drums; Potato Valdez, congas.

1. Afrodisia (Dorham)
2. Lotus Flower (Dorham)
3. Minor's Holiday (Dorham) [two takes]
4. Basheer's Dream (Gryce)

Kenny Dorham, *Afro-Cuban* (Blue Note)

SESSION NO. 42: MILT JACKSON QUARTET
MAY 20, 1955: VAN GELDER STUDIOS, HACKENSACK, N.J.

Milt Jackson, vibes; Horace Silver, piano; Percy Heath, bass; Connie Kay, drums.

1. Wonder Why (Cahn-Brodszky)
2. My Funny Valentine (Rodgers-Hart)
3. Moonray (Shaw-Madison)
4. The Nearness of You (Carmichael-Washington)
5. Stonewall (Jackson)
6. I Should Care (Cahn-Weston)

Milt Jackson Quartet (Prestige)

SESSION NO. 43: J. J. JOHNSON QUINTET
JUNE 6, 1955: VAN GELDER STUDIOS, HACKENSACK, N.J.

Hank Mobley, tenor sax; J. J. Johnson, trombone; Horace Silver, piano; Doug Watkins, bass; Art Blakey, drums.

1. Pennies from Heaven (Burke-Johnston)
2. Viscosity (Johnson)
3. You're Mine, You (Green-Heyman)
4. Daylie Double (Johnson)
5. Groovin' (Johnson)
6. Portrait of Jennie (Budge-Robinson)

J. J. Johnson, *The Eminent J. J. Johnson, Volume 2* (Blue Note)

SESSION NO. 44: KENNY CLARKE SEPTET
JUNE 28, 1955: NEW YORK CITY

Nat Adderley, cornet; Donald Byrd, trumpet; Cannonball Adderley, alto sax; Jerome Richardson, tenor sax/flute; Horace Silver, piano; Paul Chambers, bass; Kenny Clarke, drums.

1. Bohemia after Dark (Pettiford)
2. Chasm (Adderley)
3. Willow Weep for Me (Ronell)
4. Hear Me Talkin' to Ya (Adderley)
5. With Apologies to Oscar (Adderley)
6. Late Entry (Adderley)

Kenny Clarke, *Bohemia after Dark* (Savoy)

SESSION NO. 45: NAT ADDERLEY QUINTET
SEPTEMBER 6, 1955: NEW YORK CITY

Nat Adderley, cornet; Cannonball Adderley, alto sax; Horace Silver, piano; Paul Chambers, bass; Roy Haynes, drums.

1. Watermelon (Adderley)
2. Little Joanie Walks (Adderley)
3. Two Brothers (Adderley)
4. I Should Care (Cahn-Weston)
5. Crazy Baby (Adderley)
6. New Arrival (Adderley)
7. Sun Dance (Adderley)
8. Fort Lauderdale (Adderley)
9. Friday Nite (Adderley)
10. Blues for Bohemia (Adderley)

Nat Adderley, *Introducing Nat Adderley* (EmArcy)

SESSION NO. 46: GIGI GRYCE NONET
OCTOBER 22, 1955: NEW YORK CITY

Gigi Gryce, alto sax; Art Farmer, trumpet; Cecil Payne, bari sax; Eddie Bert, trombone; Julius Watkins, French horn; Bill Barber, tuba; Horace Silver, piano; Oscar Pettiford, bass; Art Blakey, drums; Ernestine Anderson, vocal.

1. Social Call (Gryce)
2. You'll Always Be the One I Love (Gryce)

Gigi Gryce, *Nica's Tempo* (Savoy)

SESSION NO. 47: GIGI GRYCE NONET
OCTOBER 30, 1955: NEW YORK CITY

Gigi Gryce, alto sax; Art Farmer, trumpet; Danny Bank, bari sax; Jimmy Cleveland, trombone; Gunther Schuller, French horn; Bill Barber, tuba; Horace Silver, piano; Oscar Pettiford, bass; Kenny Clarke, drums.

1. Smoke Signal (Gryce)
2. In a Meditating Mood (Gryce-Hendricks)
3. Speculation (Silver)
4. Kerry Dance (traditional)

Gigi Gryce, *Nica's Tempo* (Savoy)

SESSION NO. 48: JAZZ MESSENGERS
NOVEMBER 23, 1955: LIVE RECORDING FROM CAFE BOHEMIA, NEW YORK CITY

Kenny Dorham, trumpet; Hank Mobley, tenor sax; Horace Silver, piano; Doug Watkins, bass; Art Blakey, drums.

1. Blues (traditional) [rejected]
2. Like Someone in Love (Van Heusen-Burke)
3. Deciphering the Message (Mobley) [two takes]
4. I Waited for You (Fuller-Gillespie)
5. Minor's Holiday (Dorham)
6. Soft Winds (Goodman)
7. Avila and Tequila (Mobley)
8. Yesterdays (Kern-Harbach)
9. What's New (Haggart-Burke)
10. Alone Together (Dietz-Schwartz)
11. Prince Albert (Dorham) [two takes]
12. Just One of Those Things (Porter)
13. Gone with the Wind (Magidson-Wrubel)
14. Sportin' Crowd (Mobley)
15. Hank's Symphony (Mobley)
16. Lady Bird (Dameron)
17. The Theme (traditional) [two takes]

The Jazz Messengers at the Cafe Bohemia, Volumes 1 and 2 (Blue Note)

SESSION NO. 49: DONALD BYRD SEXTET
DECEMBER 2, 1955: CAMBRIDGE, MASS.

Donald Byrd, Joe Gordon, trumpet; Hank Mobley, tenor sax; Horace Silver, piano; Doug Watkins, bass; Art Blakey, drums.

1. Everything Happens to Me (Dennis-Adair)
2. Hank's Other Tune (Mobley)
3. Doug's Blues (Watkins)
4. Hank's Tune (Mobley)
5. El Sinoa (Harneefan-Mageed)
6. Crazy Rhythm (Meyer-Kahn)

Donald Byrd, *Byrd's Eye View* (Transition)

SESSION NO. 50: JOHN LAPORTA QUINTET
JANUARY 30, 1956: NEW YORK CITY

Donald Byrd, trumpet; John LaPorta, alto sax; Horace Silver, piano; Wendell Marshall, bass; Kenny Clarke, drums.

1. Budo (Powell)
2. I Married an Angel (Rodgers-Hart)
3. Jazz Message (Cadena)

Hank Mobley, *The Jazz Message of Hank Mobley, Volume 1* (Savoy)

SESSION NO. 51: JAZZ MESSENGERS
APRIL 6, 1956: COLUMBIA THIRTIETH ST. STUDIO, NEW YORK CITY

Donald Byrd, trumpet; Hank Mobley, tenor sax; Horace Silver, piano; Doug Watkins, bass; Art Blakey, drums.

1. Infra-Rae (Mobley)
2. Nica's Dream (Silver)
3. It's You or No One (Styne-Cahn)
4. Carol's Interlude (Mobley) [two takes]
5. The End of a Love Affair (Redding)
6. Ill Wind (Koehler-Arlen)
7. Late Show (Mobley)

The Jazz Messengers (Columbia)

SESSION NO. 52: RITA REYS WITH THE JAZZ MESSENGERS
MAY 3, 1956: COLUMBIA THIRTIETH ST. STUDIO, NEW YORK CITY

Rita Reys, vocals; Donald Byrd, trumpet; Hank Mobley, tenor sax; Horace Silver, piano; Doug Watkins, bass; Art Blakey, drums.

1. I Cried for You (Freed-Arnheim)
2. You'd Be So Nice to Come Home To (Porter)
3. That Old Black Magic (Arlen-Mercer)
4. Taking a Chance on Love (Latouche-Duke-Fetter)

Rita Reys, *The Cool Voice of Rita Reys* (Columbia)

SESSION NO. 53: JAZZ MESSENGERS
MAY 4, 1956: COLUMBIA THIRTIETH ST. STUDIO, NEW YORK CITY

Donald Byrd, trumpet; Hank Mobley, tenor sax; Horace Silver, piano; Doug Watkins, bass; Art Blakey, drums.

1. Ecaroh (Silver)
2. Hank's Symphony (Mobley)
3. Weird-O (Byrd)
4. Deciphering the Message (Mobley)

The Jazz Messengers (Columbia)

SESSION NO. 54: HORACE SILVER QUINTET
JULY 2, 1956: NEW YORK CITY

Joe Gordon, trumpet; Hank Mobley, tenor sax; Horace Silver, piano; Doug Watkins, bass; Kenny Clarke, drums.

1. Silver's Blue (Silver)
2. To Beat or Not to Beat (Silver)
3. How Long Has This Been Going On? (Gershwin)

Horace Silver, *Silver's Blue* (Columbia)

SESSION NO. 55: HORACE SILVER QUINTET
JULY 17, 1956: NEW YORK CITY

Donald Byrd, trumpet; Hank Mobley, tenor sax; Horace Silver, piano; Doug Watkins, bass; Art Taylor, drums.

1. I'll Know (Loesser)
2. Shoutin' Out (Silver)
3. Hank's Tune (Mobley)
4. The Night Has a Thousand Eyes (Bernier-Brainin)

Horace Silver, *Silver's Blue* (Columbia)

SESSION NO. 56: PAUL CHAMBERS SEXTET
SEPTEMBER 21, 1956: VAN GELDER STUDIOS, HACKENSACK, N.J.

Donald Byrd, trumpet; John Coltrane, tenor sax; Kenny Burrell, guitar; Horace Silver, piano; Paul Chambers, bass; Philly Joe Jones, drums.

1. Omicron (Byrd)
2. Whims of Chambers (Chambers)
3. Nita (Coltrane)
4. We Six (Byrd)

5. Dear Ann (Chambers)
6. Tale of the Fingers (Chambers)
7. Just for the Love (Coltrane)

Paul Chambers, *Whims of Chambers* (Blue Note)

SESSION NO. 57: J. R. MONTEROSE QUINTET
OCTOBER 21, 1956: VAN GELDER STUDIOS, HACKENSACK, N.J.

J. R. Monterose, tenor sax; Ira Sullivan, trumpet; Horace Silver, piano; Wilbur Ware, bass; Philly Joe Jones, drums.

1. Wee-Jay (Monterose)
2. The Third (Byrd)
3. Bobbie Pin (Monterose)
4. Marc V (Monterose)
5. Beauteous (Chambers)
6. Ka-Link (Jones)

J. R. Monterose (Blue Note)

SESSION NO. 58: LEE MORGAN QUINTET
NOVEMBER 4, 1956: VAN GELDER STUDIOS, HACKENSACK, N.J.

Lee Morgan, trumpet; Clarence Sharpe, alto sax; Horace Silver, piano; Wilbur Ware, bass; Philly Joe Jones, drums.

1. Gaza Strip (Marshall)
2. Reggie of Chester (Golson)
3. Little T (Byrd)
4. Stand By (Golson)
5. Roccus (Silver)
6. The Lady (Marshall)

Lee Morgan Indeed! (Blue Note)

SESSION NO. 59: HORACE SILVER QUINTET
NOVEMBER 10, 1956: VAN GELDER STUDIOS, HACKENSACK, N.J.

Donald Byrd, trumpet; Hank Mobley, tenor sax; Horace Silver, piano; Doug Watkins, bass; Louis Hayes, drums.

1. Enchantment (Silver)
2. Virgo (Silver)
3. Shirl (Silver)
4. Señor Blues (Silver) [two takes]

5. Camouflage (Silver)
6. Cool Eyes (Silver)
7. For Heaven's Sake (Silver)

Horace Silver, *Six Pieces of Silver* (Blue Note)

SESSION NO. 60: HANK MOBLEY SEXTET
NOVEMBER 25, 1956: VAN GELDER STUDIOS, HACKENSACK, N.J.

Hank Mobley, tenor sax; Donald Byrd, Lee Morgan, trumpet; Horace Silver, piano; Paul Chambers, bass; Charlie Persip, drums.

1. Double Whammy (Mobley)
2. Barrel of Funk (Mobley)
3. Mobleymania (Mobley)
4. Touch and Go (Mobley)

Hank Mobley Sextet (Blue Note)

SESSION NO. 61: LEE MORGAN SEXTET
DECEMBER 2, 1956: VAN GELDER STUDIOS, HACKENSACK, N.J.

Lee Morgan, trumpet; Hank Mobley, tenor sax; Kenny Rogers, alto sax; Horace Silver, piano; Paul Chambers, bass; Charlie Persip, drums.

1. Latin Hangover (Golson)
2. Whisper Not (Golson)
3. His Sister (Marshall)
4. D's Funk (Marshall)
5. Slightly Hep (Golson)
6. Where Am I? (Golson)

Lee Morgan Sextet (Blue Note)

SESSION NO. 62: MILT JACKSON SEXTET
JANUARY 1, 1957: COASTAL STUDIOS, NEW YORK CITY

Milt Jackson, vibes; Lucky Thompson, tenor sax; Joe Newman, trumpet; Horace Silver, piano; Oscar Pettiford, bass; Connie Kay, drums.

1. Ignunt Oil (Jones)
2. Blues at Twilight (Jones)
3. Sermonette (J. Adderley)
4. The Spirit-Feel (Jackson)

Milt Jackson, *Plenty, Plenty Soul* (Atlantic)

SESSION NO. 63: MILT JACKSON NONET
JANUARY 5, 1957: CAPITOL STUDIOS, NEW YORK CITY

Milt Jackson, vibes; Frank Foster, tenor sax; Cannonball Adderley "Ronnie Peters," alto sax; Sahib Shihab, bari sax; Joe Newman, trumpet; Jimmy Cleveland, trombone; Horace Silver, piano; Percy Heath, bass; Art Blakey, drums; Quincy Jones, arr.

1. Plenty, Plenty Soul (Jackson-Jones)
2. Boogity Boogity (Jones)
3. Heartstrings (Jackson)

Milt Jackson, *Plenty, Plenty Soul* (Atlantic)

SESSION NO. 64: HANK MOBLEY QUINTET
JANUARY 13, 1957: VAN GELDER STUDIOS, HACKENSACK, N.J.

Hank Mobley, tenor sax; Milt Jackson, vibes; Horace Silver, piano; Doug Watkins, bass; Art Blakey, drums.

1. Reunion (Mobley)
2. Lower Stratosphere (Mobley)
3. Don't Walk (Mobley)
4. Ultramarine (Mobley)
5. Mobley's Musings (Mobley)

Hank Mobley and His All Stars (Blue Note)

SESSION NO. 65: KENNY BURRELL QUINTET
FEBRUARY 10, 1957: VAN GELDER STUDIOS, HACKENSACK, N.J.

Kenny Burrell, guitar; Hank Mobley, tenor sax; Horace Silver, piano; Doug Watkins, bass; Louis Hayes, drums.

1. Nica's Dream (Silver)
2. D.B. Blues (Young)
3. K.B. Blues (Burrell) [two takes]
4. Out for Blood (Burrell)

Kenny Burrell, *K.B. Blues* (Blue Note)

SESSION NO. 66: CLIFFORD JORDAN–JOHN GILMORE QUINTET
MARCH 3, 1957: VAN GELDER STUDIOS, HACKENSACK, N.J.

Clifford Jordan, John Gilmore, tenor sax; Horace Silver, piano; Curly Russell, bass; Art Blakey, drums.

1. Status Quo (Neely)
2. Bo-Till (Jordan)

3. Blue Lights (Gryce)
4. Billie's Bounce (Parker)
5. Evil Eye (Jordan)
6. Everywhere (Silver)
7. Let It Stand (Jordan)

Clifford Jordan and John Gilmore, *Blowing In from Chicago* (Blue Note)

SESSION NO. 67: HANK MOBLEY QUINTET
MARCH 8, 1957: VAN GELDER STUDIOS, HACKENSACK, N.J.

Hank Mobley, tenor sax; Art Farmer, trumpet; Horace Silver, piano; Doug Watkins, bass; Art Blakey, drums.

1. Wham and They're Off (Mobley)
2. Funk in a Deep Freeze (Mobley)
3. Startin' from Scratch (Mobley)
4. Stella-wise (Mobley)
5. Base on Balls (Mobley)
6. Fin de L'affaire (Mobley)

Hank Mobley Quintet (Blue Note)

SESSION NO. 68: SONNY ROLLINS QUINTET
APRIL 14, 1957: VAN GELDER STUDIOS, HACKENSACK, N.J.

Sonny Rollins, tenor sax; J. J. Johnson, trombone; Thelonious Monk, Horace Silver, piano; Paul Chambers, bass; Art Blakey, drums.

1. Why Don't I? (Rollins)
2. Wail March (Rollins)
3. Misterioso (Monk)
4. Reflections (Monk)
5. You Stepped Out of a Dream (Brown-Kahn)
6. Poor Butterfly (Hubbel-Golden)

Sonny Rollins, Volume 2 (Blue Note)

SESSION NO. 69: HORACE SILVER QUINTET
MAY 8, 1957: VAN GELDER STUDIOS, HACKENSACK, N.J.

Art Farmer, trumpet; Hank Mobley, tenor sax; Horace Silver, piano; Teddy Kotick, bass; Louis Hayes, drums.

1. Metamorphosis (Silver)
2. No Smoking (Silver)

3. The Back Beat (Silver)
4. Soulville (Silver)
5. My One and Only Love (Wood-Mellin)
6. Home Cookin' (Silver)

Horace Silver, *The Stylings of Silver* (Blue Note)

SESSION NO. 70: HORACE SILVER QUINTET
JANUARY 13, 1958: VAN GELDER STUDIOS, HACKENSACK, N.J.

Art Farmer, trumpet; Clifford Jordan, tenor sax; Horace Silver, piano; Teddy Kotick, bass; Louis Hayes, drums.

1. The Outlaw (Silver)
2. Melancholy Mood (Silver)
3. Pyramid (Silver)
4. Moon Rays (Silver)
5. Safari (Silver)
6. Ill Wind (Arlen-Koehler)

Horace Silver, *Further Explorations* (Blue Note)

SESSION NO. 71: BILL HENDERSON AND THE HORACE SILVER QUINTET
JUNE 15, 1958: VAN GELDER STUDIOS, HACKENSACK, N.J.

Donald Byrd, trumpet; Junior Cook, tenor sax; Horace Silver, piano; Gene Taylor, bass; Louis Hayes, drums; Bill Henderson, vocal.

1. Tippin' (Silver)
2. Señor Blues (Silver) [vocal version]

Originally issued as a 45-rpm single; now available on the 2000 reissue of *Six Pieces of Silver*

SESSION NO. 72: HORACE SILVER QUINTET
JULY 6, 1958: NEWPORT JAZZ FESTIVAL, NEWPORT, R.I.

Louis Smith, trumpet; Junior Cook, tenor sax; Horace Silver, piano; Gene Taylor, bass; Louis Hayes, drums.

1. Tippin' (Silver)

Newport Jazz Festival 1958, Vol. 1: Mostly Miles (Phontastic-LP)

SESSION NO. 73: HORACE SILVER QUINTET
FEBRUARY 1, 1959: VAN GELDER STUDIOS, HACKENSACK, N.J.

Blue Mitchell, trumpet; Junior Cook, tenor sax; Horace Silver, piano; Eugene Taylor, bass; Louis Hayes, drums.

1. Finger Poppin' (Silver)
2. Juicy Lucy (Silver)
3. Sweet Stuff (Silver)
4. Swingin' the Samba (Silver)
5. Cookin' at the Continental (Silver)
6. Come on Home (Silver)
7. You Happened My Way (Silver)
8. Mellow D (Silver)

Horace Silver, *Finger Poppin'* (Blue Note)

SESSION NO. 74: HORACE SILVER QUINTET
AUGUST 29, 1959: VAN GELDER STUDIOS, ENGLEWOOD CLIFFS, N.J.

Blue Mitchell, trumpet; Junior Cook, tenor sax; Horace Silver, piano; Eugene Taylor, bass; Louis Hayes, drums.

1. Blowin' the Blues Away (Silver)
2. Break City [alternate take]
3. Peace [alternate take]
4. The Baghdad Blues (Silver)
5. Sister Sadie (Silver) [alternate take]

Horace Silver, *Blowin' the Blues Away* (Blue Note)

SESSION NO. 75: HORACE SILVER QUINTET
AUGUST 30, 1959: VAN GELDER STUDIOS, ENGLEWOOD CLIFFS, N.J.

Blue Mitchell, trumpet; Junior Cook, tenor sax; Horace Silver, piano; Eugene Taylor, bass; Louis Hayes, drums.

1. Sister Sadie (Silver)
2. Repetition (Hefti) [unreleased]
3. Peace (Silver)
4. How Did It Happen (Newey)
5. Break City (Silver)

Horace Silver, *Blowin' the Blues Away* (Blue Note)

SESSION NO. 76: HORACE SILVER TRIO
SEPTEMBER 13, 1959: VAN GELDER STUDIOS, ENGLEWOOD CLIFFS, N.J.

Horace Silver, piano; Eugene Taylor, bass; Louis Hayes, drums.

1. Melancholy Mood (Silver)
2. The St. Vitus Dance (Silver)

Horace Silver, *Blowin' the Blues Away* (Blue Note)

SESSION NO. 77: HORACE SILVER QUINTET
JULY 8, 1960: VAN GELDER STUDIOS, ENGLEWOOD CLIFFS, N.J.

Blue Mitchell, trumpet; Junior Cook, tenor sax; Horace Silver, piano; Eugene Taylor, bass; Roy Brooks, drums.

1. Me and My Baby (Silver) [unreleased]
2. Where You At? (Silver)
3. Strollin' (Silver)
4. Nica's Dream (Silver) [unreleased]
5. Without You (Newey)

Horace Silver, *Horace-Scope* (Blue Note)

SESSION NO. 78: HORACE SILVER QUINTET
JULY 9, 1960: VAN GELDER STUDIOS, ENGLEWOOD CLIFFS, N.J.

Blue Mitchell, trumpet; Junior Cook, tenor sax; Horace Silver, piano; Eugene Taylor, bass; Roy Brooks, drums.

1. Nica's Dream (Silver)
2. Horace-Scope (Silver)
3. Yeah! (Silver)
4. Me and My Baby (Silver)

Horace Silver, *Horace-Scope* (Blue Note)

SESSION NO. 79: HORACE SILVER QUINTET
SUMMER 1960: LIVE, EUROPE

Blue Mitchell, trumpet; Junior Cook, tenor sax; Horace Silver, piano; Eugene Taylor, bass; Roy Brooks, drums.

1. Nica's Dream (Silver)

Europa Jazz Live, 1960: Art Blakey, Freddie Hubbard, Horace Silver, Max Roach (Europa Jazz-LP)

SESSION NO. 80: HORACE SILVER QUINTET
MAY 19, 1961: LIVE RECORDING FROM THE VILLAGE GATE, NEW YORK CITY

Blue Mitchell, trumpet; Junior Cook, tenor sax; Horace Silver, piano; Eugene Taylor, bass; Roy Brooks, drums.

1. The Gringo (Silver) [three takes, unreleased]
2. Kiss Me Right (Silver) [three takes, unreleased]
3. Doin' the Thing (Silver)
4. Filthy McNasty/The Theme–Cool Eyes (Silver)
5. Señor Blues (Silver) [unreleased]
6. It Ain't S'posed to Be like That (Silver)
7. Filthy McNasty (Silver) [unreleased]
8. Doin' the Thing/The Theme–Cool Eyes (Silver) [unreleased]
9. It Ain't S'posed to Be like That (Silver) [two takes, unreleased]
10. Filthy McNasty/The Theme–Cool Eyes (Silver) [unreleased]

Doin' the Thing: The Horace Silver Quintet at the Village Gate (Blue Note)

SESSION NO. 81: HORACE SILVER QUINTET
MAY 20, 1961: LIVE RECORDING FROM THE VILLAGE GATE, NEW YORK CITY

Blue Mitchell, trumpet; Junior Cook, tenor sax; Horace Silver, piano; Eugene Taylor, bass; Roy Brooks, drums.

1. Cool Eyes (Silver)
2. It Ain't S'posed to Be like That (Silver) [three takes, unreleased]
3. The Gringo (Silver)
4. Filthy McNasty (Silver) [two takes, unreleased]
5. Doin' the Thing (Silver) [two takes, unreleased]
6. Kiss Me Right (Silver)
7. The Gringo (Silver) [two takes, unreleased]
8. Filthy McNasty/The Theme–Cool Eyes (Silver) [unreleased]

Doin' the Thing: The Horace Silver Quintet at the Village Gate (Blue Note)

SESSION NO. 82: HORACE SILVER QUINTET
JULY 13, 1962: VAN GELDER STUDIOS, ENGLEWOOD CLIFFS, N.J.

Blue Mitchell, trumpet; Junior Cook, tenor sax; Horace Silver, piano; Eugene Taylor, bass; John Harris Jr., drums.

1. The Tokyo Blues (Silver)
2. Ah! So (Silver) [unreleased]

3. Sayonara Blues (Silver)
4. Too Much Sake (Silver) [unreleased]

Horace Silver Quintet, *The Tokyo Blues* (Blue Note)

SESSION NO. 83: HORACE SILVER QUINTET
JULY 14, 1962: VAN GELDER STUDIOS, ENGLEWOOD CLIFFS, N.J.

Blue Mitchell, trumpet; Junior Cook, tenor sax; Horace Silver, piano; Eugene Taylor, bass; John Harris Jr., drums.

1. Ah! So (Silver)
2. Cherry Blossom (Bright)
3. Too Much Sake (Silver)

Horace Silver Quintet, *The Tokyo Blues* (Blue Note)

SESSION NO. 84: HORACE SILVER QUINTET
OCTOBER 6, 1962: OLYMPIA THEATER, PARIS

Blue Mitchell, trumpet; Junior Cook, tenor sax; Horace Silver, piano; Eugene Taylor, bass; Roy Brooks, drums.

1. Where You At? (Silver)
2. The Tokyo Blues (Silver)
3. Filthy McNasty (Silver)
4. Sayonara Blues (Silver)
5. Doin' the Thing (Silver)

Horace Silver Quintet, *Paris Blues* (Pablo)

SESSION NO. 85: HORACE SILVER TENTET
APRIL 11, 1963: VAN GELDER STUDIOS, ENGLEWOOD CLIFFS, N.J.

Blue Mitchell, Kenny Dorham, trumpet; Grachan Moncur, trombone; Julius Watkins, French horn; Junior Cook, Jimmy Heath, tenor sax; Charles Davis, bari sax; Horace Silver, piano; Eugene Taylor, bass; Roy Brooks, drums.

1. Silver's Serenade (Silver) [unreleased]
2. Sweet Sweetie Pie (Silver) [unreleased]
3. Nineteen Bars (Silver) [unreleased]
4. The Next Time I Fall in Love (Silver) [unreleased]

Horace Silver Tentet, unissued session (Blue Note)

SESSION NO. 86: HORACE SILVER TENTET
APRIL 12, 1963: VAN GELDER STUDIOS, ENGLEWOOD CLIFFS, N.J.

Blue Mitchell, Kenny Dorham, trumpet; Grachan Moncur, trombone; Julius Watkins, French horn; Junior Cook, Jimmy Heath, tenor sax; Charles Davis, bari sax; Horace Silver, piano; Eugene Taylor, bass; Roy Brooks, drums.

1. The Dragon Lady (Silver) [unreleased]
2. Let's Get to the Nitty Gritty (Silver) [unreleased]
3. Nineteen Bars (Silver) [unreleased]

Horace Silver Tentet, unissued session (Blue Note)

SESSION NO. 87/88: HORACE SILVER QUINTET
MAY 7–8, 1963: VAN GELDER STUDIOS, ENGLEWOOD CLIFFS, N.J.

Blue Mitchell, trumpet; Junior Cook, tenor sax; Horace Silver, piano; Eugene Taylor, bass; Roy Brooks, drums.

1. Silver's Serenade (Silver)
2. Let's Get to the Nitty Gritty (Silver)
3. Sweet Sweetie Pie (Silver)
4. The Dragon Lady (Silver)
5. Nineteen Bars (Silver)

Horace Silver Quintet, *Silver's Serenade* (Blue Note)

SESSION NO. 89: HORACE SILVER QUINTET
OCTOBER 31, 1963: VAN GELDER STUDIOS, ENGLEWOOD CLIFFS, N.J.

Blue Mitchell, trumpet; Junior Cook, tenor sax; Horace Silver, piano; Eugene Taylor, bass; Roy Brooks, drums.

1. Calcutta Cutie (Silver)
2. Lonely Woman (Silver)
3. Sanctimonious Sam (Kaleem)
4. Que Pasa (Silver)

Horace Silver Quintet, *Song for My Father* (Blue Note)

SESSION NO. 90: HORACE SILVER QUINTET
JANUARY 28, 1964: VAN GELDER STUDIOS, ENGLEWOOD CLIFFS, N.J.

Blue Mitchell, trumpet; Junior Cook, tenor sax; Horace Silver, piano; Eugene Taylor, bass; Roy Brooks, drums.

1. Revlis (Silver) [unreleased]
2. Sighin' and Cryin' (Silver)
3. Silver Treads among My Soul (Silver)

Horace Silver Quintet, *Song for My Father* (Blue Note)

SESSION NO. 91: HORACE SILVER QUINTET
JUNE 6, 1964: LIVE RECORDING FROM THE CORK AND BIB, WESTBURY, N.Y.

Carmell Jones, trumpet; Joe Henderson, tenor sax; Horace Silver, piano; Teddy Smith, bass; Roger Humphries, drums.

1. Filthy McNasty (Silver)
2. The Tokyo Blues (Silver)
3. Señor Blues (Silver)
4. Skinney Minnie (Silver)

Horace Silver Quintet Live 1964 (Emerald-LP)

SESSION NO. 92: HORACE SILVER QUINTET
AUGUST 15, 1964: LIVE RECORDING FROM PEP'S, PHILADELPHIA, PENN.

Carmell Jones, trumpet; Joe Henderson, tenor sax; Horace Silver, piano; Teddy Smith, bass; Roger Humphries, drums.

1. I'll Remember April (Raye-DePaul-Johnston) [unreleased]
2. The Kicker (Henderson) [five takes, unreleased]
3. Pretty Eyes (Silver) [three takes, unreleased]
4. Que Pasa (Silver) [five takes, unreleased]
5. Skinny Minnie (Silver) [two takes, unreleased]
6. Mexican Hip Dance (Silver) [three takes, unreleased]
7. The Natives Are Restless Tonight (Silver) [four takes, unreleased]

Horace Silver Quintet, unreleased live recording (Blue Note)

SESSION NO. 93: HORACE SILVER QUINTET
OCTOBER 26, 1964: VAN GELDER STUDIOS, ENGLEWOOD CLIFFS, N.J.

Carmell Jones, trumpet; Joe Henderson, tenor sax; Horace Silver, piano; Teddy Smith, bass; Roger Humphries, drums.

1. Song for My Father (Silver)
2. The Natives Are Restless Tonight (Silver)
3. Que Pasa (Silver)
4. The Kicker (Henderson)

Horace Silver Quintet, *Song for My Father* (Blue Note)

SESSION NO. 94: HORACE SILVER QUINTET
APRIL 16, 1965: LIVE RECORDING FROM THE HALF NOTE, NEW YORK CITY

Carmell Jones, trumpet; Joe Henderson, tenor sax; Horace Silver, piano; Teddy Smith, bass; Roger Humphries, drums.

1. Song for My Father (Silver)
2. The Natives Are Restless Tonight (Silver)
3. Que Pasa (Silver)

Horace Silver Quintet, *Re-Entry* (32 Jazz)

Horace Silver Quintet, *The Natives Are Restless Tonight* (Emerald/Silveto)

SESSION NO. 95: HORACE SILVER QUINTET
OCTOBER 1, 1965: VAN GELDER STUDIOS, ENGLEWOOD CLIFFS, N.J.

Woody Shaw, trumpet; Joe Henderson, tenor sax; Horace Silver, piano; Bob Cranshaw, bass; Roger Humphries, drums.

1. Pretty Eyes (Silver)
2. The African Queen (Silver)
3. The Cape Verdean Blues (Silver)

Horace Silver Quintet/Sextet, *The Cape Verdean Blues* (Blue Note)

SESSION NO. 96: HORACE SILVER SEXTET
OCTOBER 22, 1965: VAN GELDER STUDIOS, ENGLEWOOD CLIFFS, N.J.

Woody Shaw, trumpet; Joe Henderson, tenor sax; J. J. Johnson, trombone; Horace Silver, piano; Bob Cranshaw, bass; Roger Humphries, drums.

1. Nutville (Silver)
2. Bonita (Silver)
3. Mo' Joe (Joe Henderson)

Horace Silver Quintet/Sextet, *The Cape Verdean Blues* (Blue Note)

SESSION NO. 97: HORACE SILVER QUINTET
FEBRUARY 18, 1966: LIVE RECORDING FROM THE HALF NOTE, NEW YORK CITY

Woody Shaw, trumpet; Joe Henderson, tenor sax; Horace Silver, piano; Larry Ridley, bass; Roger Humphries, drums.

1. The African Queen (Silver) [two takes]

Horace Silver Quintet, *Re-Entry* (32 Jazz)

Horace Silver Quintet, *The Natives Are Restless Tonight* (Emerald/Silveto)

SESSION NO. 98: HORACE SILVER QUINTET
NOVEMBER 2, 1966: VAN GELDER STUDIOS, ENGLEWOOD CLIFFS, N.J.

Woody Shaw, trumpet; Tyrone Washington, tenor sax; Horace Silver, piano; Larry Ridley, bass; Roger Humphries, drums.

1. Mexican Hip Dance (Silver)
2. The Jody Grind (Silver)
3. Dimples (Silver)

Horace Silver Quintet/Sextet, *The Jody Grind* (Blue Note)

SESSION NO. 99: HORACE SILVER SEXTET
NOVEMBER 23, 1966: VAN GELDER STUDIOS, ENGLEWOOD CLIFFS, N.J.

Woody Shaw, trumpet; Tyrone Washington, tenor sax; James Spaulding, flute/alto sax; Horace Silver, piano; Larry Ridley, bass; Roger Humphries, drums.

1. Mary Lou (Silver)
2. Blue Silver (Silver)
3. Grease Peace (Silver)

Horace Silver Quintet/Sextet, *The Jody Grind* (Blue Note)

SESSION NO. 100: HORACE SILVER QUINTET
FEBRUARY 23, 1968: VAN GELDER STUDIOS, ENGLEWOOD CLIFFS, N.J.

Charles Tolliver, trumpet; Stanley Turrentine, tenor sax; Horace Silver, piano; Bob Cranshaw, bass; Mickey Roker, drums.

1. Serenade to a Soul Sister (Silver)
2. Psychedelic Sally (Silver)
3. Rain Dance (Silver)

Horace Silver Quintet, *Serenade to a Soul Sister* (Blue Note)

SESSION NO. 101: HORACE SILVER QUINTET
MARCH 29, 1968: VAN GELDER STUDIOS, ENGLEWOOD CLIFFS, N.J.

Charles Tolliver, trumpet; Bennie Maupin, tenor sax; Horace Silver, piano; John Williams, bass; Billy Cobham, drums.

1. Kindred Spirits (Silver)
2. Jungle Juice (Silver)
3. The Next Time I Fall in Love (Silver)

Horace Silver Quintet, *Serenade to a Soul Sister* (Blue Note)

SESSION NO. 102: HORACE SILVER QUINTET
NOVEMBER 4, 1968: CONCERT "SALLE PLEYEL," PARIS, FRANCE

Randy Brecker, trumpet; Bennie Maupin, tenor sax; Horace Silver, piano; John Williams, bass; Billy Cobham, drums.

1. The Natives Are Restless Tonight (Silver)
2. Serenade to a Soul Sister (Silver)
3. Psychedelic Sally (Silver)

Horace Silver Quintet Live (Blue Jazz-LP)

SESSION NO. 103: HORACE SILVER QUINTET
JANUARY 10, 1969: VAN GELDER STUDIOS, ENGLEWOOD CLIFFS, N.J.

Randy Brecker, trumpet; Bennie Maupin, flute/tenor sax; Horace Silver, piano; John Williams, bass; Billy Cobham, drums.

1. The Rising Sun (Silver)
2. You Gotta Take a Little Love (Silver)
3. It's Time (Silver) [unreleased]
4. Lovely's Daughter (Maupin)

Horace Silver Quintet, *You Gotta Take a Little Love* (Blue Note)

SESSION NO. 104: HORACE SILVER QUINTET
JANUARY 17, 1969: VAN GELDER STUDIOS, ENGLEWOOD CLIFFS, N.J.

Randy Brecker, trumpet; Bennie Maupin, flute/tenor sax; Horace Silver, piano; John Williams, bass; Billy Cobham, drums.

1. Brain Wave (Silver)
2. The Belly Dancer (Silver)
3. Down and Out (Silver)
4. It's Time (Silver)

Horace Silver Quintet, *You Gotta Take a Little Love* (Blue Note)

SESSION NO. 105: HORACE SILVER GROUP
APRIL 8, 1970: VAN GELDER STUDIOS, ENGLEWOOD CLIFFS, N.J.

Randy Brecker, trumpet; George Coleman, tenor sax; Horace Silver, piano; Bob Cranshaw, bass; Mickey Roker, drums; Andy Bey, vocals.*

1. The Happy Medium* (Silver)
2. That Healin' Feelin' (Silver)
3. Love Vibrations* (Silver)
4. The Show Has Begun* (Silver)
5. Peace* (Silver)

Horace Silver, *The United States of Mind, Phase I: That Healin' Feelin'* (Blue Note)

SESSION NO. 106: HORACE SILVER GROUP
JUNE 18, 1970: VAN GELDER STUDIOS, ENGLEWOOD CLIFFS, N.J.

Randy Brecker, trumpet; Houston Person, tenor sax; Horace Silver, piano; Jimmy Lewis, bass; Idris Muhammad, drums; Gail Nelson, Jackie Verdell,† vocals.*

1. Nobody Knows* (Silver)
2. Permit Me to Introduce You to Yourself† (Silver)
3. Wipe Away the Devil† (Silver)
4. There's Much to Be Done† (Silver)

Horace Silver, *The United States of Mind, Phase I: That Healin' Feelin'* (Blue Note)

SESSION NO. 107: HORACE SILVER GROUP
NOVEMBER 15, 1970: VAN GELDER STUDIOS, ENGLEWOOD CLIFFS, N.J.

Cecil Bridgewater, trumpet; Harold Vick, tenor sax; Horace Silver, piano; Richie Resnicoff, guitar; Bob Cranshaw, bass; Mickey Roker, drums; Salome Bey, vocals.

1. Big Business (Silver)
2. Total Response (Silver)
3. What Kind of Animal Am I (Silver)
4. Acid, Pot, Or Pills (Silver)

Horace Silver, *The United States of Mind, Phase II: Total Response* (Blue Note)

SESSION NO. 108: HORACE SILVER GROUP
JANUARY 29, 1971: VAN GELDER STUDIOS, ENGLEWOOD CLIFFS, N.J.

Cecil Bridgewater, trumpet; Harold Vick, tenor sax; Horace Silver, piano; Richie Resnicoff, guitar; Bob Cranshaw, bass; Mickey Roker, drums; Andy Bey, Salome Bey,† vocals.*

1. I've Had a Little Talk* (Silver)
2. Soul Searchin'† (Silver)
3. Won't You Open Up Your Senses* (Silver)
4. I'm Aware of the Animal within Me† (Silver)
5. Old Mother Nature Calls* (Silver)

Horace Silver, *The United States of Mind, Phase II: Total Response* (Blue Note)

SESSION NO. 109: HORACE SILVER GROUP
JANUARY 17, 1972: VAN GELDER STUDIOS, ENGLEWOOD CLIFFS, N.J.

Horace Silver, piano; Bob Cranshaw, bass; Mickey Roker, drums; Andy Bey, Salome Bey,† Gail Nelson,‡ vocals.*

1. Forever Is a Long Time† (Silver)
2. How Much Does Matter Really Matter‡ (Silver)
3. Cause and Effect* (Silver)
4. Who Has the Answer* (Silver)
5. From the Heart through the Mind* (Silver)

Horace Silver, *The United States of Mind, Phase III: All* (Blue Note)

SESSION NO. 110: HORACE SILVER GROUP
FEBRUARY 14, 1972: VAN GELDER STUDIOS, ENGLEWOOD CLIFFS, N.J.

Cecil Bridgewater, trumpet; Harold Vick, tenor sax; Horace Silver, piano; Richie Resnicoff, guitar; Bob Cranshaw, bass; Mickey Roker, drums; Andy Bey, Salome Bey, Gail Nelson, vocals.

1. Summary (Silver)
2. The Merger of the Minds (Silver)
3. The Soul Is My Computer (Silver)
4. Horn of Life (Silver)
5. All (Silver)

Horace Silver, *The United States of Mind, Phase III: All* (Blue Note)

SESSION NO. 111: HORACE SILVER QUARTET
OCTOBER 6, 1972: VAN GELDER STUDIOS, ENGLEWOOD CLIFFS, N.J.

Dave Friedman, vibes; Horace Silver, piano; Bob Cranshaw, bass; Mickey Roker, drums.

1. Summer in Central Park (Silver)
2. Strange Vibes (Silver)
3. Kathy (Santos-Livingston-Evans)
4. In Pursuit of the 27th Man (Silver)

Horace Silver Quartet/Quintet, *In Pursuit of the 27th Man* (Blue Note)

SESSION NO. 112: HORACE SILVER QUINTET
NOVEMBER 10, 1972: VAN GELDER STUDIOS, ENGLEWOOD CLIFFS, N.J.

Randy Brecker, trumpet; Michael Brecker, tenor sax; Horace Silver, piano; Bob Cranshaw, bass; Mickey Roker, drums.

1. The Liberated Brother (Irvine)
2. Nothin' Can Stop Me Now (Silver)
3. Gregory Is Here (Silver)

Horace Silver Quartet/Quintet, *In Pursuit of the 27th Man* (Blue Note)

SESSION NO. 113: HORACE SILVER QUINTET
JULY 15, 1973: PESCARA JAZZ FESTIVAL, PESCARA, ITALY

Randy Brecker, trumpet; Michael Brecker, tenor sax; Horace Silver, piano; Will Lee, bass; Alvin Queen, drums.

1. Gregory Is Here (Silver)

It Happened in Pescara (1969–1989) (Philology-LP)

SESSION NO. 114: HORACE SILVER QUINTET
JANUARY 10, 1975: A&R STUDIOS, NEW YORK CITY

Tom Harrell, trumpet; Bob Berg, tenor sax; Horace Silver, piano; Ron Carter, bass; Al Foster, drums.

Overdub: *Oscar Brashear, Bobby Bryant, trumpet; Jerome Richardson, Buddy Collette, flute/alto sax; Vince De Rosa, French horn; Frank Rosolino, trombone; Maurice Spears, bass trombone; Wade Marcus, arr.*

1. Barbara (Silver)
2. Dameron's Dance (Silver)

3. Adjustment (Silver)
4. Mysticism (Silver)

Horace Silver, *Silver 'n Brass* (Blue Note)

SESSION NO. 115: HORACE SILVER QUINTET
JANUARY 17, 1975: A&R STUDIOS, NEW YORK CITY

Tom Harrell, trumpet; Bob Berg, tenor sax; Horace Silver, piano; Bob Cranshaw, bass; Bernard Purdie, drums.

Overdub: *Oscar Brashear, Bobby Bryant, trumpet; Jerome Richardson, Buddy Collette, flute/alto sax; Vince De Rosa, French horn; Frank Rosolino, trombone; Maurice Spears, bass trombone; Wade Marcus, arr.*

1. Kissin' Cousins (Silver)
2. The Sophisticated Hippie (Silver)

Horace Silver, *Silver 'n Brass* (Blue Note)

SESSION NO. 116: HORACE SILVER QUINTET
NOVEMBER 7, 1975: A&R STUDIOS, NEW YORK CITY

Tom Harrell, trumpet; Bob Berg, tenor sax; Horace Silver, piano; Ron Carter, bass; Al Foster, drums.

Overdub: January 2–3, 1976, Los Angeles, Calif.
Lanny Morgan, alto sax; Jerome Richardson, soprano sax; Buddy Collette, Fred Jackson, flute; Jack Nimitz, bari sax; Bill Green, bass sax; Garnett Brown, trombone.

THE TRANQUILIZER SUITE

1. Keep on Gettin' Up (Silver)
2. Slow Down (Silver)
3. Time and Effort (Silver)
4. Perseverance and Endurance (Silver)

Horace Silver, *Silver 'n Wood* (Blue Note)

SESSION NO. 117: HORACE SILVER QUINTET
NOVEMBER 14, 1975: A&R STUDIOS, NEW YORK CITY

Tom Harrell, trumpet; Bob Berg, tenor sax; Horace Silver, piano; Ron Carter, bass; Al Foster, drums.

Overdub: January 2–3, 1976, Los Angeles, Calif.

Lanny Morgan, alto sax; Jerome Richardson, soprano sax; Buddy Collette, Fred Jackson, flute; Jack Nimitz, bari sax; Bill Green, bass sax; Frank Rosolino, trombone.

THE PROCESS OF CREATION SUITE

1. Motivation (Silver)
2. Activation (Silver)
3. Assimilation (Silver)
4. Creation (Silver)

Horace Silver, *Silver 'n Wood* (Blue Note)

SESSION NO. 118: HORACE SILVER QUINTET
SEPTEMBER 24, 1976: A&R STUDIOS, NEW YORK CITY

Tom Harrell, trumpet; Bob Berg, tenor sax; Horace Silver, piano; Ron Carter, bass; Al Foster, drums.

Overdub: October 19 and 22, 1976, Los Angeles, Calif.

Monica Mancini, Avery Sommers, Joyce Copeland, Richard Page, Dale Verdugo, Alan Copeland, vocals.

1. Togetherness (Silver)
2. Mood for Maude (Silver)
3. New York Lament (Silver)
4. All in Time (Silver)

Horace Silver, *Silver 'n Voices* (Blue Note)

SESSION NO. 119: HORACE SILVER QUINTET
OCTOBER 1, 1976: A&R STUDIOS, NEW YORK CITY

Tom Harrell, trumpet; Bob Berg, tenor sax; Horace Silver, piano; Ron Carter, bass; Al Foster, drums.

Overdub: October 19 and 22, 1976, Los Angeles, Calif.

Monica Mancini, Avery Sommers, Joyce Copeland, Richard Page, Dale Verdugo, Alan Copeland, vocals.

1. Out of the Night (Silver)
2. I Will Always Love You (Silver)

3. Incentive (Silver)
4. Freeing My Mind (Silver)

Horace Silver, *Silver 'n Voices* (Blue Note)

SESSION NO. 120: HORACE SILVER QUINTET
JULY 9, 1977: AHUSFESTIVAL SONMARLUST KRISTIANSTAD JAZZ FESTIVAL

Tom Harrell, trumpet; Larry Schneider, tenor sax; Horace Silver, piano; Chip Jackson, bass; Eddie Gladen, drums.

1. Time and Effort (Tranquilizer Suite No. 3) (Silver)
2. Mood for Maude (Silver)
3. Out of the Night (Came You) (Silver)
4. The Sophisticated Hippie (Silver)

Horace Silver Quintet, unreleased live recording (Swedish Broadcast Radio)

SESSION NO. 121: HORACE SILVER SEPTET
NOVEMBER 12, 1977: VAN GELDER STUDIOS, ENGLEWOOD CLIFFS, N.J.

Tom Harrell, trumpet; Larry Schneider, tenor sax; Horace Silver, piano; Ron Carter, bass; Al Foster, drums; M. Babatundo Olatunji, Ladji Camara, percussion.

Overdub: November 25 and 30, 1977, Los Angeles, Calif.

Fred Hardy, Lee C. Thomas, Fred Gripper, Bob Barnes, Bobby Clay, Peter Oliver Norman, voices; Chapman Roberts, dir.

AFRICAN ASCENSION

1. The Gods of Yoruba (Silver)
2. The Sun God of the Masai (Silver)
3. The Spirit of the Zulu (Silver)

Horace Silver, *Silver 'n Percussion* (Blue Note)

SESSION NO. 122: HORACE SILVER SEPTET
NOVEMBER 17, 1977: VAN GELDER STUDIOS, ENGLEWOOD CLIFFS, N.J.

Tom Harrell, trumpet; Larry Schneider, tenor sax; Horace Silver, piano; Ron Carter, bass; Al Foster, drums; M. Babatundo Olatunji, Ladji Camara, percussion.

Overdub: November 25 and 30, 1977, Los Angeles, Calif.
Fred Hardy, Lee C. Thomas, Fred Gripper, Bob Barnes, Bobby Clay, Peter Oliver Norman, voices; Chapman Roberts, dir.

THE GREAT AMERICAN INDIAN UPRISING

1. The Idols of the Incas (Silver)
2. The Aztec Sun God (Silver)
3. The Mohican and the Great Spirit (Silver)

Horace Silver, *Silver 'n Percussion* (Blue Note)

SESSION NO. 123: HORACE SILVER QUINTET
NOVEMBER 3, 1978: VAN GELDER STUDIOS, ENGLEWOOD CLIFFS, N.J.

Tom Harrell, trumpet; Larry Schneider, tenor sax; Horace Silver, piano; Ron Carter, bass; Al Foster, drums, Gregory Hines, vocals.*

THE PHYSICAL SPHERE: THE SOUL AND ITS EXPRESSION

1. The Search for Direction (Silver)
2. Direction Discovered (Silver)
3. We All Have a Part* (Silver)

Horace Silver, *Silver 'n Strings Play the Music of the Spheres* (Blue Note)

SESSION NO. 124: HORACE SILVER QUINTET
NOVEMBER 10, 1978: VAN GELDER STUDIOS, ENGLEWOOD CLIFFS, N.J.

Tom Harrell, trumpet; Larry Schneider, tenor sax; Horace Silver, piano; Ron Carter, bass; Al Foster, drums.

Overdub:* *Guy Lumia, Aaron Rosand, Marvin Morganstern, Peter Dimitriades, Paul Winter, Lewis Eley, Louann Montesi, Harry Glickman, violin; Harold Coletta, Harry Zaratzian, Seymour Berman, Theodore Israel, viola; Seymour Barab, Jonathan Abramowitz, cello; Gene Bianco, harp; Wade Marcus, arr.*

THE SPIRITUAL SPHERE: THE SOUL IN COMMUNION WITH THE CREATOR

1. Communion with the Creator (Silver)
2. The Creator Guides Us* (Silver)

3. Progress through Dedication and Discipline* (Silver)
4. We Expect Positive Results (Silver)

Horace Silver, *Silver 'n Strings Play the Music of the Spheres* (Blue Note)

SESSION NO. 125: HORACE SILVER GROUP
OCTOBER 26, 1979: VAN GELDER STUDIOS, ENGLEWOOD CLIFFS, N.J.

Tom Harrell, trumpet; Larry Schneider, tenor sax; Horace Silver, piano; Ron Carter, bass; Al Foster, drums, Carol Lynn Maillard, Chapman Roberts,† Brenda Alford,‡ vocals.*

Overdub: *Guy Lumia, Aaron Rosand, Marvin Morganstern, Peter Dimitriades, Paul Winter, Lewis Eley, Louann Montesi, Harry Glickman, violin; Harold Coletta, Harry Zaratzian, Seymour Berman, Theodore Israel, viola; Seymour Barab, Jonathan Abramowitz, cello; Gene Bianco, harp; Wade Marcus, arr.*

THE MENTAL SPHERE, SUBCONSCIOUS MIND: THE PYGMALION PROCESS

1. Inner Feelings† (Silver)
2. Friends* (Silver)
3. Empathy† (Silver)
4. Optimism* (Silver)
5. Expansion‡ (Silver)

Horace Silver, *Silver 'n Strings Play the Music of the Spheres* (Blue Note)

SESSION NO. 126: HORACE SILVER GROUP
NOVEMBER 2, 1979: VAN GELDER STUDIOS, ENGLEWOOD CLIFFS, N.J.

Tom Harrell, trumpet; Larry Schneider, tenor sax; Horace Silver, piano; Ron Carter, bass; Al Foster, drums, Gregory Hines, Brenda Alford, Chapman Roberts, Carol Lynn Maillard,† vocals.

Overdub:* *Guy Lumia, Aaron Rosand, Marvin Morganstern, Peter Dimitriades, Paul Winter, Lewis Eley, Louann Montesi, Harry Glickman, violin; Harold Coletta, Harry Zaratzian, Seymour Berman, Theodore Israel, viola; Seymour Barab, Jonathan Abramowitz, cello; Gene Bianco, harp; Dale Oehler, arr.*

THE PHYSICAL SPHERE: THE SOUL AND ITS PROGRESS THROUGHOUT THE SPHERES

1. Self Portrait No. 1* (Silver)
2. Self Portrait No. 2* (Silver)
3. Portrait of the Aspiring Self* (Silver)

THE MENTAL SPHERE, CONSCIOUS MIND:
THE SOUL'S AWARENESS OF CHARACTER

1. The Soul (Character Analysis)†
2. Negative Patterns of the Sub-Conscious (Silver)
3. The Conscious and Its Desire for Change (Silver)

Horace Silver, *Silver 'n Strings Play the Music of the Spheres* (Blue Note)

SESSION NO. 127: HORACE SILVER QUINTET
SEPTEMBER 18, 1981: HOLLYWOOD, CALIF.

Eddie Harris, tenor sax; Joe Diorio, guitar; Horace Silver, piano; Bob Magnusson, bass; Roy McCurdy, drums; Bill Cosby, voice; Weaver Copeland, Mahmu Pearl, vocals.

1. Accepting Responsibility (Silver)
2. Reaching Our Goals in Life (Silver)
3. Learning to Be Unselfish (Silver)
4. Helping Others (Silver)

Horace Silver Quintet, *Guides to Growing Up* (Silveto-LP)

SESSION NO. 128: HORACE SILVER QUINTET
SEPTEMBER 29, 1981: HOLLYWOOD, CALIF.

Eddie Harris, tenor sax; Joe Diorio, guitar; Horace Silver, piano; Bob Magnusson, bass; Roy McCurdy, drums; Bill Cosby, voice; Weaver Copeland, Mahmu Pearl, vocals.

1. Finding Good Rules to Live By (Silver)
2. Honesty and Self Control (Silver)
3. Managing Your Money (Silver)
4. The Things That Really Matter (Silver)

Horace Silver Quintet, *Guides to Growing Up* (Silveto-LP)

SESSION NO. 129: HORACE SILVER QUINTET
JANUARY 19, 1983: HOLLYWOOD, CALIF.

Bobby Shew, trumpet; Eddie Harris, Ralph Moore, tenor sax; Horace Silver, piano; Bob Maize, bass; Carl Burnett, drums.

1. Smelling Our Attitude (Silver)
2. Seeing with Perception (Silver)
3. The Sensitive Touch (Silver)
4. Exercising Taste and Good Judgment (Silver)

5. Hearing and Understanding (Silver)
6. Moving Forward with Confidence (Silver)

Horace Silver Quintet, *Spiritualizing the Senses* (Silveto-LP)

SESSION NO. 130: HORACE SILVER GROUP
AUGUST 25, 1983: HOLLYWOOD, CALIF.

Weaver Copeland, Mahmu Pearl, vocals; Bobby Shew, trumpet; Eddie Harris, tenor sax, vocals; Horace Silver, piano, vocals; Bob Maize, bass; Carl Burnett, drums.

1. I Don't Know What I'm Gonna Do (Silver)
2. Don't Dwell on Your Problems (Silver)
3. Everything's Gonna Be All Right (Silver)
4. There's No Need to Struggle (Silver)

Horace Silver, *There's No Need to Struggle* (Silveto-LP)

SESSION NO. 131: HORACE SILVER QUINTET
SEPTEMBER 1, 1983: HOLLYWOOD, CALIF.

Bobby Shew, trumpet; Eddie Harris, tenor sax, Horace Silver, piano; Bob Maize, bass; Carl Burnett, drums.

1. Seeking the Plan (Silver)
2. Discovering the Plan (Silver)
3. Fulfilling the Plan (Silver)
4. Happiness and Contentment (Silver)

Horace Silver, *There's No Need to Struggle* (Silveto-LP)

SESSION NO. 132/133: HORACE SILVER GROUP
MARCH 25 AND 28, 1985: HOLLYWOOD, CALIF.

Carl Saunders, flügelhorn; Buddy Collette, Ray Pizzi, Ernie Watts, Don Menza, flute; Horace Silver, piano; Bob Maize, bass; Carl Burnett, drums; Andy Bey, Maxine Waters, Julia Waters, vocals; Chuck Niles, voice; Los Angeles Modern String Orchestra, William Henderson, cond.

1. Message from the Maestro, Part 1 (Silver)
2. Message from the Maestro, Part 2 (Silver)
3. Message from the Maestro, Part 3 (Silver)
4. In Tribute, Part 1 (Silver)
5. In Tribute, Part 2 (Silver)
6. In Tribute, Part 3 (Silver)

Horace Silver, *Continuity of Spirit* (Silveto-LP)

SESSION NO. 134: HORACE SILVER QUINTET
MARCH 31, 1988: HOLLYWOOD, CALIF.

Clark Terry, flügelhorn, vocal; Junior Cook, tenor sax; Horace Silver, piano; Ray Drummond, bass; Billy Hart, drums; Andy Bey, vocals.*

1. Prologue (Silver)
2. Hangin' Loose* (Silver)
3. The Respiratory Story (Silver)
4. Tie Your Dreams to a Star (Silver)
5. Music to Ease Your Disease (Silver)
6. The Philanthropic View (Silver)
7. What Is the Sinus Minus (Silver)
8. Epilogue (Silver)

Horace Silver Quintet, *Music to Ease Your Disease* (Silveto-LP)

SESSION NO. 135: HORACE SILVER OCTET
JUNE 10 AND 11, 1991: SAGE AND SOUND STUDIOS, HOLLYWOOD, CALIF.

Rickey Woodard, Ralph Brown, tenor sax; Michael Mossman, trumpet; Andy Martin, Bob McChesney, trombone; Bob Maize, bass; Carl Burnett, drums; Horace Silver, piano; Andy Bey, Dawn Burnett,† vocals.*

1. Satchmo's Song† (Silver)
2. A Ballad for Hawk* (Silver)
3. The Skunky Funky Blues* (Silver)
4. Sunday Mornin' Prayer Meetin'† (Silver)
5. The Righteous Rumba* (Silver)
6. Rockin' with Rachmaninoff*† (Silver)

Horace Silver, *Rockin' with Rachmaninoff* (Bop City)

SESSION NO. 136: HORACE SILVER OCTET
AUGUST 14 AND 15, 1991: SAGE AND SOUND STUDIOS, HOLLYWOOD, CALIF.

Rickey Woodard, Doug Webb, tenor sax; Bob Summers, trumpet; Andy Martin, Bob McChesney, trombone; Bob Maize, bass; Carl Burnett, drums; Horace Silver, piano.

1. Rocky's Overture (Silver)
2. Rocky Meets the Duke (Silver)
3. Monkeyin' Around with Monk (Silver)

4. Hallelujah to Ya (Silver)
5. Lavender Love (Silver)

Horace Silver, *Rockin' with Rachmaninoff* (Bop City)

SESSION NO. 137/138: HORACE SILVER AND THE SILVER BRASS ENSEMBLE
FEBRUARY 8 AND 9, 1993: OCEAN WAY STUDIOS, LOS ANGELES, CALIF.

Ron Stout, Oscar Brashear, Bob Summers, trumpet; Bob McChesney, Maurice Spears, trombone; Suzette Moriarty, French horn; Eddie Harris, Red Holloway, Branford Marsalis, sax; Horace Silver, piano; Bob Maize, bass; Carl Burnett, drums; Andy Bey, vocals.*

1. Funky Bunky (Silver)
2. Dufus Rufus* (Silver)
3. Lunceford Legacy (Silver)
4. Hillbilly Bebopper* (Silver)
5. The Walk Around—Look Up and Down Song (Silver)
6. It's Got to Be Funky* (Silver)
7. Basically Blue (Silver)
8. Song for My Father* (Silver)
9. When You're in Love (Silver)
10. Put Me in the Basement (Silver)
11. Little Mama (Silver)
12. Yo' Mama's Mambo (Silver)

Horace Silver, *It's Got to Be Funky* (Columbia)

SESSION NO. 139/140: HORACE SILVER AND THE SILVER BRASS ENSEMBLE
JANUARY 10 AND 11, 1994: OCEAN WAY STUDIOS, LOS ANGELES, CALIF.

Ron Stout, Oscar Brashear, trumpet; George Bohannon, Maurice Spears, trombone; Suzette Moriarty, French horn; Eddie Harris, Red Holloway, James Moody, Rickey Woodard, sax; Horace Silver, piano; Bob Maize, bass; Carl Burnett, drums; O. C. Smith, vocals.*

1. Pencil Packin' Papa (Silver)
2. I Got the Dancin' Blues* (Silver)
3. Soul Mates* (Silver)
4. I Need My Baby (Silver)

5. My Mother's Waltz (Silver)
6. Red Beans and Rice* (Silver)
7. Blues for Brother Blue
8. Let It All Hang Out* (Silver)
9. Señor Blues (Silver)
10. Viva Amour (Silver)

Horace Silver, *Pencil Packin' Papa* (Columbia)

SESSION NO. 141: DEE DEE BRIDGEWATER
DECEMBER 1994: PLUS XXX STUDIOS, PARIS

Stephane Belmondo, trumpet; Lionel Belmondo, tenor sax; Horace Silver, piano; Hein Van DeGeyn, bass; Andre "Dede" Ceccarelli, drums; Dee Dee Bridgewater, vocals.

1. Nica's Dream (Silver)
2. Song for My Father (Silver)

Dee Dee Bridgewater, *Love and Peace: A Tribute to Horace Silver* (Verve)

SESSION NO. 142/143: HORACE SILVER SEPTET
FEBRUARY 29 AND MARCH 1, 1996: THE POWER STATION, NEW YORK CITY

Claudio Roditi, trumpet; Michael Brecker, tenor sax; Steve Turre, trombone; Ronnie Cuber, bari sax; Horace Silver, piano; Ron Carter, bass; Lewis Nash, drums.

1. I Want You (Silver)
2. Hippest Cat in Hollywood (Silver)
3. Gratitude (Silver)
4. Hawkin' (Silver)
5. I Got the Blues in Santa Cruz (Silver)
6. We've Got Silver at Six (Silver)
7. Hardbop Grandpop (Silver)
8. Lady from Johannesburg (Silver)
9. Serenade to a Teakettle (Silver)
10. Diggin' on Dexter (Silver)

Horace Silver, *The Hardbop Grandpop* (Impulse!)

SESSION NO. 144/145: HORACE SILVER QUINTET
MAY 6 AND 7, 1997: AVATAR STUDIOS, NEW YORK CITY

Randy Brecker, trumpet; Michael Brecker, tenor sax; Horace Silver, piano; Ron Carter, bass; Louis Hayes, drums.

1. Prescription for the Blues (Silver)
2. Whenever Lester Plays the Blues (Silver)
3. You Gotta Shake That Thing (Silver)
4. Yodel Lady Blues (Silver)
5. Brother John and Brother Gene (Silver)
6. Free at Last (Silver)
7. Walk On (Silver)
8. Sunrise in Malibu (Silver)
9. Doctor Jazz (Silver)

Horace Silver Quintet, *A Prescription for the Blues* (Impulse!)

SESSION NO. 146/147: HORACE SILVER QUINTET
DECEMBER 17 AND 18, 1998: AVATAR STUDIOS, NEW YORK CITY

Jimmy Greene, tenor, soprano sax; Ryan Kisor, trumpet; Horace Silver, piano; John Webber, bass; Willie Jones III, drums.

1. Satisfaction Guaranteed (Silver)
2. The Mama Suite (Silver): Part I: Not Enough Mama, Part II: Too Much Mama, Part III: Just Right Mama
3. Philley Millie (Silver)
4. Ah-Ma-Tell (Silver)
5. I Love Annie's Fanny (Silver)
6. Gloria (Silver)
7. Where Do I Go from Here? (Silver)

Horace Silver Quintet, *Jazz Has a Sense of Humor* (Verve)

RECORDINGS HONORING HORACE SILVER

Oddbjorn Blindheim Trio, *Horace Hello* (Gemini, Norway)

Dee Dee Bridgewater, *Love and Peace: A Tribute to Horace Silver* (Verve)

The Bronx Horns, *Silver in the Bronx* (Timeless)

David Hazeltine Trio, *Señor Blues* (Venus, Japan)

Andy LaVerne, *Serenade to Silver: A Tribute to Horace Silver* (Steeplechase)

Hideo Shiraki, *Hideo Shiraki Plays Horace Silver* (King, Japan)

Silvermine, *The Funky Bluesy Groovy Soul Jazz of Horace Silver* (Recycling, Germany)

Various artists, *The Jazz Giants Play Horace Silver: Opus de Funk* (Prestige)

A SELECT BIBLIOGRAPHY OF MUSIC PUBLICATIONS

PUBLICATIONS BY HORACE SILVER

Silver, Horace. *Horace Silver: The Art of Small Combo Jazz Playing, Composing, and Arranging.* Milwaukee: Hal Leonard, 1995.

———. *Horace Silver Collection: Artist Transcriptions, Piano.* Transcribed by Alex Smith. Milwaukee: Hal Leonard, 1996.

———. *Shoutin' Out!: The Music of Horace Silver.* New Albany, Ind.: Jamey Aebersold, 1998. Contains "Doodlin'," "Hardbop Grandpop," "Juicy Lucy," "Jungle Juice," "Mary Lou," "Moon Rays," "Penny," "Pretty Eyes," "Serenade to a Soul Sister," "Señor Blues," "Shoutin' Out," "Tokyo Blues."

———. "Sister Sadie": *Professional Editions for Jazz Ensemble.* Arranged by Michael Abene. Milwaukee: Hal Leonard, n.d.

———. "Song for My Father": *Jazz Classics for the Young Ensemble.* Arranged by Mark Taylor. Milwaukee: Hal Leonard, n.d.

———. "Strollin'." [Band orchestration.] Arranged by Terry White. Portland, Maine: Manduca Music, 1996.

PUBLICATIONS CONTAINING MUSIC BY HORACE SILVER

The Best Chord Changes for the Best-Known Songs. Milwaukee: Hal Leonard, 1995. Contains "Song for My Father."

The Big Book of Jazz. Milwaukee: Hal Leonard, 1992. Contains "Song for My Father."

Classic Jazz Standards: Fifty-six Jazz Essentials. Milwaukee: Hal Leonard, n.d. Contains "Song for My Father."

Dunlap, Larry, and Chuck Sher, eds. *The Standards Real Book.* Petaluma, Calif.: Sher Music, 1991. Contains "Doodlin'," "The Tokyo Blues," "Too Much Sake."

Edstrom, Brent, arr. *Hard Bop.* Milwaukee: Hal Leonard, n.d. Contains "Nica's Dream," "Song for My Father."

Fifty Essential Bebop Heads. Milwaukee: Hal Leonard, 1996. Contains "Mayreh," "Quicksilver."

The Hal Leonard Real Jazz Book. Milwaukee: Hal Leonard, n.d. Contains "Filthy McNasty," "Me and My Baby," "Peace," "Strollin'."

Jazz Classics: Fifty Favorites of the Bebop Era and Beyond. Milwaukee: Hal Leonard, n.d. Contains "Song for My Father."

Laverne, Andy, arr. *Tunes You Thought You Knew: Reharmonized Standards.* New Albany, Ind.: Jamey Aebersold, 1998. Contains "Song for My Father."

Mike Stern: Standards. Transcribed by Greg Varlotta. n.p.: Greg Varlotta, 1996. Contains "Peace."

Rubin, Dave, ed. and arr. *The Guitar Style of George Benson.* Milwaukee: Hal Leonard, 2000. Contains "Song for My Father."

Sher, Chuck, and Bob Bauer, eds. *The New Real Book.* Vol. 2. Petaluma, Calif.: Sher Music, 1991. Contains "Ecaroh," "Filthy McNasty," "Gregory Is Here," "Horace-Scope," "Moon Rays," "The Natives Are Restless Tonight," "Nica's Dream," "Nutville," "Peace," "Quicksilver," "Señor Blues," "Silver's Serenade," "Song for My Father," "Strollin'," "Summer in Central Park."

———. *The New Real Book.* Vol. 3. Petaluma, Calif.: Sher Music, 1991. Contains "Lonely Woman," "Metamorphosis," "Opus de Funk," "Pyramid."

Sher, Chuck, and Larry Dunlap, eds. *The All-Jazz Real Book.* Petaluma, Calif.: Sher Music, 2001. Contains "Shoutin' Out," "Yeah!"

Sher, Chuck, and Michael Zisman, eds. *The Real Easy Book: Tunes for Intermediate Improvisors.* Vol. 2. Petaluma, Calif.: Sher Music, 2003. Contains "Barbara," "Come on Home," "Enchantment," "Peace," "Room 608," "Silver's Serenade," "Split Kick."

Zisman, Michael, ed. *The Real Easy Book: Tunes for Beginning Improvisors.* Vol. 1. Petaluma, Calif.: Sher Music, 2003. Contains "The Jody Grind," "Sister Sadie," "Song for My Father."

AWARDS

1954	*Downbeat* New Star, Jazz Critics' Poll, Piano
1958	Budweiser Award
1959	Blue Note Records Award
1963	Schaefer Award for Outstanding Achievement as an Exponent of Modern Jazz
1964	The Jazzmobile Certificate of Appreciation (New York City)
1977	City of Los Angeles Proclamation: Horace Silver Month (February)
	Jazz Heritage Foundation Award
1979	Silver Anniversary, Blue Note Records
1985	City of Los Angeles Proclamation: Horace Silver Day (March 22, 1985)
1989	City of Los Angeles Proclamation: Horace Silver Day (September 10, 1989)
1990	Black Heritage Association of Palos Verdes Award (California)
1991	Cape Verdeans of Southern California Achievement and Recognition Award
	U.S. House of Representatives Tribute to Horace Silver (May 14, 1991)

County of Los Angeles Commendation (June 24, 1991)

California Legislative Assembly, Certificate of Recognition (June 24, 1991)

California State Senate, Certificate of Recognition

1992 Rutgers University Jazz Hall of Fame (May 1, 1992)

1993 Visionary 3M Award: Artist/Producer for *It's Got to Be Funky* (album)

1994 *Academie du jazz* award, Paris, France

National Endowment for the Arts: Jazz Masters Fellowship Grant

1995 International Association of Jazz Educators: For Outstanding Service to Jazz Education

City of Los Angeles Commendation (June 13, 1995)

1996 International Association of Jazz Educators: For Outstanding Service to Jazz Education (January 11, 1996)

The American Society of Music Arrangers and Composers: For Consistent Achievement in Music, Arranging, Orchestration, and Composition (March 20, 1996)

Norwalk (Connecticut) High School Wall of Honor, Class of 1947 (November 17, 1996)

Downbeat Magazine Sixty-first Annual Readers' Poll: Hall of Fame

Honorary Doctorate: Berklee School of Music

NARAS Grammy Nomination for *The Hardbop Grandpop* (album)

1998 Los Angeles Jazz Society: Jazz Tribute Honoree

2000 The Larry Gales Fifth Annual Music Achievement Award (July 4, 2000)

2001 New Jersey Performing Arts Center: Jazz for Teens Award (May 19, 2001)

Juke Joint Cafe Award, San Diego, California (May 25, 2001)

Charles R. Drew University of Medicine and Science, Los Angeles, California: Jazz at Drew Living Legend/Lifetime Achievement Award (October 6, 2001)

INDEX

Designer: Nola Burger
Text: 10/15 Janson
Display: Stymie Condensed
Compositor: Integrated Composition Systems
Indexer: Patricia Deminna
Printer and binder: Thomson-Shore